D0296939

1

1

EXPLORING THE FRENCH LANGUAGE

R. ANTHONY LODGE, NIGEL ARMSTRONG, YVETTE M. L. ELLIS AND JANE F. SHELTON

CRPYK

ARNOLD

A member of the Hodder Headline Group
LONDON • NEW YORK • SYDNEY • AUCKLAND

First published in Great Britain 1997 by
Arnold, a division of The Hodder Headline Group,
338 Euston Road, London NW1 3BH

Distributed exclusively in the USA by
St. Martin's Press, Inc.
175 Fifth Avenue, New York, NY 10010

British Library Cataloguing in Publication Data
A catalogue record for this book is available from the British Library

Library of Congress Cataloging-in-Publication Data
A catalog record for this book is available from the Library of Congress

ISBN 0 340 67662 0 (pb)
ISBN 0 340 67661 2 (hb)

Typeset in 10/12pt Sabon by Phoenix Photosetting, Chatham, Kent
Printed and bound in the United Kingdom by J. W. Arrowsmith Ltd, Bristol

Contents

Preface

One of the problems currently facing French studies in higher education is the widening gap between the approaches to language practised there and those which have been developed in university departments of Linguistics and English Language: the advances made in the latter during the past 25 years have not filtered through sufficiently to the former. The explanation lies principally in the already crowded curricula of Modern Language degrees, combining as they do practical language-learning with the study of literature, area studies and cultural studies as well as language-study. Part of the responsibility rests too, it has to be said, with the highly theoretical and often sectarian attitudes of specialists in linguistics which have deterred many of the most well-meaning students of Modern Languages from entering their area.

Given the centrality of language in the discipline of Modern Languages, this separation has been detrimental. The present volume cannot attempt to transform the situation, but we would like it to contribute to change in a modest way by helping students in the early stages of degrees in French to an understanding of the approach to language adopted so productively by specialists in the various branches of linguistics. It should be stressed, however, that this book is not conceived as an introduction to linguistics. Many excellent books with this aim have been published over the past 25 years. Our aims are more limited: our prime focus is upon French, rather than language in general, and even here we do not pretend to offer a general description of the language. Our goals are simply to show how analytical frames and terminology developed in linguistics can lead to a heightened interest in the French language and to encourage students to further exploration of the subject.

To this end, the bibliographical references placed at relevant points in the text are integral to our aims: they indicate not all the main treatises concerning the different parts of the discipline, but simply key introductory works which beginners should find interesting and which they can be reasonably expected to understand. They are all grouped together in the general bibliography to be found at the end of the volume. We feel that this mode of presentation will give more precise guidance to the reader than classified lists placed at the end of each chapter. Each chapter in fact concludes with a set of suggestions for seminar activities. No key to the 'right' answers is provided for these, as their prime function is to open the door to discussion not to close it.

The authors would like to thank several first-year cohorts of French Honours students in Newcastle and St Andrews Universities who have taught us which features of French linguistics we need to be clear about, and we extend particular gratitude to Aidan Coveney of Exeter University whose comments on our text have been invaluable.

St Andrews, May 1996

Acknowledgements

The authors and publishers wish to thank the following for their permission to use copyright material:

Geoffrey Bremmer for material from the *Aberystwyth Word Lists*.

Cambridge University Press for material from *Sociolinguistics and Contemporary French* by Dennis Ager, 1990.

Hachette for material from *Et si l'on écrivait correctement le français?* by Michel Massian, 1985.

Hodder and Stoughton Educational for material from *Travaux pratiques* by David Hartley (ed.), 1987, and from *Le français en faculté* (Audio Course) by Brian Farrington, 1980.

Larousse-Bordas for material from *Dictionnaire du français contemporain*, 1971 by Dubois et al., and from *Le parfait secrétaire* by Georges Vivien and Véronique Arné, 1996.

Macmillan for material from *Varieties of Contemporary French* by Malcolm Offord, 1990.

Presses Universitaires de France for material from *Dictionnaire étymologique de la langue française* by Oscar Bloch and Walther von Wartburg, 1991.

Routledge for material from *French: From Dialect to Standard* by R. Anthony Lodge, 1993.

Editions du Seuil for material from *La liaison avec et sans enchaînement* by Pierre Encrevé, 1987.

1

Lay-persons versus linguists

Most people interested in foreign languages are concerned primarily to use them for business purposes, for foreign travel, for reading a foreign literature, and so on. At school, pupils learn French with the same practical aim, that of communicating with speakers from the French-speaking world. There comes a time, however, when advanced learners of the language perceive that a simple practical knowledge of the language is insufficient. It is not enough for them to know how to use the language, they need to know *about* it too. Why should this be? An immediate answer might be that such knowledge about the French language may well enhance their learning of it from a practical standpoint, but the issues run deeper.

The French language is more than just a tool for communication, it has a crucial role to play in the way native-speakers of French think about the world and about themselves. Language is central to thought (have you ever considered, for instance, how much thinking you can carry out without the help of words?) and it is central to cultural identity (is language not one of the most basic features distinguishing French civilisation from that of the Germans or Italians?). As a result, if you want to penetrate seriously the way French speakers think, if you want to understand in a non-superficial way the nature of French culture (using this term not just in its aesthetic sense, but also in its broad anthropological sense of 'customs and civilisation of a particular group'), it is important to develop an understanding of what the French language is and how it works. This book is designed to help you with the first steps along this road.

The discipline concerned with the scientific study of language in general is linguistics. This book is not conceived as an introduction to linguistics, for many such books are currently available (see Yule 1985, Hudson 1984). However, what we would like to offer is an introduction to looking at the French language from a linguistic point of view. The fundamental aim of linguistics has been defined as 'to present in a precise, rigorous and explicit form facts about language which those who speak it as a native-speaker know intuitively'. If you think about this statement, you will see that the linguist's approach to language is very different from that of the lay-person. Thus, in this introductory chapter we will begin by highlighting aspects of the lay-person's attitude to language, and then contrast them with the linguist's approach, in the hope that the reader will thereafter want to follow us down the linguist's route.

1.1   The lay-person's approach to language

The lay-person does not normally spend much time and effort thinking about language. The very deep-seated nature of a speaker's knowledge of their language means that it is very difficult for them to become consciously aware of it and to speak about it. They normally take language completely for granted, often regarding discussions about language as so much time-wasting pedantry. 'Language is for talking about something, it is not something to be talked about.' They tend to be impatient with people examining the way a particular bit of language functions (e.g. the meaning of a particular word or the structure of a particular phrase), and they can afford to be so since language is primarily about getting things done in the practical sphere of our everyday existence. For them it is a tool rather than a structure to be explored. However, the specialist in languages does not have the luxury of dismissing the core of his specialism in such a cavalier fashion.

The fact that the lay-person takes language for granted means that when they are called upon to talk about a feature of language (e.g. what is Geordie/Cockney speech like?), they are usually at a loss to say anything sensible, (a) because they have no terminology or 'metalanguage' to talk precisely about language and (b) because they have no solid theoretical framework within which to develop ideas. However, this inability to pronounce articulately on language matters does not mean that the lay-person has no ideas about language and that they make no implicit assumptions about the subject – language is too central to all of our lives for any of us to get away with that. What it does mean is that the assumptions the lay-person makes are often light-years away from the position taken by linguists after serious reflection.

It is possible to characterise the difference by saying that the lay-person's approach to language is subjective and unsystematic and the linguist's approach is (in theory at least) objective and methodical. Let us look first at subjective attitudes to language current in our society, before tackling the way linguistics approaches the analysis of language.

1.1.1 Subjective attitudes to language

A lay-person's attitudes to language are on the whole not objective or detached, but are conditioned by a set of cultural factors which make them subjective, evaluative, prescriptive, i.e. they predispose the lay-person towards making value judgements or statements about what they think is good or bad about a piece of language rather than describing in a detached way what is actually there. The most deeply engrained subjective attitudes to language current in our society usually reflect our attitudes to the people who speak particular languages or dialects and our notions of what is and is not correct, bestowing particular status upon writing as distinct from speech. Let us look at some of the crazy things people say about different languages and varieties of language. You will find further examples in French in Yaguello (1988).

NATIONAL, RACIAL AND SOCIAL STEREOTYPING

Consider the following clichés about particular languages:

- 'Italian is a very musical language'
- 'German is a harsh and guttural language'
- 'Spanish is a very romantic language'

Such statements are frequently trotted out in everyday talk about language, but if you examine them you will see that they tell us nothing at all about the structure of Italian, German and Spanish. What they do reveal, however, is the way we tend to stereotype the speakers of those languages: in the British popular imagination, Italians are still widely associated with opera, Germans with jackboots and Spaniards with guitars and flamenco dancing. Have you ever heard tell of a German complaining to one of his compatriots about how 'harsh' is their mother-tongue upon the ear?

Now consider the following statement taken from Yaguello (1988: 131):

> Ah, vous faites du Wolof [Senegalese language]. Ça doit être une langue assez simple, non?

Lay-persons commonly assume that languages spoken by people in undeveloped countries are in some sense simpler, more primitive languages than our own. British explorers travelling, say, in Uganda in the late nineteenth century, may be described as speaking a 'language' (i.e. English), whereas their native-bearers speak only 'dialect' (i.e. Luganda). When linguists analyse these 'primitive' languages they invariably discover that there is nothing simple or primitive about their internal structure at all, and that in this respect all languages are in fact equally complex. Those people who speak about simple, primitive languages in Africa or in South America are usually basing their approach on racial stereotypes and a naive belief in the superiority of Western culture.

In a similar way, when lay-persons discuss different varieties of their own language (e.g. Brummie English, Geordie English, Cockney), they often speak of them not in a detached way, but in an evaluative, hierarchical way, invariably regarding some varieties as 'better' than others. Low value is attributed to the speech of groups in our society with low power and status, and vice versa. Thus, the girl from middle-class suburbia will be said to speak 'nicely', while her working-class cousin on the council estate will have 'slovenly', 'lazy' speech. Rural varieties are regarded more favourably than lower-class urban ones – in Britain at least, though in France attitudes to rural varieties are often less favourable. What constitutes 'good' and 'bad' in English? There is nothing objectively better about the Queen's English than about Geordie English (nor, come to that, between American Standard English and Black English Vernacular). It is just that in our society we have been brought up to believe that the Queen's English is 'better' in view of her superior social position. This tells us more about social stratification in our society than the linguistic properties of particular dialects (see Milroy and Milroy 1991).

Subjective attitudes to language like these have no sound intellectual basis, but they can have disturbing social consequences if they are not recognised and controlled. A report was made about a lecturer who gave an identical lecture on two consecutive evenings. On the first evening he spoke standard English and was roundly congratulated for the excellence of his ideas. On the second evening he pronounced exactly the same words, but in a Brummie accent. Certain members of the audience left after a few minutes. Others complained bitterly at the end of the lecture about the foolishness of the lecturer's ideas. For further information on subjective attitudes to varieties of English see Giles (1970), and to varieties of French see Gueunier *et al.* (1978) and Hawkins (1993).

One often hears lay-persons declaring very confidently that 'English is a very beautiful language' and that French is particularly 'clear' and 'logical'. Witness the following statement made by President Mitterrand, while opening an exhibition devoted to the French language:

> A propos de la langue française, il est difficile d'ajouter, après tant d'autres des éloges tant de fois répétés sur sa rigueur, sa clarté, son élégance, ses nuances, la richesse de ses temps et de ses modes, la délicatesse de ses sonorités, la logique de son agencement.
>
> (quoted by Yaguello 1988: 122–23)

Statements like this raise issues beyond those of social or national stereotyping, and reveal the lay-person's inability to make an important distinction: between language as a system and language in use. By language as a system we mean the abstract set of phonological, lexical and grammatical rules which a speaker subconsciously puts into practical application (use) when he/she speaks. It is impossible to demonstrate the superiority of one language system (e.g. French, English) over another: no language system can be inherently more beautiful, more clear, more logical than another. What does differ, however, is the ability of individual speakers to make use of the system: some people are very proficient users of the language, others less so. Some people can write very beautiful poetry, most of us cannot. For more ideas on this topic see Milroy and Milroy (1991: 15). It brings us to the second set of subjective attitudes to language current among lay-persons, namely the belief in the superiority of written over spoken use of language.

SPEECH, WRITING AND PRESCRIPTIVISM

Deeply engrained in European consciousness is the belief that writing is a superior form of language to speaking. With the spread of literacy in Europe in the eighteenth and nineteenth centuries the ability to read and write became a touchstone of the educated, even of the intelligent person. So, a person who cannot write properly is nowadays regarded as educationally and even, in some way, cognitively deficient. In this connection, a high premium is set on the ability to spell correctly, particularly in France where spelling competitions have become something of a national spectator sport. Attribution of a high value to writing has meant a corresponding reduction in the value attributed to speaking – speaking is regarded by many people as an inferior form of language to writing. We ought allegedly to speak as we write, but since most of us are not able to do this, our speech is regarded as a corrupt, degenerate version of writing. Statements like the following are commonly heard, even on the lips of teachers of Modern Languages: 'Speaking is *less grammatical* than writing.' A formulation like this is much more problematic than it seems, not only because of the implication it unthinkingly carries of the superiority of writing over speech, but also because of the woolliness and lack of precision in its use of the word 'grammatical'. The terms 'grammatical' and 'grammar' are frequently bandied about by lay-persons pontificating on the decline in educational standards, but their own use of these terms is often highly confused. Let us consider some of the meanings attributed to the word 'grammar' in contemporary English (for further discussion see Palmer 1971: 11–13):

1 'She finds learning Russian difficult because she does not have much *grammar*.' – here the word means terms for talking about language, 'linguistic terminology' or 'metalanguage'.
2 'She'll never get on in the Civil Service because her *grammar* is so bad.' – here the word means the 'norms of correct English usage'.
3 'English doesn't have much *grammar*, but German and Latin have a lot.' – here the word implies complex verb and noun systems (conjugations and declensions).
4 '*Grammar* is a systematic description of a language as found in a sample of speech or writing' – a linguist's definition of the term (see Crystal 1991 (3rd edn): 141).

Clearly, the word 'grammar' in modern English (and in French too) is open to a range of interpretations, so it is important to make it clear which meaning we intend, whenever we use it. Speaking may be 'less grammatical than writing' if we take definition (2), since the normative rules of correct English usage tend to be based on writing rather than speech, but it would constitute an absurd claim, if we were to take definition (4), for all language (written and spoken) is of necessity systematic and rule-governed: if it were not, no two people could understand one another (all speakers of the same language have to follow more or less the same system).

In this way, dealing with the meanings of the word 'grammar' also forces us to confront different uses of the word 'rule': a 'prescriptive' (or 'normative') rule lays down the law about how you think something ought to be organised; a 'descriptive' rule is a statement about how something actually is organised. Speech is no less rule-governed than writing (in the 'descriptive' sense). It just happens that the rules governing speech are not the same as the rules governing writing. We will be looking at the differences in the next chapter. Linguists are not centrally concerned with 'prescriptive rules', that is to say that they are not interested in showing the superiority of one form of language use over another. What do preoccupy them, however, are descriptive rules: how are they to describe in the neatest and most powerful way the linguistic systems which people use?

In order to make progress in linguistics, it is important to shed a lot of the lay-person's subjective attitudes to language. We need to accept that all varieties of language are equally valid as communication, provided they are used in the appropriate milieu and for the appropriate purpose. We need to be objective in our approach and methodical in our analysis.

1.2   The linguist's approach to language

Linguists have to begin their analysis by divesting themselves of the subjective assumptions about language we have just described. They must try to 'get back to basics'. This involves making explicit statements about things which speakers do intuitively, without thinking. The lay-person can find this sort of activity rather frustrating and tedious but we hope language students will find it more congenial. In this section we will first of all explore some of the basic characteristics of human languages, then examine how linguists organise their study of the phenomenon through the various branches of their discipline.

1.2.1   *The basic characteristics of human languages*

Speech is a faculty possessed by human beings, and it is often said that it is language which distinguishes man from beasts. However, man is not the only living creature which possesses the means of communicating with his fellows. So what is so special about human languages?

We need first of all to distinguish between two different types of signal – *informative* signals (involving 'natural meaning') and *communicative* signals (involving 'non-natural' meaning). The difference between them is one of intentionality. For example, dishevelled hair and bags under her eyes signal to me that student X has had a bad night and that she hasn't managed to finish her essay. Her signals are informative, but they were probably not intentional. Student Y, on the other hand, declares openly 'Could I have an extension on my essay? I've been very busy recently and it's not finished yet.' This signal is communicative, and it is only this type of signal which is involved in language.

What are the characteristics of human languages which set them apart from animal communication systems? Linguists have identified five basic features (see Aitchison 1992: 25–30).

1 *learnability*: Human children are born with the ability to acquire language, though after the age of 10 this ability declines rapidly. More-over, they can learn any human language. A French child reared in a Chinese-speaking environment will grow up speaking perfect Chinese. Animals and birds, on the other hand, can acquire no language other than the one transmitted from their parents. Human beings can of course learn several human languages, and linguists often distinguish between 'first language acquisition' (what you did when you were a baby) and 'second language learning' (what people do at school or evening classes).

2 *cultural transmission*: the capacity to acquire language is innate in humans, that is, it is part of our genetic make-up. However, the actual language we acquire depends on the people who bring us up, that is, it is transmitted 'culturally'. The calls of birds and animals on the other hand are species-specific and are broadly the same the world over. They are transmitted genetically.

3 *displacement*: the messages communicated by animals and birds relate only to the immediate needs of and environment inhabited by the creature in question. Human languages can refer to entities totally dis-placed from the immediate situation. They can refer to other places, other times and, indeed, to abstract concepts which have no physical existence anywhere at all.

4 *arbitrariness*: some signs in language are directly linked to or 'motivated by' the things they stand for, e.g. *coucou, cocorico, chuchoter*. These are onomatopeic words which stand in *iconic* relationship with what they refer to, i.e. they reproduce in their sound the sounds they stand for. However, onomatopeic words are the exception rather than the rule in human languages. Most words are conventional and arbitrary, that is to say that there is no natural connection between the sounds of a word and

the thing it stands for. This quality of arbitrariness endows human languages with great flexibility, but it also leads to the great diversity which exists between the languages of the world.

5 *creativity, productivity*: man has been described as 'the articulate mammal'. Animals and birds have their communication systems, but the number of messages they can transmit is extremely limited. Normally each call carries its own message (e.g. fear, anger, desire to mate, etc.), but it cannot be broken down into smaller components which can be re-used in different combinations to produce new individualised messages. It is true that much human language is formulaic and ritualistic. 'How do you do?' looks like a question, but people would look oddly at you if you replied with a description of your state of health. That said, most language can be analysed into smaller components which can in turn be re-used in new permutations to produce, to create an unlimited number of messages never transmitted before. The French linguist André Martinet (1970: 13–15) drew attention to what he calls *la double articulation du langage* whereby each human language selects a limited number of basic sounds ('phonemes' – French has 34 of them). These have no meaning in themselves and represent the 'first articulation'. At a second stage these basic sound units are strung together ('articulated' as in 'articulated lorry') in diverse combinations (words, phrases, clauses and sentences) to generate an unlimited number of messages.

1.2.2   *The priority of speech*

We shall be looking in some detail at the differences between speech and writing in the next chapter. Here we will simply point out that, unlike lay-persons, linguists give no special priority to the written language. Indeed, for a variety of reasons they have to give priority to speech:

- 75 per cent of the world's languages have no written form;
- historically, writing developed many thousands of years after the development of speech;
- children learn to speak before they can write and many never learn to write at all;
- much more speech 'happens' than writing;
- writing is ultimately derived from speech and not the other way round.

1.2.3   *The branches of linguistics*

In order to analyse such a complex thing as human language linguists need to be not only as objective as possible, but also as rigorous and methodical as they can. This means, among other things, that the terminology they employ has to be clear and unambiguous. The technical terms they use can be off-putting, but this is no cause for alarm. A glossary of linguistic terms is to be found at the back of this book, and there exist excellent tools like the *Dictionary of Linguistics and Phonetics* which can be of great assistance (see Crystal 1991).

Language can be looked at from two very different perspectives – as *system* and as *behaviour*. The first is concerned with the internal structuring of a language, the second with the psychological and social behaviour of human beings when they make use of language.

LANGUAGE AS SYSTEM

We have just seen how human languages contrive to generate an unlimited number of utterances on the basis of a strictly limited number of basic sounds (Standard French has 34 phonemes, Standard English has 44). They succeed in this because they are profoundly systematic, structured and patterned. Linguists generally distinguish three levels of patterning:

I	sound patterns	>	phonetics phonology
II	word patterns	>	lexicology morphology syntax
III	meaning patterns	>	semantics

Let us look briefly at each of these in turn.

I   Sound patterns

Phonetics and phonology are both concerned with the sounds of a language, but in significantly different ways. *Phonetics* looks to provide a scientific description of the raw sounds used in speech. Various instruments are available to enable us to analyse speech sounds very precisely, e.g. labiograms, palatograms, etc. The former, for instance, plots the shape of the lips during speech and the latter allows us to produce accurate pictures of tongue contact with the roof of the mouth. At an early stage in the development of phonetics as a science it was realised that the traditional way of representing speech in writing (spelling) was inadequate for scientific purposes. Sometimes the same sound receives different spellings (e.g. *vers, vert, verre*); sometimes the same spelling represents different sounds (e.g. *cough, through, thought, plough*). As a result, phoneticians have designed special systems which provide a one-to-one equivalence of sound and letter. The most widely used phonetic system is the International Phonetic Alphabet (IPA) and you can find it being used to set out the speech sounds of French at the beginning of most French dictionaries.

Phonology looks at the sounds of language in a more abstract way. Phoneticians are able to detect very subtle distinctions between the various speech sounds used in natural language. Did you know, for instance, that the [p] in *pin* is not quite the same as the [p] in *spin*? The first [p] is slightly aspirated, i.e breathed, whereas the latter is not. Such distinctions are of great importance to phoneticians, but matter less to phonologists. Phonologists are interested only in those distinctions of sound which are used by a particular language to differentiate meaning.

II Word patterns

Lexicology is the branch of linguistics devoted to the study of words: what are the words which exist in a particular language? Where do they come from? How are they formed? An important part of lexicology is *lexicography* (the science of compiling dictionaries). No dictionary is a simple list of words. Dictionaries are human creations reflecting the preoccupations and prejudices of the people who compile them. No two dictionaries are the same. They all differ in the way they select, classify and explain the words they contain. It is, therefore, unhelpful to say 'I found this word in the dictionary.' We need to know which dictionary.

Morphology is concerned with the way words are built up from smaller elements known as 'morphemes'. There are two types of morphology: *derivational morphology* and *inflectional morphology*. The former is a branch of lexicology and is concerned to find out how different words are made up in a particular language out of the morphemes available. Words are composed of roots and affixes (prefixes and suffixes), e.g. *anti/ ségrégationn/ iste*. Inflectional morphology is related to syntax and is concerned with the way one and the same word varies its form according to the syntactic function it is performing. Thus the verb *venir* changes shape according to person, tense and mood. For example,

(1)
> *je viens*
> *tu viens*
> *il vient*
> *nous venons*
> *vous venez*
> *ils viennent*

The word *syntax* is derived from two Greek words meaning 'together joining'. This branch of linguistics is concerned with the rules for combining words into higher units (phrases, clauses and sentences) in a particular language. It is about the structure of sentences. A question you might ask is where does *grammar* fit into all this. The grammar of a language is the set of linguistic rules which speakers know intuitively and which they activate when they use their language. For some linguists the rules of grammar cover everything (pronunciation, syntax and vocabulary), but for most, grammar involves essentially morphology and syntax.

III Meaning patterns

The 'deepest' of the three levels of structure in language is that of meaning. There are many facets to the concept of 'meaning': we can talk of the meaning of individual words (lexical meaning), the meaning added when words are put into sentences (grammatical meaning) and the meaning acquired by utterances when they are used in particular social contexts (social meaning).

The branch of linguistics concerned centrally with meaning is *semantics*. Semanticists are concerned with different types of meaning (word meaning versus sentence meaning, conceptual versus associative meaning, linguistic versus contextual meaning). They confront issues such as the role of language in the way we formulate ideas – is it possible to think without words? If it is, how do words help us clarify our thoughts? Do all languages analyse the world in the same way? If they don't, how much of our world-view stems from the language we speak?

LANGUAGE AS BEHAVIOUR

A second way of looking at language is to see it not as an internal system but as a form of human behaviour. Linguistic behaviour can be observed at the level of the minds of individual speakers and at the level of human groups, even whole societies.

I Psycholinguistics

This is the branch of linguistics concerned with what happens in an individual's brain when he or she speaks. There are two directions of study here: (1) What is the role of language in our normal thought processes? Is there part of the brain which is reserved for the 'faculty' of language? (2) What are the mental processes underlying the planning, production, perception and comprehension of speech? How do we acquire language as infants? What happens when we attempt to learn a second or third language? For an introduction to this subject see Aitchison (1992).

II Sociolinguistics

This branch of linguistics looks at linguistic behaviour not in terms of an individual's psychological mechanisms but in terms of the social groups to which he/she belongs. What are the ways in which language affects society and how does society affect language? In what ways does a language vary according to who is using it? – different groups of speakers (different social classes, different sex- and age-groups, different ethnic groups) produce their own varieties of a language (inter-speaker variation). In what ways does a language vary according to what it is being used for? – individual speakers will vary their use of the language according to the situation in which they find themselves (intra-speaker variation). Closely linked with sociolinguistics is *dialectology* which examines in particular the way a language varies across geographical space. For an introduction to this subject see Trudgill (1995).

III Pragmatics

This branch of linguistics brings together the two aspects of language, system and behaviour. It investigates the relationship between language and context, laying bare 'the nature of the assumptions participants [in a conversation] are making, and the purposes for which utterances are being made' (Levinson 1983: 53). If the linguist is to uncover the rules which govern a person's speech, they must work out their grammatical competence (i.e. their internalised knowledge of the linguistic system). However, the linguist must also uncover the rules which govern the speaker's ability to function in society and apply language to real-life situations (communicative competence and linguistic behaviour). 'The goal of a broad theory of (language) competence can be said to be to show the ways in which the systemically possible, the feasible and the appropriate produce actually occurring cultural behaviour' (Hymes 1971: 286). How do we utilise the linguistic system in our everyday social behaviour? How do we make what we say appropriate to the situational context in which we are saying it and to the people we are addressing? What functions do we ask language to perform in our daily lives and what linguistic mechanisms do we activate to enable us to perform them?

Some linguists include within the general area of 'pragmatics' the two related activities of *discourse analysis* (what regularities can be discovered in chunks of text larger than individual sentences?) and *conversation analysis* (how do conversations work?). It is within this area too that we can locate the study of *stylistics*: the investigation of the configuration of linguistic features which characterise particular written texts (often literary, but not necessarily).

HISTORICAL LINGUISTICS

An essential feature of human languages is that they are constantly changing. A language which has ceased to change is a dead language, a language with no speakers. All aspects of a language we have sketched in above can then be looked at from two points of view: from the point of view of the language as it functions at a given point in time, and from that of the language as it changes over the course of time. The former approach is referred to as 'synchronic' and the latter as 'diachronic'. Explaining how and why a language changes is one of the central goals of linguistics. For an introduction to this subject see Aitchison (1981).

Seminar exercises

1.   Assemble as many other clichés about language as you can and attempt to see what hidden subjective attitudes lie behind them.

2.   To what extent can linguistics be regarded as a 'science'?

3.   Explain what the term *arbitrariness* means as it is used to describe a property of human language.

2

Varieties of French

In countries like Britain and France with long traditions of literacy, the population is very strongly aware of the existence of the standard language. A standard language is a set of rules or norms prescribing what is and what is not correct in all aspects of language (pronunciation, spelling, grammar and vocabulary). The standard forms of English and French are what are taught to foreign learners, in the initial stages at least. They took many centuries to be developed and codified, and are based historically on the usage of the most powerful people in society (in English we still talk about 'the Queen's English') and upon the written form of the language (we are often enjoined to speak as we write since writing is widely felt to be 'more correct'). In France the 'ideology of the standard' (the belief that everyone should use the language in the same prescribed way) is particularly strong, no doubt in view of the role of the French language in definitions of French national identity, see Lodge (1993: 2–3).

Defenders of the French standard language, guardians of usage like school-teachers of French, the *Académie française*, operate on the assumption that the ideal state for a language is one of uniformity and that everyone should speak (and write) in the same way. They appear to believe there is only one acceptable form of the language and that deviations from that norm should be suppressed. They usually maintain that the standard form of the language is inherently better (i.e. clearer, more logical, more beautiful) than other varieties and should, therefore, always be adhered to. Sometimes such people are referred to as 'purists', i.e. people who want to keep linguistic usage free of contamination from new forms (neologism), low-status forms (e.g. slang) and foreign elements (e.g. anglicisms).

It is of course essential in modern societies that there exists a standard language, for reasons of communicative efficiency. However, it is illusory to believe that linguistic norms are anything but artificial constructs, that the standard variety is linguistically 'better' than non-standard varieties, and that complete linguistic uniformity can ever be brought about. Living languages are by definition languages which people are using all the time and which they are constantly modifying to suit their changing needs and circumstances. Living languages are characterised by inherent variability, that is to say that language variation is not something exceptional and untoward, but is fundamental and permanent. A fixed, invariant language would be simply incapable of meeting the diverse needs of its users. In this chapter, therefore, we will look very rapidly at some of the ways in which the French language varies.

In order to structure our discussion, we will make a basic distinction: between *inter-speaker variation* (variation between speakers, i.e. according to user) and *intra-speaker variation* (variation within the same speaker, i.e. according to use). The first of these categories concerns the way French varies according to the social characteristics of its different users, and goes under the general heading of *social dialect*. It covers language varieties which correlate with different categories of speaker (e.g. regional and class dialects, differences between ethnic groups, between the speech of males and females, and between young and old). The second concerns the way French varies according to the different uses to which one and the same speaker may wish to put it (intra-speaker variation). It is referred to as *register* (or 'stylistic') variation and covers language varieties which correlate with different situations of language use (e.g. speech versus writing, formal situations versus informal situations, etc.). For purposes of exposition we will treat them separately, but throughout the discussion we need to bear in mind that the two axes of variation operate conjointly and not independently (see Labov 1972: 192).

2.1 Inter-speaker variation (social dialects)

Let us look first of all at different varieties of French which can be correlated with such factors as geography, social class and ethnicity. To these we will then add the basic speaker-characteristics of age and sex, for both of these materially affect the way people speak. Ultimately, every individual speaker has his/her own personal variety of the language, depending on his/her social origins, age, sex, etc. The linguistic system of an individual speaker is referred to as his/her *idiolect*.

2.1.1 Geography

French is spoken not only in France, but also in other countries in Europe (notably Belgium and Switzerland), in Francophone Africa, in the Caribbean and in Canada. The non-European areas in particular have developed their own strikingly divergent varieties of the language which are of considerable interest to linguists (see Fig. 2.1).

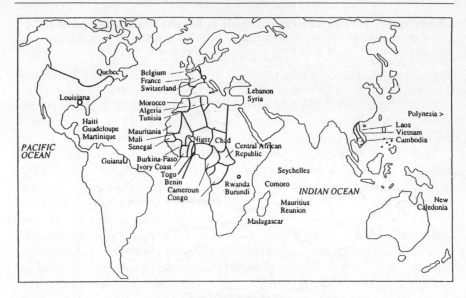

Fig. 2.1 The French-speaking world
Source: Ager 1990

Limitation of space prevents us from examining these non-European varieties here in the detail they require. We will simply refer the reader to the relevant chapters in Sanders (1993), where sound analyses and valuable indications of further reading are to be found. In this chapter we will restrict ourselves to examination of metropolitan varieties.

After many centuries of political and economic centralisation based on Paris, France still presents a linguistic map which is far from uniform. On the peripheries of the country, languages which, in terms of language families, are very remote from French can still be heard: Flemish, Alsatian, Basque and Breton. To these can be added two languages which like French are of Romance origin (i.e. developed out of the speech of the Romans), but which are not normally intelligible to speakers of French: Corsican and Catalan. All of these are referred to as *les langues régionales*.

In the main part of the country, in rural areas, you can still occasionally find old country-folk who speak dialects largely unintelligible to speakers of Parisian French, which are referred to, often pejoratively, as *patois*. Here, as an example, is a short passage written in a spelling system devised to represent the speech of one of the *patois* of Picardy:

> Deux grands ferlapeux d'gouttes, Baloufe épi José, is étaient allés insanne à l'mon d'un marchand d'eue-de-vie en grous, pour en acater un tchout baril, à meilleure compte, de l'pus forte – chelle-lo qui vous gratte l'gasiou comme si qu'os avaloit du vitriol – et aussi dins l'idée d'n'en r'céder, *avu bénéfice*, à cheuss' d'leus amis qui n'en voudraint.

[Deux grands buveurs de gouttes, Baloufe et Joseph, étaient allés ensemble chez un marchand d'eau de vie en gros, pour en acheter un petit baril, à meilleur marché, de la plus forte – celle qui vous gratte le gosier comme si vous avalez du vitriol – et aussi dans l'idée d'en revendre *avec bénéfice*, à ceux de leurs amis qui en voudraient.]

Fig. 2.2 The linguistic map of France
Source: Offord 1990

It will be seen that this text differs from standard French not simply in terms of 'accent' or pronunciation, but also in terms of vocabulary and grammar.

The French *patois* survive most strongly in the south of the country where they are the last relics of the language sometimes called Provençal, but now more generally referred to as Occitan. Varieties of Occitan were familiar to almost everyone living south of a line running from Bordeaux to Geneva until the end of the nineteenth century. Sadly, despite valiant attempts to keep the old *patois* alive, the whole peasant way of life which sustained them has now been virtually destroyed and it will not be long before they have disappeared completely.

The influence of the *patois* and regional languages will live on, however, for as speakers shifted from the *patois* to the standard language (largely over the past century and a half), they brought over into their realisation of the standard language various reminiscences of their previous speech-habits. These have given rise to language varieties which are referred to as the various *français régionaux*. On this topic see Walter (1988: 155–78) and Hawkins (1993). Regional variation affects all levels of language. Here are some examples.

> Grammar: in the north of France you might hear people say *il faut qu'il vient* instead of *il faut qu'il vienne*.
> Vocabulary: in Belgium and Switzerland you are likely to hear *septante*, *octante* and *nonante* instead of *soixante-dix*, *quatre-vingts* and *quatre-vingt-dix*.
> Pronunciation: in the south of the country a phrase like *Je me le demande* is likely to be pronounced with all the *e*'s sounded and with the *a* articulated without nasalisation.

The result of all this is that French still varies substantially from one region to another, for any language with a reasonably large number of speakers will develop dialects, especially if there are geographical barriers separating groups of people from each other, or if there are divisions of social class. This brings us to a second factor in inter-speaker variation.

2.1.2   Social class variation

The definition of 'social class' is interesting and highly controversial, but we do not have the space here to elaborate on the issues involved. Under this heading we simply wish to discuss language variation which can be correlated with factors involved in social stratification (occupation, income level, education, residence, lifestyle, etc.). In Britain it has been commonly observed that the further down the social scale you go, the more you find that speech is marked by regional features: put crudely, this often means that the stronger your regional 'accent', the lower your social status (see Trudgill 1995: 29–30). In France, class-bound differences in language are evaluated on a slightly different basis: pronunciation variables are less strongly coded than in Britain, while more importance is attached to grammar and vocabulary.

Lower-class speech in France traditionally receives the label *français populaire*, but this term is fraught with problems (see Gadet 1992). The word *populaire* does not normally mean 'popular' in the sense of 'well liked'; it means rather 'pertaining to the people', and the 'people' (*le peuple*) in this context denotes 'the working classes', especially those resident in Paris. The prescriptive tradition in France attributes certain speech-forms to the working classes. For example, lexical items like *bagnole* = *voiture*, *fric* = *argent*, *mec* = *homme*, and grammatical forms like *La pièce qu'il est entré dedans* and *C'est-ti que tu viens?* However, this sort of exercise is highly problematic, for two reasons. First, it is difficult to arrive at an objective definition of who are the working classes: the term does not cover a homogeneous social group and the boundary between the working class and the lower middle class is entirely fluid. Second, many of the speech-forms traditionally ascribed to the working classes are frequently also found in the informal style of members of higher social groups. In this way it can be seen that variation along the social axis cannot be easily separated from variation along the axis of register (or 'style'), as we indicated earlier.

What seems to happen is that linguistic variants are conventionally allocated particular social values. Low-value items (e.g. slang) are attributed conventionally to the lower social groups, high-value items (e.g. literary language) to the higher. Low-value items are used in informal social contexts while high-value items are reserved for formal occasions. If there is a difference between the speech of low- and high-class speakers in France, it derives from their participating in different sorts of social activity: the lifestyle of the lower groups takes them chiefly into informal contacts with a tight network of familiar people, whereas that of the higher social groups takes them additionally into formal contacts with a looser network of semi-strangers. It has been claimed that lower-class people operate essentially with what is referred to as 'restricted code', whereas upper-class speakers have greater access to 'elaborated code' (see Bernstein 1971).

2.1.3   Language and ethnicity

Divisions in society come about as a consequence of geography and stratification into classes, but they can also come about through movement of populations, i.e. immigration. France is host to a very large immigrant population, some of which is of European origin (Poles, Italians, Spaniards and Portuguese), and some of which comes from Africa (North Africans and Black Africans). All immigrant groups have linguistic problems and problems of identity – do they belong to their country of origin or to their country of adoption? – and these difficulties are exacerbated by poverty and unemployment. The immigrant community currently faced with the most serious problems of integration are the North Africans, whose first language is or was in most cases Arabic. French hostility towards them has been endemic since the Algerian War of Independence (1954–62) and has not been reduced by the recent revival of Muslim fundamentalism.

The great wave of North African immigration came in the 1950s, but it is the offspring of the original migrants whose problems are now of particular concern, given the current situation of poverty and unemployment among young people in Europe. Whereas bilingualism in the first generation of immigrants was heavily weighted in favour of Arabic – their knowledge of French was in many cases rudimentary – with the second generation the situation is reversed. These young people, like all oppressed minorities, use language as an identity shield, but instead of opting for the language of their parents, they choose instead the most vernacular variety of French (cf. the development of Black Vernacular English in the USA and Britain). One of the most salient features of this vernacular is the use of *verlan* – the creation of new words by inverting the sounds/syllables of existing words. In this way *l'envers* → *verlan, femme* → *meuf, fête* → *teuf* and *Arabe* → *Beur*. This last word has in fact been adopted as the name for North African immigrants of the second generation.

2.1.4   Language and sex

Men and women do not speak in the same way. As well as the self-evident fact that women speak at a higher pitch than men, it has also been demonstrated that they speak slightly faster and that they produce a higher number of syllables between breaths (see Müller 1985: 177). However, these differences are probably biological in origin. What is of more interest to us here are cultural differences.

In conversational interaction, women are apparently more co-operative than men: they interrupt less, they use more hedging and politeness formulae. Perhaps the most widely attested feature differentiating the speech of males and females in advanced Western societies is the greater tendency among females to move their speech in the direction of high-prestige norms. Put simply, this means that females tend to speak more 'correctly' than males. This 'sociolinguistic gender pattern' (as Fasold 1990: 92 calls it) can be clearly seen in Figure 2.3 which is based on a survey where informants in Clermont-Ferrand were asked to report on their personal use of French slang vocabulary (see Lodge 1989). The horizontal axis represents the age of the informants, while the vertical axis indicates the average 'slang-score' (readiness to use slang terms with strangers).

Various reasons have been proposed to explain this tendency in females – masculine status in society is allegedly demonstrated by men's

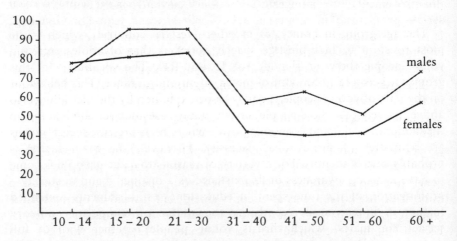

Fig. 2.3 Average 'slang scores' correlated with age and sex

professional occupation, whereas females, with less access to real power, have to fall back on appearances and self-presentation; females are allegedly more socially docile, whereas males are more ready to reject constraints and to behave in a rebellious and aggressive manner, particularly in all-male company. However, neither of these explanations is particularly satisfactory, partly because they generally assume that male speech-behaviour is normal and that it is female behaviour which is odd and requires explanation. It may be that the problem should be seen the other way round, concentrating efforts on explaining the 'deviant' behaviour of males, or, better still, seeing each sex as dependent on the other, seeking a sexual identity in speech patterns whose essential characteristic is to be different from those adopted by the opposite sex.

2.1.5   *Language and age*

It is quite clear that the speech of an individual changes as he/she moves through the various stages of life. This is referred to in sociolinguistic literature as 'age-grading'. During the first 10 years of life the child gradually acquires control of their first language in the form of the vernacular – the language of home and the child's immediate circle of intimates (the 'restricted code' we referred to earlier). As the child moves out into a wider range of social contacts – especially through school – they graft on to their vernacular a more formal 'elaborated code'. The extent of their control of 'elaborated code' will vary with the sorts of professional activity subsequently engaged in. The higher they move up the ladder of power and social status, the more their ability to manipulate the publicly legitimated varieties of language will matter to them. When they step off the economic ladder in retirement the importance of the formal code diminishes. This goes some way to explaining the age-related differences visible in the graph given above.

The age-group in France, as in other Western countries, which is the most resistant to high-prestige speech norms is that of adolescents and young people (between the ages of 13 and 21). The vocabulary of this group attracts a large amount of media attention in France. This behaviour on the part of young people is partly to be explained by the fact alluded to above, namely that these people have in many cases not yet climbed far up the ladder of social and economic power where high-prestige speech norms are a matter of professional necessity. However, the main factor is probably one of identity. For a variety of reasons this age-group has come to have a strong awareness of its existence as a distinct group in society – prolongation of the time spent in educational establishments (extended further in France until recently by the system of compulsory military service for males) which thrusts young people together without full exposure to the rigours of adult professional life; or the 'cult of youth' by commercial interests keen to exploit the spending-power of young people without family responsibilities.

It is traditionally assumed that the prime function of language is the communication of 'ideas'. While no-one could dispute that this is one of its basic functions, it is by no means the only one. What has emerged in this section is the importance of a second function of language: the creation and expression of personal and group identity. A uniform variation-free language may be the ideal form for the communication of ideas, but it becomes something of a liability when speakers seek to use it for the expression of who they are in terms of their social, ethnic, sexual and age-group affiliation. The social variation in French we have looked at here demonstrates the elasticity of natural language.

2.2   Intra-speaker variation (register)

In this section we offer a very general overview of the way French varies not according to the social characteristics of its different users (inter-speaker variation), but according to the different uses to which one and the same speaker may wish to put it (intra-speaker variation). Each speaker of French has a range of language varieties at his/her disposal (their 'verbal repertoire') which they draw upon according to the situational context, their communicative purpose, their relationship with the other participant(s), etc. It must be borne in mind here that the range of factors which come into play is large and that they operate conjointly rather than independently. They also vary, of course, with the social factors we looked at in section 1. We will use the terminology developed by the British linguist M. A. K. Halliday (1964) who distinguishes between '*mode of discourse*' and '*manner of discourse*'.

2.2.1   Mode of discourse

This term designates the medium or channel of communication – speech or writing. It is a truism to assert that speaking and writing are very different linguistic activities. For many centuries it was believed in Europe that the written language represented the real language while speech was an imperfect attempt to replicate it orally. Linguists in our century have ceased to be interested in demonstrating the superiority of one form over the other. They are more interested in exploring and describing how each operates in its own domain. Table 2.1 summarises some of the essential differences between speech and writing.

In speech the interlocutors negotiate meaning with each other with reference to their shared physical location and situational context, enabling them to make significant use of paralinguistic features like gestures and

Table 2.1 Fundamental differences between speech and writing

	Speech	Writing
Medium	sound phonemes intonation	sight letters punctuation
Space	speakers together use of body language shared context	speakers apart message must be explicit no shared context

Time	transmission and receipt
	   simultaneous
	spontaneity (false starts,
	   hesitations, incomplete
	   sentences)
		time-lapse between
		   transmission and receipt
		planned discourse (complete
		   sentences, complex structures)

facial expression. In writing both of these extra-linguistic factors are absent, so communication relies exclusively on explicit, visual linguistic mechanisms.

SPEAKING AND WRITING IN FRENCH

The French writing system is an old one, and it started to become fixed into something like its present form as early as the fourteenth century. No such fixation has taken place in the French spoken language, however, and the result has been an ever-growing gap between French spelling and pronunciation. Consider, for instance, the word: *beau*. It is likely that 600 years ago the word was pronounced: [beaw] and that in its written form each of the letters represented a distinct sound. Since then, sound-changes have modified the pronunciation of this word to [bo], and the close sound–letter relationship present in the medieval spelling has been lost. Many French speakers are dismayed at the lack of congruence between modern pronunciation and the writing system, and this has led to strong and highly controversial calls for spelling reform (see Catach in Sanders 1993).

However, the issues run deeper than the surface issue of spelling, and involve fairly fundamental differences between the grammar of speech and the grammar of writing. Traditionally, it is the grammar of the written language which is taught in schools, but its rules are often unhelpful for learners attempting to master the French spoken language. For instance, it is normally explained that to make a noun or adjective plural, an *s* is added to the singular, and that for verbs one adds the ending -*ent*. In the following example '+' indicates the plural-marker:

(1)   *Les enfants mangent des poires*
        +   +   +   +   +

We can see here that the plural is marked on each of the words in the sentence. The written language is in fact characterised by the presence of a high level of 'redundancy'. If now we pronounce this same sentence out loud, we will hear that the word-endings play no part at all in indicating plurality, and that this job is carried out solely by the articles *les* and *des*.

A similar problem arises in connection with the marking of gender on French adjectives. In order to distinguish masculine from feminine, traditional grammar takes the masculine form as the base and calls for the addition of an *e* to give the feminine form. Thus *grand* → *grande*, *petit* → *petite*, *gros* → *grosse*. If, however, we want to explain how the spoken language works, we will soon discover that this rule is quite unhelpful. If we pronounce these pairs out loud, we will hear that the written *e* has no corresponding sound in the spoken word, and that what marks the difference between masculine and feminine in speech is the presence or absence of the final consonant. Indeed, from the point of view of the spoken language, the simplest way of formulating the rule for gender-marking on French adjectives would be to take the feminine form as the base (rather than the masculine) and delete the final consonant to form the masculine.

The differences between speech and writing do not arise solely from the medium used (sight versus sound), but also from the very different circumstances in which communication takes place in each of the 'modes'. In spoken discourse the participants are normally together in both time and space, whereas in writing they are apart. Modern inventions like telephones and television blur this distinction, but the principle remains valid for the vast majority of acts of communication.

Most spoken language is produced in everyday conversations where speakers respond spontaneously to the words of the other participants. They do not have the time to produce carefully planned utterances. To illustrate this, identify the linguistic features in the following extract which indicate that this is a transcript of naturally occurring speech rather than a sample of normal written language:

- Et ce qui se passe c'est que / il y a eu une réforme gouvernementale / c'est-à-dire que après le / le / les élections 1981 et le changement de pouvoir politique / il y a les socialistes ont décidé de / de carrément briser / euh l'école publ l'école euh / privée / en mettant des bâtons dans les roues de de ces /

- il dit n'importe quoi /

- tu permets que je termine /

- mais attends

- c'est-à-dire que ils veulent / ce qu'ils veulent faire / c'est faire passer l'école privée au même titre que l'école libre / c'est-à-dire que les gens / qui euh gèrent les écoles / par exemple les les des oblats / des des prêtres / n'aient plus la possibilité / d'orienter / euh / le le le type d'étude et de formation qui est donné en accord évidemment avec euh / les programmes les programmes de l'éducation nationale / comme ils l'entendent / et donc euh

/ en fait euh il va y avoir une indifférenciation / entre ce type d'école /
l'école privée et l'école et l'école euh / et l'école publique / c'est tout //

(taken from Hartley 1987)

One of the most striking features of this text is its apparent lack of planning: in everyday conversation speakers quite normally produce a large amount of repetition, hesitation, false starts, and so on. There is nothing incompetent or reprehensible in producing spontaneous speech with these characteristics: in everyday conversation meanings are negotiated between the participants through co-operative interaction. This contrasts starkly with the characteristics of written language: because the writer has time and does not have to respond instantly to what his/her interlocutor has just said, the writer can plan what he/she is writing, editing out hesitations and so on and organising the text in the most effective way.

The fact that participants in conversations are together in space as well as in time means that they are automatically able to use more than words and sentences to get their message across. They make use of subtle nuances of intonation and stress. They exploit a range of devices available in body language (kinesic features) – smiles, frowns, gestures, etc. They can point to particular features of the environment without having to refer to them explicitly. All of these elements are denied to the writer who has, in consequence, to rely solely on words and sentences. The writer has to be entirely explicit in what is put down on paper. Since writer and recipient do not share the same situational context, the writer has to create a context in the written message which will enable the reader to understand. All of us have had experiences of how difficult it is to avoid misunderstandings in the messages we send by writing.

Before closing this section it might be worth reminding the reader that we have purposely chosen to contrast typical acts of speech with typical acts of written communication. There exists of course a number of intermediary forms like reading aloud and speaking from notes, where writing-like speech is produced, and where this contrast is blurred, not to mention the great transformations coming about as a result of on-line communication.

2.2.2   *Manner of discourse*

A major factor influencing the language variety a speaker adopts, outside the basic speech–writing opposition, is the nature of the relationships holding between the various participants. They may all be members of the same in-group, or alternatively, communication may be taking place with a stranger (with all the degrees of acquaintance which lie in between). The participants may all be equal in power, or alternatively, one or more of them may have power over the others. The act of communication may be taking place in public, or alternatively it may be happening in private. All of these factors are likely to affect the level of formality of the language variety used.

The term commonly used by linguists to refer to the varying levels of formality is *style*.

In French the distance between formal and informal style can often be very great, as illustrated by the following realisations of the same speech act – an invitation to drinks (taken from Farrington 1980):

(a) **Formal**
- Allô.
- 73 35 93 61?
- Oui.
- Excusez-moi de vous déranger. Je voudrais parler à M. Legrand, s'il vous plaît.
- C'est moi-même.
- Ah, bonjour monsieur. C'est Françoise Rousseau à l'appareil.
- Bonjour Mademoiselle. Comment allez-vous?
- Très bien, merci. Et vous même?
- Très bien. Et avez-vous eu des nouvelles de vos parents dernièrement?
- Oui, je viens justement de recevoir une lettre où ils m'annoncent leur visite pour dans quelques jours.
- Quelle bonne nouvelle! J'espère bien avoir le plaisir de les voir.
- Eh bien, je vous téléphonais justement pour vous demander si vous et Mme Legrand pourriez venir prendre l'apéritif chez moi vendredi prochain.
- C'est une excellente idée.
- C'est à l'occasion de la visite de mes parents. J'ai organisé une petite réunion d'amis et cela me ferait plaisir si vous pouviez être des nôtres.
- C'est très aimable à vous mademoiselle, et nous serons ravis de vous voir.
- Alors, c'est entendu. Nous vous attendons vendredi vers 7h.
- C'est cela. Au revoir, mademoiselle, et merci pour votre invitation.
- Je vous en prie. Au revoir, Monsieur.

(b) **Informal**
- Allô.
- le 73 92 29 85?
- Oui.
- C'est toi, Dominique? Ici, Claude.
- Tiens, bonjour Claude. Comment ça va?
- Bien, et toi?
- Ah, ça va. Alors quoi de neuf? Et ces vacances?
- Très bien passées. Il faudrait que je te raconte ça.
- Ah oui, dis donc. On pourrait se voir un de ces jours?
- J'ai justement des copains qui viennent à la maison prendre un pot jeudi soir. Tu peux venir?
- Attends.
  Jeudi soir tu dis? Oui, j'ai rien de spécial.
- Tu verras. J'ai rapporté de Londres des disques tout nouveaux.
- Formidable! Et puis ça sera bien de retrouver toute la bande.
- Alors à jeudi vers les 9h.
- D'accord. A jeudi. Au revoir.
- Salut, Dominique.

In French shifting style from informal to formal usually involves changes in pronunciation. For instance, in formal style speakers are more likely to produce more liaisons like *Je vais»aller»en Suisse*, they are less likely to simplify consonant clusters like *problème* > *pro'lème* or delete 'mute e' in phrases like *Je ne le sais pas* > *Ché pas*. It also involves modifications to syntax. For instance, negation is almost invariably expressed in informal style not with *ne ... pas*, but with *pas* alone, e.g. *Je viens pas demain*. Inversion of the normal Subject – Verb order, which is quite common in formal style, is virtually absent from informal style, even in questions. Thus:

(2) *Où vas-tu?* > *Où tu vas?*
     Où est-ce que tu vas? > *Où c'est que tu vas?*

A whole set of tenses (the past historic, the past anterior and the imperfect subjunctive) are available for use in formal style (usually in writing), but would be highly unusual in informal contexts. French, like many other European languages, distinguishes *tu* and *vous* forms in the verbal system to signal degrees of solidarity.

It is in vocabulary choices, however, that the differences between formal and informal style in French are most clearly and consciously signalled. French possesses hundreds of paired items for commonly referred to objects, one for use in informal contexts, the other in formal situations:

bagnole – voiture	fric – argent
bahut – lycée	frousse – peur
boulot – travail	godasse – chaussure
bouquin – livre	mec – homme
bringue – fête	môme – enfant
con – bête	pépin – ennui
démerder (se) – se débrouiller	piaule – chambre
dingue – fou	saoul – ivre
emmerder – embêter	sèche – cigarette
flic – agent de police	taule – prison

In many instances speakers are not faced with a simple binary choice, but with a range of near synonyms spread out along a scale of formality. French dictionaries conventionally use the following labels to indicate the stylistic level:

(3) *vulgaire* > *argotique* > *populaire* > *familier* > *courant* > *cultivé*.

Other labels are also used, as can be seen in Table 2.2.

This example illustrates an important characteristic about style-shifting in French vocabulary: the various stylistic levels shade into one another to form a continuum without a sharp natural break. The notion of continuum is an important one when we attempt to describe natural language. Here we have an example of a stylistic continuum. Similarly, we can observe geographical continua in language as one dialect shades imperceptibly into the next. We can observe social continua as we move up the social scale from Lower Working Class > Upper Working Class > Lower Middle Class > Upper Middle Class.

Table 2.2 A chacun son français

Précieux (snob, poétique, désuet)	Soutenu (littéraire)	Courant (commercial), public, administratif	Familier (privé, populaire)	Argotique (snob, jeune, vulgaire)
Le chef	La tête	La figure	La bobine, la bouille, la binette, la caboche, la bille	La gueule, la tronche, la trombine, la margoulette
Un mortel	Un homme	Un individu	Un type, un gars, un pékin, un zèbre	Un mec, un gonze, un zig, un gazier
Cocasse	Amusant	Drôle	Rigolo, tordant, gondolant, fendant	marrant, bidonnant, poilant, à 's'tap'
Le véhicule	L'automobile	La voiture	L'auto, la bagnole	La tire, la caisse
Il chuta	Il tomba	Il est tombé	Il s'est cassé la figure, il a pris un billet de parterre	Il s'est cassé la gueule, il a ramassé une gamelle
Qu'il manque d'intelligence!	Qu'il est sot!	Qu'il est bête!	Quel idiot! Quel crétin!	Quelle andouille! Quel couillon! Quel cul! Quel con!
Il est béni des dieux	Il est né sous une bonne étoile	Il a de la chance	Il a de la veine, il a du pot	Il a du bol, du cul, il est beurré, il l'a bordé de nouilles
Il fait preuve de pusillanimité	Il est rempli de crainte	Il a peur	Il a la frousse, il se dégonfle, il panique	Il a la trouille, les chocottes, les jetons, les grelots, le trouillomètre à zéro
Tu m'agaces	Tu me fatigues	Tu m'ennuies	Tu m'embêtes, tu me fais suer, tu m'enquiquines	Fais chier, tu me les casses, tu m'emmerdes
Suffit!	Assez!	Par-dessus la tête!	Plein le dos!	Ras-le-bol! Plein le cul! Y en a marre!

Source: Merrien (1985)

In some speech communities, however, style-shifting involves a much more abrupt change than we can observe in French. In Arabic-speaking countries, in Greece, in Paraguay, in German-speaking Switzerland, there are current throughout society two distinct language varieties, distributed not socially but functionally. People need to know two languages if they are to participate in the full range of activities taking place in their society. This situation is referred to as one of diglossia (see Fasold 1984: 34–60).

Table 2.3 Specialisation of functions of H and L in diglossia

	High	Low
Sermon in church or mosque	•	
Instruction to servants, waiters, workmen, clerks		•
Personal letter		•
Speech in parliament, political speech	•	
University lecture	•	
Conversation with family, friends, colleagues		•
News broadcast	•	
Radio soap opera		•
Newspaper editorial, news story, caption on picture	•	
Caption on political cartoon		•
Poetry	•	
Folk literature		•

In diglossic communities a H(igh) language variety is used for 'important', dignified functions like public administration, the law, education, religion, formal writing, etc., and a L(ow) variety is used in everyday conversation, shopping, personal correspondence, 'folk' literature, etc., see Table 2.3. It would not be accurate to describe France as a diglossic society: despite the fact that there has developed a very marked difference between the formal, codified variety and the informal colloquial forms of the language, the space between them is occupied by a stylistic continuum, i.e. there exist linguistic items which, stylistically speaking stand midway between the H and the L forms of the language. However, the sociolinguistic situation in French is probably more diglossia-like than in other European languages where the guardians of usage have had less success in arresting the development of the H variety, thereby allowing it to evolve and keep pace with the ever-changing L variety.

Conclusion

In this chapter we have seen how the French language, as it is used by its 70 million European speakers, is far from being a simple, homogeneous entity, but is instead an accumulation of many forms varying according to the diverse social characteristics of its speakers and according to the infinite array of different situations in which they need to use it. There exists a standardised form of the language which for historical and institutional reasons exerts a powerful influence on speakers. This standard language is best seen as an abstract set of norms rather than a real variety, and is found in its most invariant form in the written language. In speech its norms exert varying amounts of pressure according to the social and situational factors we have looked at in this chapter. It is important for foreign learners to be able to handle this standardised form, but the closer they wish to approach native-speaker competence, the more they need to be able to handle (if only receptively) a range of non-standard varieties too.

There comes a point, however, when the linguist has to ask where, in all this variability, is the French language. The French language is one sense the sum of the idiolects and dialects of its speakers, but what is it that allows us to say of all these variant forms that they are nevertheless French, rather than Spanish or Latin or English? The Swiss linguist Ferdinand de Saussure, working at the beginning of the twentieth century, distinguished between language as expressed by individual speakers in concrete utterances on specific occasions (which he called *parole*), and language as the underlying system stored in the minds of all members of the speech community, which they activate in their own individual way every time they speak (which he called *langue*). More recently an American linguist Noam Chomsky has made a similar though not identical distinction between *performance* and *competence* – the former stands for the linguistic output produced by an individual speaker in particular utterances, while the latter designates the set of rules stored in their mind which enable them to generate an infinity of such utterances.

Linguists working in the tradition of Saussure and Chomsky give priority not to exploring the variability of language through concentration on acts of *parole* and 'performance' – which they regard as external and superficial – but to finding out about the abstract and invariant systems of *langue* and 'competence' which lie behind them. Access to *langue* can only be had through analysis of acts of *parole*, but for these linguists it is *langue* which takes priority. Not all speakers of a language participate in the rules of *langue* to the same degree (they do not all possess exactly the same rules of competence), but there is sufficient overlap to permit them to understand what other speakers of the language are saying (see Durand 1993). It is at this point that we discover that we eventually have to shift focus from the 'externals' of language in order to examine the 'internals' – words, sounds and sentences. This is what we will be doing in the next six chapters.

Seminar exercises

1.   Elicit from native-speakers of French with whom you come into contact those linguistic features they regard as give-aways (a) for particular regional accents in French, and (b) uneducated usage.

2.   Collect as many examples as you can of *verlan*, and attempt to formulate the rules which French speakers use in order to generate these forms.

3.   What linguistic features visible in the transcription given on p. 24 indicate that we are dealing here with natural rather than with scripted language? Is this speaker speaking 'badly' in your view?

4.   Compare the transcripts of the two telephone conversations given on p. 26 and describe the linguistic features which show the difference between formal and informal style in French.

3

Word formation and etymology

For the lay-person, 'words' are the linguistic units which they recognise intuitively and which seem to them to be the most closely synonymous with 'language'. Learners of any foreign language realise quite early on that the part of it they need to control the most effectively is its vocabulary. If their mastery of the pronunciation and grammar of the target-language is quite sound, they will not get very far, communicatively speaking, without knowing a reasonable number of words. Linguists, on the other hand, have a rather perverse tendency to locate lexicology outside the central core of their discipline, probably because the thousands of words in a language cannot be embraced by 'rules' in the same way as its phonological or grammatical systems. However, in this book, which is designed to take the reader from the situation of the layman to that of the linguist, we will begin with vocabulary before looking at the other levels of language structure.

The branch of linguistics concerned with the study of the vocabulary (or the lexicon) is *lexicology*. It has a related discipline known as *lexicography* (the 'science' of dictionary writing). Lexicology is concerned with language-analysis not at the level of sounds (phonetics and phonology), nor at the level of phrases, clauses and sentences (grammar and syntax), but at a level situated in between, that of 'words'. We suggested above that 'rules' in lexicology do not enjoy the same status within linguistics as phonology and syntax, and this must have something to do with the sheer size of the lexicon. Whereas we can easily put a figure on the number of phonemes in Standard French (34), no-one can say how many words there are in the language. The phonemes of the language constitute a 'closed set', while the lexicon is an 'open set', that is to say the inventory of words in a living language can never be exhaustive, for the list is constantly changing as new words come in and old words drop out.

You might think that an exhaustive list is contained in 'the dictionary', but such a statement is in fact meaningless since, if you compare dictionaries of contemporary French with one another (e.g. *Petit Larousse*,

Le Petit Robert, Lexis), you will see that they all list differing numbers of items and that none of them is definitive. The *Grand Larousse* dictionary, for instance, lists several hundred thousand items in French, but there is no reason to believe that even this inventory is complete. No two dictionaries take an identical approach to the lexicon and no two contain the same inventory of items. It is for this reason that there has grown up, as a sub-branch of lexicology, the science (or is it an art?) of lexicography (see Matoré 1968). Dictionaries are human creations and need to be used critically and not naively or passively. If you need convincing on this point, see Yaguello (1978) for a revelation of the sexist bias present in most of the current dictionaries of French.

Words are two-sided entities: they have a form (a shape, a sound) and a content (a meaning). In this chapter we will look in particular at the form of words in French (word formation) and where they come from (etymology). In the following chapter we will look at word meaning (lexical semantics).

3.1   The 'word' and word formation

One of the difficulties facing anyone listening to an unfamiliar language is recognising where the word divisions come in what speakers of that language are saying. For the linguist this difficulty reflects a theoretical problem: how do we decide what constitutes a 'word' in a particular language? This might seem a pedantic question, but it is quite an important one as we shall see, and the answer is not as self-evident as the layman assumes. We could perhaps say: 'Words are sequences of letters separated by spaces in print.' This definition works in a rough-and-ready fashion when we are looking at written languages, but it begs the question as to how printers or dictionary-writers decide where to put the spaces in the first place. And how could we operate this definition with languages and dialects possessing no written form? The linguist can approach the problem from three directions: phonological, semantic and grammatical. Let us see which one works best.

3.1.1   The phonological approach

Words are units of sound, that is sequences of sounds with a beginning, middle and end. But the question we are trying to answer is: where does one word end and the next one begin? If there were audible boundaries between the words existing in a particular language this would solve a lot of the language-learner's difficulties in aural comprehension, and it would give the linguist a phonological means of defining its words. This is to an extent possible in certain languages, e.g. Polish and Czech where each word has its own independent stress. But what about French? Listen to a French person saying *Il est avec sa petite amie*. The French person will run all these words together in an uninterrupted sequence with the main stress coming on the last syllable of the *phrase*, not on any individual word. In French, then, there are no audible word boundaries and it is not possible to define what French words are purely in terms of pronunciation.

3.1.2   *The semantic approach*

Words are units of meaning. Could we use that as our criterion for deciding what a word is in French? Whereas individual sounds (or **'phonemes'** as we shall be calling them) like /m/, /e/, /t/, /R/, /o/ have no meaning, when we arrange them into larger units – words – they become meaningful, e.g. *métro*. The problem here is that phrases (e.g. *sa petite amie*) and sentences (e.g. *Il est avec sa petite amie*) are also meaningful sequences of phonemes, and because they are made up of groups of words, we would not want to call them 'words'. Perhaps we could say then that 'words are the *smallest* units of meaning in a particular language'. But unfortunately, this is not the case either for we can subdivide words into smaller meaningful units (e.g. *in/accept/able*, *(il) ven/ait*). There exist in languages units of meaning which are smaller than words and which are called **morphemes**. The examples we have just quoted contain 3 and 2 morphemes respectively.

Before going on, let us say a few things about morphemes. Morphemes are the smallest meaningful units existing in a particular language: you can chop up any word into its component morphemes (though, of course, some words consist of only one morpheme, e.g. *femme, garçon*), but if you chop up a morpheme into smaller units you end up with phonemes which have no specific meaning (e.g. /g/, /a/, /R/, etc.). Size or number of syllables is not a useful guide in identifying morphemes, some consist of several syllables, others of just one. It is possible to distinguish two different types of morpheme. Take the English words *big/ger* and *kill/ed*. In each of these cases the first of the two morphemes can stand on its own (e.g. *She is a big girl*, *I'm going to kill you*), and so is referred to as a 'free' morpheme. The second of the two (*-ger* and *-ed*) cannot, so they are referred to as 'bound', that is they can only be found attached to another morpheme. Some bound morphemes are lexical (derivational) and are used for the creation of new words (e.g. *re-* combined with *venir* produces a 'new' word *revenir*), while others are grammatical (inflectional) and serve to modify the grammatical function of what remains the 'same' word (e.g. *-ons* added to the verb-stem *travaill-* produces the first person plural, present indicative). For more on this distinction see pp. 115–20. We would say then that the bound morphemes *in-* and *-able* in *inacceptable* are derivational (they tend to be listed in French dictionaries), whereas *-ait* in *il venait* is inflectional (these are listed in French grammar books).

Some words consist of just one morpheme (e.g. *moi, petit, homme*) while others are made up of a sequence of morphemes (e.g. *inacceptable, pare-brise, viendrait*). This brings us back to our original question: how can we tell whether a particular sequence of morphemes (e.g. *intolérable, chasse-neige, chemin de fer, il est parti*) is to be regarded as one word or several? It is grammatical rather than semantic factors which are going to help us most.

3.1.3   *The grammatical approach*

A definition of a word in grammatical terms would go something like this: 'A word is a morpheme or series of morphemes possessing internal cohesion and positional mobility.' What does this mean? Internal cohesion means that the series of morphemes in question cannot be interrupted through the insertion of any other element, i.e. nothing can be inserted between the morphemes making up the following words: *in/accept/able* and *aim/er/i/ons*. These sequences therefore can be recognised as 'words' in French. Positional mobility means that a particular morpheme or sequence of morphemes is free to range about the sentence, it is not bound always to occur stuck on to some other morpheme. Thus the morpheme *de* fits our definition of 'word' because it can occur in a wide range of contexts, e.g. before a verb (*avant de partir*), after a verb (*partir de chez lui*), after and before a noun (*histoire de France*).

3.1.4   *Different types of word*

We can classify the different types of word present in a language according to a number of different criteria. We could, for instance, categorise them on the basis of meaning, e.g. words denoting people and places, words denoting things, or according to grammatical function, making a broad distinction between 'full words' (nouns, adjectives, verbs and adjectives), and 'grammatical words' (prepositions, determiners, pronouns, conjunctions, etc.). However, here we will classify them on the basis of the way in which they are formed. Three basic types of word formation are found in French: simple words, derived words and compounds. Let us look at each of these in turn.

SIMPLE WORDS

Words are said to be 'simple' from a morphological point of view when they contain just one lexical morpheme and cannot be broken down into smaller lexical units, e.g. *nom, enfant, venir*. This last example can be divided into a lexical morpheme *ven-* and a grammatical morpheme *-ir*, but from the lexical point of view *venir* remains a 'simple' word.

DERIVED WORDS

Derivatives are formed by the addition of affixes to roots (these may be 'simple' words or 'derived' words), see Fig. 3.1.

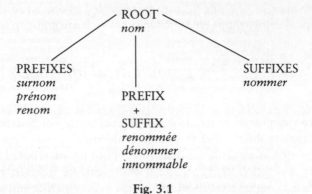

Fig. 3.1

In theory there is no limit to the number of affixes that can be added to roots. Consider, for instance the English word *anti/dis/establish/ment/arian/ism*. Prefixes and suffixes are said to be 'productive' so long as they continue to be available to speakers for the creation of new words (neologisms), e.g. *déindustrialisation*, *bipolariser*. Productive affixes are listed at the beginning of dictionaries. Figure 3.2 is the list offered by the *Dictionnaire du français contemporain* (ed. Dubois *et al.* 1971).

Over the course of time affixes go out of fashion. In Old French nouns could be made from verbs by adding *-aison* to the stem, e.g. *conjugaison*, *terminaison*, *pendaison*. This suffix is no longer productive.

suffixes et préfixes

suffixes

Les *suffixes*, placés après le radical, sont utilisés pour passer d'un type de phrase à un autre, sans variation de sens, ou d'un mot à un autre terme de même catégorie, avec changement de sens. Le même suffixe peut servir à plusieurs usages.

● 1. Transformation d'un verbe en un substantif (nom d'action ou d'état).

-age	*arroser le jardin*	*l'arrosage du jardin*
-issage	*l'avion atterrit*	*l'atterrissage de l'avion*
-ment	*remembrer une propriété*	*le remembrement de la propriété*
-issement	*ses enfants s'assagissent*	*l'assagissement de ses enfants*
-(i)tion	*punir un coupable*	*la punition du coupable*
-(a)tion	*les prix augmentent*	*l'augmentation des prix*
-ure	*lire un roman*	*la lecture d'un roman*
suffixe zéro	*reporter un rendez-vous*	*le report d'un rendez-vous*
(déverbal)	*la troupe marche*	*la marche de la troupe*

Fig. 3.2 List of French suffixes and prefixes

● 2. Transformation d'un adjectif en un substantif (nom de qualité, de système, d'état).

-(i)té	*le malade est docile*	*la docilité du malade*
-(e)té	*la pièce est propre*	*la propreté de la pièce*
-ie	*les hommes sont fous*	*la folie des hommes*
-erie	*le procédé est fourbe*	*la fourberie du procédé*
	son discours est pédant	*le pédantisme de son discours*
-isme	*cette construction est archaïque*	*l'archaïsme de cette construction*
	ses conceptions sont pessimistes	*le pessimisme de ses conceptions*
-eur	*ses joues sont pâles*	*la pâleur de ses joues*
(féminin)	*cette analyse est profonde*	*la profondeur de cette analyse*
-ance	*sa tenue est élégante*	*l'élégance de sa tenue*
-ence	*ses propos sont incohérents*	*l'incohérence de ses propos*
-ise	*cet homme est sot*	*la sottise de cet homme*
-esse	*sa constitution est robuste*	*la robustesse de sa constitution*
-(i)tude	*les parents sont inquiets*	*l'inquiétude des parents*

● 3. Transformation d'un verbe (et de son sujet) en un substantif (nom d'agent ou d'instrument ; nom de personne exerçant un métier).

-eur	*personne qui moissonne*	*un moissonneur*
(masculin)	*appareil qui bat (les mélanges)*	*un batteur*
-ateur, -teur	*personne qui décore (les appartements)*	*un décorateur*
-trice	*machine qui perfore (les cartes)*	*une perforatrice*
-euse	*machine qui arrose (les rues)*	*une arroseuse*
-ier, -ière	*personne qui cuisine*	*un (une) cuisinier(-ère)*
	avion qui bombarde	*un bombardier*
-ant	*personne qui milite*	*un militant*
-ante	*machine qui imprime*	*une imprimante*
-aire	*personne qui signe une lettre*	*le signataire d'une lettre*
-oir	*appareil qui ferme (un sac)*	*un fermoir*
-oire	*ustensile qui passe une substance*	*une passoire*
-iste	*personne qui anesthésie*	*un anesthésiste*

● 4. Transformation d'un substantif en un adjectif (dans les types de phrases : nom + complément de nom ; *avoir* + nom ; etc.).

-al, -ale	*une douleur de (à) l'abdomen*	*une douleur abdominale*
-el, -elle	*le voyage du président*	*le voyage présidentiel*
-ien, -ienne	*la politique de l'Autriche*	*la politique autrichienne*
-ais, -aise	*le vin des Charentes*	*le vin charentais*
-in, -ine	*les poètes d'Alexandrie*	*les poètes alexandrins*
-ois, -oise	*l'industrie de Grenoble*	*l'industrie grenobloise*
-ain, -aine	*le commerce de l'Amérique*	*le commerce américain*
-if, -ive	*elle a de l'attention*	*elle est attentive*
-oire	*le choc de l'opération*	*le choc opératoire*
-aire	*le budget a un déficit*	*le budget est déficitaire*
-eux, -euse	*il a le cafard*	*il est cafardeux*
-ant, -ante	*elle a du charme*	*elle est charmante*
-ier, -ière	*il fait des dépenses*	*il est dépensier*
-ique	*il a de l'ironie*	*il est ironique*
-u, -ue	*il a une barbe*	*il est barbu*
-é, -ée	*il a son domicile à Paris*	*il est domicilié à Paris*
	petit déjeuner au cacao	*petit déjeuner cacaoté*
-esque	*une œuvre de titan*	*une œuvre titanesque*

● 5. Transformation d'un verbe en un adjectif (équivalence entre un groupe verbal avec *pouvoir* et le verbe *être* suivi d'un adjectif).

-able	*cette proposition peut être acceptée*	*cette proposition est acceptable*
in[...]able	*on ne peut croire cette histoire*	*cette histoire est incroyable*
-ible	*l'issue peut en être prévue*	*l'issue est prévisible*

Fig. 3.2 (Continued)

● 6. Transformation d'un adjectif en un verbe (équivalence entre *rendre, faire*, suivis d'un adjectif, et le verbe).

-iser	*rendre uniformes les tarifs*	*uniformiser les tarifs*
-ifier	*faire plus simple un exposé*	*simplifier un exposé*
suffixe zéro	*rendre une feuille noire*	*noircir une feuille*
	rendre épais un mélange	*épaissir un mélange*

Cette transformation peut se faire au moyen de préfixes.

a...	*rendre plus grande une pièce*	*agrandir une pièce*
é...	*faire plus large un trou*	*élargir un trou*

● 7. Transformation de l'adjectif en un verbe (équivalence entre *devenir,* suivi d'un adjectif, et le verbe). Cette transformation se fait en général avec le suffixe zéro.

suffixe zéro	*devenir grand*	*grandir*
	devenir rouge	*rougir*
	devenir bleu	*bleuir*

● 8. Transformation d'un substantif en un verbe (*faire*, ou autre, suivi d'un substantif, équivalent du verbe).
Elle se fait au moyen du suffixe zéro.

suffixe zéro	*la réforme de l'État*	*réformer l'État*
	le supplice d'un condamné	*supplicier un condamné*
	le programme d'un spectacle	*programmer un spectacle*
	se servir du téléphone	*téléphoner*
	donner des armes à une troupe	*armer une troupe*

Transformation d'un adjectif en adverbe.

-ment	*une expression vulgaire*	*s'exprimer vulgairement*
même forme	*une voix fausse*	*chanter faux*

● 9. Transformation d'un substantif en un autre substantif, d'un adjectif en un autre adjectif, avec variation de sens (elle se fait dans les deux sens).

— / **-ier**	groupe/personne	*il fait partie d'une équipe*	*un équipier*
-eur / **-orat**	personne/métier	*il est professeur*	*exercer le professorat*
— / **-at**		*il est interprète*	*il fait de l'interprétariat*
-ie / **-ien**		*il fait de la chirurgie*	*il est chirurgien*
-ique/ **-ien**		*il fait de l'électronique*	*il est électronicien*
-erie/ **-ier**		*il tient une charcuterie*	*il est charcutier*
— / **-aire**	objet/commerce	*il vend des disques*	*il est disquaire*
— / **-iste**		*il fait des affiches*	*il est affichiste*
— / **-ier**		*il fait des serrures*	*il est serrurier*
— / **-ier**	fruit/arbre	*arbre qui porte des abricots*	*abricotier*
— / **-aie**	arbre/collection d'arbres	*groupe de chênes*	*une chênaie*
— / **-ée**	objet/contenu	*le contenu d'une assiette*	*une assiettée*
— / **-iste**	nom/disciple	*disciple d'Hébert*	*hébertiste*
— / **-ette (-et)**	terme neutre/plus petit	*une petite maison*	*une maisonnette*
-eur / **-ard**	terme neutre/péjoratif	*un mauvais chauffeur*	*un chauffard*
— / **-aud**		*un homme lourd*	*un lourdaud*
— / **-âtre**	terme neutre/atténuatif	*une lueur rouge*	*rougeâtre*

Fig. 3.2 (Continued)

préfixes

Les préfixes, qui ne modifient pas la classe des mots, établissent un rapport entre le terme simple et le terme préfixé.

● Préfixes des verbes portant sur l'action.

dé- (dés-)	privatif	*dépoétiser,* enlever le caractère poétique *déshabituer,* enlever l'habitude
en-	factitif	*engraisser,* faire devenir gras
entre-	réciproque	*s'entr'égorger, s'entretuer*
re-, ré-, r-	réitératif, répétition	*refaire,* faire de nouveau, une seconde fois *réimprimer,* imprimer de nouveau *rajuster,* ajuster de nouveau

● Préfixes privatifs et intensifs

in- **(il-, im-, ir-)** **a-, an-** **sans-**	privatifs	*inaltérable, illisible, immangeable, irréel apolitique, anormal sans-abri*
archi- **extra-** **hyper-** **super-** **sur-** **ultra-**	intensifs	*archifou ; archisot extra-fin ; extra-souple hypersensible ; hypertension supermarché ; supercarburant surabondant ; suralimentation ultracolonialiste ; ultra-court*

● Préfixes indiquant un rapport de position (espace, hiérarchie ou temps).

après- **post-**	postériorité	*après-demain ; après-guerre postface ; postscolaire*
avant- **pré-** **anté-**	antériorité	*avant-hier ; avant-guerre préétabli ; préhistoire antédiluvien*
co-, con-	simultanéité,	*co-auteur ; concitoyen*
hors-	position	*hors-jeu*
outre-	au-delà de	*outremer*
entre-	réunion, position	*entre-deux ; entre-deux-guerres*
inter-	au milieu	*interocéanique*
extra-	hors de	*extra-territorialité*
intra-	au-dedans de	*intramusculaire*
ex-	qui a cessé d'être	*ex-député ; ex-sénateur*
trans-	à travers	*transsibérien ; transocéanique*
vice-	à la place de	*vice-amiral*

● Préfixes indiquant la sympathie, l'hostilité, l'opposition ou la négation.

anti-	hostilité, opposition protection	*antidémocratique antituberculeux*
contre-	réaction	*contre-attaque*
mal-	négation	*malcommode*
non-	négation, refus	*non-violence*
pro-	partisan	*procommuniste*

Fig. 3.2 (Continued)

Before leaving derivation we should also mention other devices for deriving new words from existing ones: 'back-formation' which involves the removal rather than the addition of suffixes, e.g. *frapper* → *frappe*, *geler* → *gel*; 'SIGLES' or acronyms like *l'ONU* (*Organisation des Nations Unies*), *le PS* (*Parti Socialiste*), *les SDF* (*Sans Domicile Fixe*); portemanteau words like *le franglais*, *le francitan*, etc.

Now do the exercises 1–5 on p. 47.

COMPOUNDS

These are formed when two (or more) existing words are run together into one, e.g. *grand-mère*, *chasse-neige*. In the written language compounds are often written with a hyphen between the component elements, e.g. *wagon-restaurant* (restaurant car), *pare-choc* (car bumper), *tire-fesses* (t-bar on ski lift), *sourd-muet* (deaf-mute), *nu-pieds* (barefoot). Whereas German makes very extensive use of compounding, e.g. *Flugzeug* ('flying thing'), *Untergrundbahn* ('under-ground way'), French is often said not to use it much. This may be a misconception arising from the fact that many compounds in French are not recognised as such because they are not punctuated with hyphens.

Let us consider, for instance, commonly occurring sequences like *chemin de fer* (railway), *pied à terre* (a place to stay), *chambre à air* (inner tube). In these cases, we may ask: are we dealing with groups of three separate words (two independent nouns linked by *à* or *de*), or with a single lexical item which is a compound noun (head + post-modifier)? If we apply the criteria explained above for the definition of a 'word' – internal cohesion and positional mobility – we will see that the groups just quoted as examples actually behave as single words (i.e. they are compounds).

The case of sequences like *chemin de fer* is a tricky one, however, for, while sometimes two nouns linked by *de/à* make a single compound noun, sometimes they remain as two independent nouns. Let us take for example the following: we might want to say that *le chien de berger* is a compound noun (meaning 'sheepdog'), but we can also find *le chien du berger*, with a definite article inserted before the second noun, and here we would say we are dealing with two separate nouns (meaning 'the dog of the shepherd'). The interruption of the sequence by inserting the article makes all the difference. Broadly speaking, we can say that if the second noun refers to a specific individual, then the definite article should be inserted, e.g. *porte de la voiture* (= the door of a specific car); if, on the other hand, the identity of the individual referred to by the second noun is generic and unspecified, the second noun acting merely as a sort of adjective qualifying the first, then *de* alone is used (without being followed by *le* or *la*), e.g. *porte de voiture* (= car door).

Often it is difficult to know whether a particular NOUN + *de/à* + NOUN sequence can or cannot be interrupted by, say, an adjective after the first noun or by an article before the second. Not all of such phrases can be interrupted in this way. Some definitely cannot, e.g. *pomme de terre*, *chemin de fer*, *pied à terre*; some definitely can, e.g. *le chien du berger*. With others, however, usage is variable, e.g. *vedette (française) de cinéma* ('film star'), *poste (portatif) de radio* ('radio set'), *voiture (anglaise) de tourisme* ('private car'). Some French speakers feel they can insert adjectives in these examples, others prefer to place the adjective after the second noun, thus preserving the phrase as an uninterruptible sequence. It is a question of time and of frequency of usage: it depends on how often these particular groups of NOUN + *de/à* + NOUN occur together in actual usage.

Groups of words which very commonly co-occur will become fused into a single word, i.e. they will become 'lexicalised' as a single compound noun. If the phrase does not 'catch on' as an expression, the two words will remain independent. Word boundaries clearly fluctuate over time, as we can see with the following: *ainz né* ('first born' → *aîné*), *plus tost* ('more soon' → *plutôt*), *des or mais* ('from now forward' → *désormais*).

In this section we have looked at the ways in which different types of words in French are formed. We have seen that from a core of 'simple' words there radiates a constant output of new words formed primarily by derivation and composition, giving the vocabulary of the language an essentially dynamic quality (see Guilbert 1975). Just as speakers have built into their linguistic competence a set of 'rules' allowing them to generate an infinite set of unique sentences, so they also possess the capacity to constantly modify their vocabulary to meet their changing communicative needs. If we look at the way the French lexicon has changed over the past centuries we enter the domain of 'etymology'.

3.2   Etymology

Etymology is the branch of linguistics concerned with the origins and history of words. In the second part of this chapter we will be asking where French words come from and how the French lexicon has developed over the centuries. In our answer we will look briefly at the history of the language and draw upon some of the concepts we have just explored in 'word formation'. We will see that, etymologically speaking, French words can be placed into one of three categories: *inherited* words, *created* words and *borrowed* words.

French is a member of the Romance group of languages, that is one of the dozen or so languages which emerged 1000 years ago out of the speech of the Romans (Latin). The principal Romance languages (in order of number of speakers) are: Spanish, Portuguese, French, Italian, Rumanian, Catalan, Occitan, Sardinian and Rheto-Romance, see Fig. 3.3.

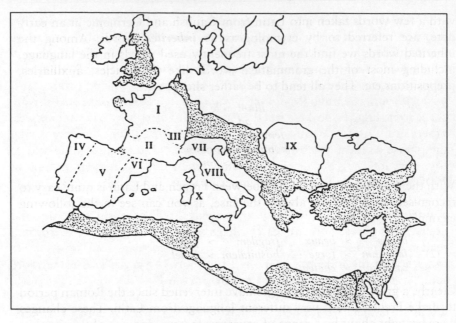

Fig. 3.3 The Romance languages

Key: I   French
        II   Occitan
        III   Franco-Provençal
        IV   Portuguese
        V   Castilian
        VI   Catalan
        VII   Rheto-Romance
        VIII   Italian
        IX   Rumanian
        X   Sardinian
Source: Lodge 1993

Many people refer to Latin as a 'dead language', and in one sense they are right, for there are no longer any native-speakers of the Classical Latin taught in schools and universities. However, in another sense they are quite wrong, for French is nothing other than Modern Latin as spoken in France, just as Spanish is Modern Latin as spoken in Spain, etc. The fact that Modern French speakers cannot understand Latin indicates that a great number of changes have come about in that language since the time when France (or Gaul as it was then called) was part of the Roman Empire, but it does not alter the fact that the line of descent from Latin to the Romance languages has never been broken.

So, as a starting-point, we can say that the core vocabulary of French comes from Latin. Those words in the French lexicon which have always been in the language in an unbroken line of descent from Latin, together with a few words taken into Latin from Gaulish and Germanic at an early date, are referred to by etymologists as *inherited* words. Among the inherited words we find the most frequently used words in the language, including most of the grammatical words like the articles, auxiliaries, prepositions etc. They all tend to be rather short , e.g.

	illum	>	*le*
	ad	>	*à*
(1)	*feminam*	>	*femme*
	hominem	>	*homme*
	bonum	>	*bon*

With the words just cited the link between French and Latin is quite easy to recognise, but this is not always the case, as you can see in the following examples:

	bellos	>	*beaux*	*fragilem*	>	*frêle*
(2)	*fabricam*	>	*forge*	*hospitalem*	>	*hôtel*
	castellum	>	*château*			

Clearly, a great number of changes have intervened since the Roman period to make French into a very different language from Latin. These changes were brought about by a range of causative factors, and one of the simplest to understand, though by no means the most significant, is interference from other languages. In the early history of French these external influences came first from Gaulish and later from Germanic.

Latin was by no means the first language to have been spoken in Gaul. From the eighth century BC and for about 1000 years, the inhabitants of Gaul spoke a Celtic language (Gaulish) which was related to Ancient British (Welsh) and to Scots and Irish Gaelic. The Romans began colonising Gaul in the first century BC and during the course of the next 500 years led the inhabitants gradually to shift language from Gaulish to Latin. As the Gauls shifted language, it appears that they brought over into their Latin a Gaulish 'accent' and a certain number of Gaulish words which have remained in the language ever since, e.g.:

	brucaria	>	*bruyère*
(3)	*carrum*	>	*char*
	dunam	>	*dune*

In the fifth century AD the Roman Empire finally collapsed, engulfed by massive inward migrations of Germanic-speaking 'barbarians'. Britain was invaded by Angles and Saxons, northern Italy by Lombards, Spain by Vandals (giving rise to the name *Andalucia*), southern Gaul by the Visigoths, eastern Gaul by the Burgunds and northern Gaul by the Franks (who eventually renamed the country *Francia > France*). The Germanic peoples who settled in Gaul quickly assimilated to the native population and adopted their language, but as they did so, they introduced into the Latin of Gaul a large number of Germanic words, e.g. *bleu, blond, brun, haie, haïr, hache, guerre, garder*.

The disruption created by the Germanic invasions led to the wholesale dialectalisation of the Latin spoken in Gaul. That is to say that while most of the inhabitants of Gaul continued to speak Latin, because of disrupted communications their speech developed differently in different regions. Spoken Latin thus lost its unity and became fragmented into numerous regional dialects, of a southern type (*langue d'oc*) and of a northern type (*langue d'oil*), see Fig. 2.2, p. 17. A similar process of dialectalisation took place in all the countries of the Roman Empire where Latin was spoken, and in this way, new (Romance) languages came into being between the fifth and the ninth centuries in Spain, Gaul, Italy and Rumania. By the first half of the ninth century, in northern Gaul at least, the gap between the written form of Latin (which had remained relatively stable since Imperial times) and the many spoken forms of the language had become so wide that mutual intelligibility became increasingly difficult. People gradually came to the realisation that the language spoken in Gaul could no longer be appropriately called Latin.

Throughout the Middle Ages (ninth century–fifteenth century) France was a diglossic society (see above p. 29), with Latin performing the H functions and 'Old French' the L functions. The sociolinguistic history of French over this period traces the emergence of a new standard language, replacing Latin. We can distinguish four processes at work in language standardisation:

1. Selection of norms
2. Elaboration of functions
3. Codification
4. Acceptance

Let us use these as the basis for our periodisation of the history of French vocabulary.

1. *Selection of norms*: between the ninth and the thirteenth centuries the inhabitants of northern Gaul gradually came to regard the speech of Paris and the area around it (Ile-de-France) as having more status than other dialects. The dialect of Ile-de-France was unconsciously selected as the norm, not because of any linguistic qualities which made it inherently 'better' than other dialects in northern France, but because of its association with the rich and powerful in the burgeoning city of Paris. In traditional histories of French, this period is referred to as the Old French period.

2. *Elaboration of functions*: from the fourteenth century onwards the dialect spoken by the King and his court gradually acquired greater prestige and began to replace Latin as the language of writing, government and education. This is to say that the King's French now took on new H functions in society over and above its basic L function as an ordinary vernacular (the language of everyday conversation). As it did so it had to

increase its linguistic resources in grammar and vocabulary to enable it to perform its new role. The period between the fourtcenth and sixteenth centuries is often referred to in histories of the language as the 'Middle French' period.

As the language entered new domains of use previously occupied by Latin, it borrowed heavily from Latin to acquire the words which it did not as yet possess, e.g.:

	fragilem	>	*fragile*
(4)	*hospitalem*	>	*hôpital*
	fabricam	>	*fabrique*

Words borrowed from Latin at a date subsequent to the beginning of the Old French period (ninth century) are called *learnèd borrowings*, for Latin (and later Greek too) were the languages of learning and high culture. You will have noticed, perhaps, that the same Latin word can come down to us in French in two forms:

	frêle	~	*fragile*
(5)	*hôtel*	~	*hôpital*
	forge	~	*fabrique*

The first is the inherited or 'popular' form and the second is the learnèd, borrowed form. You will have noticed too that the learnèd form remains much closer in sound/spelling to the Latin etymon (= source-word).

3. *Codification*: implicit in the notion of standardisation is that of imposing a common measure on a group of items with the aim of suppressing variation and producing uniformity. In language the process of stating explicitly what is correct and what is not is known as 'codification'. This task is performed by prescriptive grammarians and by lexicographers (compilers of dictionaries), and in France the movement reached its height in the seventeenth and eighteenth centuries (the period referred to in histories of the language as 'Classical French'). A key date here is 1635 when the Académie française was set up with a brief to produce a rhetoric, a grammar and a dictionary of French. The first edition of its dictionary was published in 1694, and along with many others published at this time, its function was threefold: first, to establish the inventory of officially recognised words in French (this inevitably meant the exclusion of a large number of items); second, to specify their meanings; and third, to indicate the stylistic level to which they belonged with such labels as *populaire*, *familier*, *poétique*, etc.

4. *Acceptance*: by the end of the eighteenth century, the French language had been provided with a standardised form, based ultimately on the speech of the social elite in Paris. However, outside Paris and, indeed, among the uneducated proletariat in the capital itself, there were few people who were very familiar with it. Most of the French population lived on the land in small rural communities, speaking regional dialects and *patois*. The

nineteenth and twentieth centuries have seen the development of an urban, industrial society which has required the acceptance by the whole population of the standard language, killing off the old dialects and *patois* in the process.

During all of these massive social and cultural changes, the French lexicon has had to keep pace. How has it managed to renew itself at every stage in its history? An element of stability is provided by the core vocabulary of *inherited* words. Renewal has come about partly through *borrowing* (which we considered briefly above), and partly through the *creation* of new words either by the processes of derivation and composition discussed above (section 3.1.4), or by semantic change (i.e. by giving existing words new meanings).

Word *borrowing* is the easiest of these processes to understand. Throughout the history of the language French has been copying words from other languages with which it has been in contact, particularly from those whose culture was at the time perceived to be more advanced (see Walter 1997). Right down to the present day the greatest source of foreign borrowings in French has been Latin (and to a lesser extent Greek). However, since the Middle Ages, borrowings from other languages have become frequent too. In the sixteenth century Italy was probably the richest and most advanced country in Europe, so that period sees a considerable number of borrowings into French from Italian, e.g. *arcade, balcon, banque, bulletin* (see Hope 1971). Since the eighteenth century, provided we leave the 'learnèd languages' out of account, English has taken over as the chief supplier of foreign borrowings into French (see Haugen 1950 and Spence 1976). Borrowings from foreign languages into French are relatively easy to spot, e.g. *le building, le snack-bar, le management*, and tend to generate a lot of emotion in linguistic 'purists' (see Etiemble 1964) and politicians (see Toubon 1994), but their importance in the overall development of the lexicon should not be exaggerated. Many of the English words borrowed into French in the 1960s have already fallen out of use.

Of far greater importance is the production of words from native resources. This happens when new words are *created* from existing French words through derivation and compounding (word formation processes which we looked at in the first part of this chapter), e.g. *déindustrialiser, bipolariser, pare-choc*, and when existing words are used in new senses. Space does not allow us to explore here the intricacies of semantic change. Examples of it are very numerous: the word *bourgeois* in the twelfth century meant essentially the inhabitant of a *bourg*, but now it is covered with a host of social and political overtones; the word *maîtresse* implied a perfectly legitimate sexual relationship in the seventeenth century, but nowadays it necessarily involves adultery; *une navette* at one time meant simply 'a shuttle' used in weaving, but nowadays it also designates 'a bus shuttling to and fro from an airport to a passenger terminal'. Although semantic changes are less conspicuous than foreign borrowings, they are much more pervasive and ultimately more interesting.

Seminar exercises

1. Take a monolingual French dictionary like the *Petit Larousse* and try to find examples of unequal treatment of males and females (a) in the language itself (e.g. in the various *noms de métier* like *médecin, dactylo*), and (b) in the way lexicographers attempt to describe and exemplify usage.

2. On the basis of Figure 3.2 compile a list of affixes which change the grammatical category ('part of speech') of a word. For each affix you choose state:
(a) which word category it can combine with and which word category the combination creates;
(b) which of the affixes can be combined with only one word category and which can be combined with more than one;
(c) which of the affixes create only one word category and which can create more than one.

3. Compile a list of several common affixes which do not change the grammatical category of the word. For each of these state:
(a) whether they are inflectional or derivational affixes;
(b) which word categories they can be affixed to.

4. Which word category in French has the widest range of derivational affixes? Which noun suffixes are related to gender marking? Is gender marking the only interpretation of these suffixes? If not, what else do they indicate?

5. Provide a morphological breakdown of the following words. (NB: this includes identifying morphemes) and give the order in which affixes have been attached.

abattre	enfin	préoccupation
conséquence	suivant	emprisoner
malheureux	gentillesse	encadrement
rougissant	utilisation	inaltérabilité
affaiblir	disproportionné	impossibilité
inutilement	embouteillage	routières
automobiliste	naturellement	ingéniosité
infatigablement	individualisation	réorganisation

6. In order to gain an overview of the points made in this chapter about the history of French vocabulary, look in detail at a single page drawn at random from O. Bloch and W. von Wartburg's *Dictionnaire étymologique de la langue française* (Fig. 3.4).

L

LA, nom de la sixième note, v. **gamme.**

LÀ. En a. fr. en outre *lai*. Lat. *illāc* ; v. çà. It. *là*, esp. *allá*. — Comp. : delà, xiie.

LABARUM, 1556. Empr. du lat. impérial (du ive s.), d'origine obscure.

LABEL, 1906. Empr. de l'angl. *label* « étiquette », empr. lui-même de l'a. fr. *label*, v. **lambeau.**

LABEUR, xiie ; souvent fém. jusqu'au xve s., d'après le genre normal des subst. en -*eur* ; **laborieux**, vers 1200. Empr. du lat. *labor* « effort, fatigue », *laboriosus* « pénible » et déjà « actif », avec francisation des suffixes -*or*, -*osus* sur le modèle des nombreux mots fr. en -*eur*, -*eux.*

LABIAL, 1605 ; **labiée**, fin xviie (Tournefort). Dér. sav. du lat. *labium* « lèvre ».

LABILE, xive. Empr. du lat. de basse ép. *labilis* (de *labi* « glisser »).

LABORANTINE, 1934. Empr. de l'all. *Laborantin*, formé d'après *Laboratorium* « laboratoire ».

LABORATOIRE, 1612. Dér. sav. du lat. *laborare* « travailler ».

LABOURER, x^e *(Fragment de Valenciennes)*, au sens de « se don ner de la peine, travailler », sens maintenu jusqu'au début du xviie s., souvent sous la forme *labeurer*, d'après *labeur*. Empr. du lat. *laborare* « se donner de la peine, travai ler ». A été pris de bonne heure pour le travail de la terre, au détriment du verbe *arer* (lat. *arāre*), usuel jusqu'au xvie s. It. *arare*, esp. *arar* ; mais l'a. pr. a une forme pop. de *labŏrāre*, *laurar*, encore vivante. *Arer* survit dans les parlers de la Franche-Comté, de la Suisse romande. de la Savoie et du Sud-Est. — Dér. : **labour**, vers 1180 ; **labourable**, 1368 ; **labourage**, vers 1200, a eu aussi le sens de travail (en général) jusqu'au xvie s., cf. : « Par excellence le mot de labourage a esté donné à la culture des bleds, encores qu'il soit communiqué à tout autre travail », O. de Serres ; **laboureur**, « travailleur, ouvrier » au moyen âge, l'on trouve jusqu'au xve s. *laboureur de mains, de bras.*

LABRE, 1754. Empr. du lat. des naturalistes *labrus*, tiré arbitrairement du lat. *labrum* « lèvre », parce que le labre a des lèvres épaisses.

LABYRINTHE, 1418 (alors *lebarinthe*), au sens propre ; sens fig. dès le xvie s. Empr. du lat. *labyrinthus* (du grec *labyrinthos*, mot égéen).

LAC, vers 1120. Empr. du lat. *lacus* la forme pop. *lai* a eu peu de vitalité.

LACER. Lat. *laqueāre* « serrer avec un lacet ». It. *lacciare*, a. pr. *lassar*. — Dér. et Comp. : **lacis**, xiie ; **délacer**, vers 1080 *(Roland)* ; **enlacer**, xiie, **enlacement**, *id.* ; **entrelacer**, *id.*, **entrelacs**, *id.*, **entrelacement**, *id.*

LACÉRER, xive (Bersuire) ; **lacération**, *id.* Empr. du lat. *lacerare, laceratio.*

LACERON, 1393. Nom dialectal de la région centrale, du laiteron, cf. aussi le normanno-picard *lucheron.* Elargissement de *lasson*, attesté en a. fr. xive (E. Deschamps) et aujourd'hui en lorrain ; pour les suff. comp. *liseron* ; *lasson*, représente un lat. pop. *°lacteōnem*, acc. de *°lacteō*, dér. de l'adj. *lacteus* « laiteux », le laiteron est en effet une plante lactescente.

LACET, v. **lacs.**

LÂCHE, v. **lâcher.**

LÂCHER, vers 1080 *(Roland)*. Lat. de basse ép. *laxicare* « détendre », dér. de *laxare*, id., v. **laisser** ; *laxicare* est devenu *°lascare* par dissimilation des deux *k* dans *laksikare.* — Dér. : **lâche**, xiiie, comp. a. pr. *lasc*, **lâcheté**, xiie ; **lâcheur**, 1858 ; **lâchage**, 1839 ; **relâcher**, xiiie ; **relâche**, 1539 (une première fois vers 1170) ; **relâchement**, vers 1170.

LACINIÉ, 1676. Empr. du lat. *laciniatus* « fait de morceaux » (de *lacinia* « morceau d'étoffe »).

LACONIQUE, 1529. Empr. du grec *lakōnikós* « bref, concis », propr. « de Laconie », les Lacédémoniens ou Laconiens ayant été célèbres pour leur manière de parler brève. — Dér. : **laconisme**, 1556 (le grec *lakōnismos* avait un autre sens).

LACRYMAL, xvie (Paré ; déjà vers 1300 comme subst. sous la forme *lacrimel*) ; **lacrymatoire**, 1690. Le premier est un dér. sav. du lat. *lacryma*, autre orthographe de *lacrima* « larme », le deuxième de *lacrymari*, pour *lacrimari* « verser des larmes », à l'imitation des nombreux mots en -*atoire.*

LACS. Aujourd'hui seulement littéraire. Anciennement *laz, las*, orthographié *lacs* vers le xve s., d'après *lacer.* Lat. *laqueus.* It. *laccio*, esp. *lazo.* — Dér. : **lacet**, 1315.

LACTATION, 1747 ; **lacté**, xive ; **lactescent**, 1792 ; **lactique**, 1787. *Lactation* est empr. du lat. de basse ép. *lactatio* (de *lactare* « allaiter »), *lacté* du lat. *lacteus, lactescen*,

Fig. 3.4

Here is an expansion of the abbreviations used in this extract:

acc.	= accusatif
a. fr.	= ancien français
a. pr.	= ancien provençal
all.	= allemand
angl.	= anglais
comp.	= composé/comparez
dér./dér. sav.	= dérivé
empr.	= emprunté
ép.	= époque
esp.	= espagnol
fém.	= féminin
fig.	= figure (figurative)
id.	= idem (the same)
it.	= italien
lat.	= latin
pop.	= populaire
s.	= siècle
subst.	= substantif (noun)
suff.	= suffixe

Consider the 48 words printed in **bold** in this specimen page and classify them according to whether they are 'inherited', 'borrowed' (from which languages), and 'created'. Place words labelled *dér.* and *dér. sav.* in your 'created' category. Produce a bar-chart indicating the numbers of first attestations in each century since 1100. What does this tell us about the history of French vocabulary?

7.   Here is a random passage of French where 50 words are occurring in context, rather than in a dictionary. The following abbreviations are used: *i* = inherited, *b* = borrowed, *c* = created.

> De toute évidence, l'homme était fou. Fou comme un baromètre. 'Le
> i   i   b   i i   i   i   i   i i   c   i
> dragon! Le dragon!' criait-il en gesticulant vers le ciel orageux.
>   i   i   i   i   i i   b   i i i   c
> Autour de lui, déjà la foule s'assemblait. Ses yeux immenses, ses
>   c   i i   c   i i   b   i i   b   i
> narines dilatées, sa bouche béante exprimaient la plus vive terreur;
>   b   b   i   i   b   i i   i i
> on la lisait même dans ....
> i i i   i   i

How does this exercise help correct the impression about the etymological structure of French which you may have derived from exercise 6?

8.   The following is a list of 25 new words (neologisms) entering the language during the 1970s and 1980s. Where do new words come from in French in our own day?

> **accroche** (nf) draw, hook (marketing).
>   l'accroche commerciale ... deux personnes ne paient qu'une place pendant le weekend du 22 septembre.

anticohabitationniste (nm) opponent of 'cohabitation' (q.v.).

antinucléaire (nm) antinuclear campaigner.

archivage (nm) storage (computer).

archiver (vt) store (computer).

 dans chacune des disquettes sont archivées environ 80 pages dactylographiées.

autodiagnostic (nm) diagnostics, self-diagnosis (photocopying).

base de données (nf) data base.

bipolariser (vr) (bi)polarize.

 le jeu politique ne peut que se bipolariser entre les deux grandes coalitions.

bureautique (nf) office automation, office technology.

calculette (nf) pocket calculator.

cinéphilique (adj) related to cinematic merit.

 leurs (Cannes and Venice) sélections tiennent plus à des considérations géopolitiques qu'à des choix cinéphiliques.

cohabitation (nf) situation where the President of the Republic is in political opposition to the majority in the National Assembly.

cohabitationniste (nm) supporter of 'cohabitation'.

cohabiter (vi) see 'cohabitation'.

 cohabiter, c'est bel et bien partager le pouvoir.

compact disc (nm, pl compact discs) compact disc.

copieur (nm) photocopier.

déchoquage (nm) treatment for shock.

 le blessé fut transporté à l'hôpital au service neurologique dans la section de déchoquage.

décrispation (nf) relaxing of tension.

 la décrispation entre Hanoi et Pékin.

désindustrialisation (nf) de-industrialisation.

 ce département en voie de déindustrialisation.

disque souple (nm) floppy disc.

disquette (nf) floppy disc.

fifty-fifty (adv) fifty fifty.

 un contrat d'association: fifty-fifty sur les droits commerciaux et publicitaires.

floppy disc (nm, pl floppy discs) floppy disc.

friqué (adj) well-off (qui a du fric).

 une jeune bourgeoise friquée et romantique.

guerre des étoiles (nf) star wars.

(taken from Bremner 1986–1993)

4

Word meaning

In Chapter 3 we looked at French vocabulary from the point of view of the form of the words in the language. Now we shall consider words from the point of view of their meaning. The branch of linguistics concerned with this topic is 'lexical semantics'.

One of the most fascinating aspects of learning a second language is the progressive realisation of how differently the vocabulary of the second language behaves from that of one's own. An important fact which gradually becomes clear to learners is that there are very few words in one language which have their exact equivalent in the other. It is not difficult to see how this principle might apply when we are dealing with two languages which are historically unrelated to each other, like English and Japanese. However, it also holds good when we compare two languages like English and French, whose histories have been closely bound up with one another for 1000 years. The central aim of this chapter will then be to explore in what ways French words possess not only a French form, but also distinctively French meanings. At the same time, however, we must not forget that at a fundamental level, despite these differences, the lexicons of human languages also have a great deal in common.

4.1   Lack of lexical symmetry between languages

How is it that the meaning and value of words in one language fail to overlap completely with those of words in another? We can distinguish two very general ways in which this observation applies: (1) the number of lexical items available to 'cover' a particular sector of human experience may not be the same in one language as in the other; (2) the combination possibilities of a word in one language may not be identical to those of an 'equivalent' word in the other language. Let us look at a few examples from English and French to make these ideas clearer.

First, it is rather unusual to find two languages having the exactly same number of words to 'cover' the same area of human experience – semanticists refer to this as a 'semantic field' – and even when they do, they rarely divide up the 'field' in exactly the same way. For instance, whereas English has two words *sheep* and *mutton* which enable it to make a lexical distinction between the living animal and the meat, French has only the one word *mouton* to cover both senses. The lexical choices open to speakers of one language tend not to be exactly the same as those available to speakers of another. Because of this, it is not possible to claim that the meaning of English *sheep* is exactly the same as that of French *mouton*. This particular lack of symmetry between the two languages does not reflect some cultural difference between France and Britain. If anything, the stereotypical French love of food might predispose the French to make more lexical distinctions in this area than English speakers, rather than the other way round as here. The dissymmetry results from an etymological accident: the French lexicon is fundamentally Romance in origin (producing the word *mouton* from Latin *moltonem*), but English, since the Norman Conquest in the eleventh century, has drawn on both Germanic (*sheep*) and Romance (*mutton*) elements. Cases abound where, in a largely arbitrary and unpredictable way, one language has inherited a different number of words from another to cover a given 'semantic field'. Compare English *river* with French *rivière* and *fleuve*, and English *know* with French *savoir* and *connaître*.

Not all such dissymmetries come about in so arbitrary a fashion. Many do reflect cultural differences between the two speech communities: it is not difficult to find a large number of culture-specific English words which have no exact lexical equivalent in French, and vice versa. A *surveillant* in a French *lycée* may carry out many of the duties performed in a British school by a *prefect*, but the meanings of the two words reflect major institutional and, indeed, philosophical differences between British and French education. Have you ever tried explaining the rules of cricket to a monolingual speaker of French? Speakers in one speech community need more words in areas which are culturally important to them, in order to express finer distinctions (either semantic, social or stylistic), than speakers of the other language, for whom these areas are of lesser interest. To take a banal example, the French vocabulary of wine-tasting is likely to be more extensive (and more widely known) than the equivalent vocabulary in English, because of the traditional importance of wine in French culture.

Dissymmetries of this kind do not occur solely on the level of the conceptual meaning of words: certain French vocabulary items possess social and stylistic values reflecting the particular sociolinguistic state of French, and as a consequence differ significantly from apparently 'equivalent' English words, which have a different sociostylistic value allocated to them. We saw in Chapter 2, for instance, that French has a wide range of words to designate a car, e.g. *véhicule, automobile, voiture, auto, bagnole, tire, caisse.* The distinctions between these terms are stylistic rather than semantic: they can be arranged, as on p. 28, on a scale of formality. English, on the other hand, has a rather more limited set of words to choose from in this area, e.g. *vehicle, car, motor, banger,* so we could argue that none of the English words is the *exact* stylistic equivalent of any of the French words.

So far we have seen how the vocabulary of one language differs from that of another as a result of differences in the range of lexical choices available to speakers of each language. We shall now see that lexical differences between languages exist on a second level too: the combination possibilities of a word in one language are not normally the same as those of an 'equivalent' word in another language. A quick look at the definitions provided in a monolingual dictionary like the *Dictionnaire du français contemporain* will show that a high proportion of the words in French as in most languages have more than one meaning. Thus *garçon* is listed as meaning: (1) *Enfant mâle,* (2) *Homme célibataire,* (3) *Jeune ouvrier travaillant chez un patron artisan.* For example:

(1)   Ils ont trois *garçons* et une fille.
(2)   Cet homme veut toujours rester *garçon.*
(3)   Le *garçon* est chargé de servir la clientèle.

When we say that the word *garçon* has a different meaning in each of these contexts, we are saying that in combinations with certain words *garçon* is to be interpreted one way, while in other combinations it has to be interpreted in another. If we now take the English 'equivalent' of the French *garçon,* that is *boy,* and attempt to use it in English, making similar combinations to those available to the French word *garçon,* we will quickly come up with pieces of English which carry a different meaning from the French:

(4)   They have three *boys* and a girl.
(5)   *This man still wants to remain a *boy.*
(6)   *The *boy* is responsible for serving the customers.

[* = unacceptable as a translation of the French sentences quoted above. Elsewhere we use the * to indicate that a structure or word within a structure is not grammatically correct in French.] This example demonstrates that the combination possibilities of even a common French word like *garçon* are not 100 per cent the same as those of the 'equivalent' English word.

So, an important part of knowing the meaning of a word in a foreign language consists of knowing what are the particular combinations of words (i.e. contexts) in which it may occur, and what interpretations to give to the word in these different combinations. We shall see that this combinatorial question has important implications for language-learning, for what do we mean by 'She speaks very idiomatic French', if not that she succeeds in finding for each context exactly the word a native-speaker would choose.

4.2　The structural approach to meaning

An important point which we hope has emerged from the preceding section is that it is not very profitable to try to work out the meaning and value of a word in a foreign language simply by scouring bilingual dictionaries in search of an English equivalent. Even more importantly, the meaning and value of a word in a particular language are not to be revealed by consideration of that word *on its own*, in isolation from other words in the language. Words belong in structures and they derive much of their meaning and value from their place in a network of relationships with other words. In the preceding section we hinted at two types of relationships which can be seen to hold between linguistic items in a language. Let us now explore them further. Structural linguists refer to them as *paradigmatic* relations and *syntagmatic* relations.

Paradigmatic relations are links which are forged between linguistic items in speakers' minds. The words we have stored in our heads do not lie there in individual, hermetically sealed boxes: our brains seem to group them together and organise them into larger sets of associated items. These mental structures are referred to as 'paradigms'. Grammarians frequently use the term 'paradigm' in the context of morphology. For instance, verb conjugations constitute paradigms, e.g.:

	suis	chante
	es	chantes
(7)	est	chante
	sommes	chantons
	êtes	chantez
	sont	chantent

as do noun and adjective declensions, e.g.:

	Latin	Nominative (subject case)	bonus
		Vocative (addressing case)	bone
(8)		Accusative (direct object case)	bonum
		Genitive (possessing case)	boni
		Dative (indirect object case)	bono
		Ablative ('taking away from' case)	bono

The lexicon is not structured in such a rigid way as the grammar, but it is possible to argue none the less that in our minds words too are organised into sets or paradigms, based either on the form of the words in question (as we saw above, p. 36, with the derivational family constructed around *nom*), or on their conceptual content. A simple example of a lexical paradigm is shown in Fig. 4.1.

Lexical paradigms are like folders in a filing cabinet. We associate words together in a folder which is filed away in a particular part of the cabinet until the need arises to select and extract a particular item for use in a particular utterance.

The expression 'particular utterance' brings us to the notion of *syntagma*.

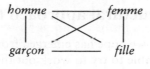

Fig. 4.1

This word, like its cognate term *syntax*, derives from Greek elements meaning 'joining together'. When we take words out of the 'filing cabinet' (the paradigm) and join them up with other words to create a 'chain' of words (a phrase, a sentence), we have created a syntagma. In real-life use of language, a word almost never occurs on its own, in isolation from other words. It invariably occurs in the context of other words, that is in a chain or syntagma. Syntagmatic relations are the patterns which can be observed in the ordering of linguistic items into longer sequences.

To sum up then, paradigmatic relations operate *in the mind* and they involve us in making choices between items stored there. Syntagmatic relations operate *in the context of utterance* and they involve us in constructing sequences or chains of linguistic items. Paradigmatic relations are relationships of *choice*. Syntagmatic relations are relationships of *chain*. The two axes operate conjointly and not independently of one another, as you can see in Figure 4.2.

Fig. 4.2

In what follows we will apply this distinction to our discussion of lexical meaning, dealing with paradigms in section 4.3 and syntagmas in section 4.4.

4.3 Lexical 'paradigms'

What sorts of mental, conceptual structures could exist to enable our brains to keep track of our vocabulary and allow us to have the right word ready for use when we need it? If we wanted to tackle this subject in any depth, we would have to engage seriously with the research conducted in the field of psycholinguistics (see Aitchison 1987). Here our ambitions must be more limited: we simply wish to illustrate some of the main lexical structures (paradigms) which may exist in our minds and which structure our lexical choices, and hence affect word meaning. We need to be aware, however, that the term paradigm, when applied to vocabulary, does not have the same rigour and fixity which it possesses in inflectional morphology: every speaker associates words in his/her mind in his own individual and rather personal way.

4.3.1   Meaning and choice

The question of choice is of critical importance in semantics, for the meaning of all linguistic items depends crucially upon it: if we have no choice, no option but to use a particular item in a particular context, we have to say that, in that context, the item has no meaning. For example, imagine a situation where all road traffic-lights contain not three bulbs with three different colours (red, yellow and green), but only one colour, say red. This would mean that when the lights 'change', they go from red to red to red. Such a situation would leave drivers more than a little confused: does the red light mean, 'stop', 'get set' or 'go'? For the red light to have any meaning the motorist requires the possibility of finding a yellow or a green light instead. The red light has no meaning unless there exists a *choice* between it and a yellow or green light.

Another example of this principle could be constructed around the words *yes* and *no*. Imagine that the English language had only the word *yes* and no word to express *no*. This would mean that whenever anyone asked you a *yes/no* question, you would have to answer *yes*. So, if you were asked 'Is Jane intelligent?', you would answer *yes*, and if you were then asked by someone else 'Is Jane rather a dim-wit?', you would have to give the same answer. This would make nonsense of what is said, for *yes* can have no meaning without the possibility of choosing between it and a word for *no*. Without a choice between *yes* and *no*, the word *yes* has no meaning. Meaning implies choice and the more choice we have about using a particular word in a particular context, the more meaning it conveys. Conversely, the less choice we have (i.e. the more predictable the word), the less meaning it brings to the overall message.

When we look at the structure of different languages we can observe that the choices on offer differ significantly from language to language, even on an apparently simple issue like *yes* and *no* (see Catford 1965: 40–41). For example, see Table 4.1.

We can see from Table 4.1 that the choices available to speakers of English, French and Japanese, even in such a basic area as *yes* and *no*, are different. This means that a different value 'has to be given to the word for *yes* in each of the languages.

4.3.2   Linguistic relativity

Examples like this one illustrate a principle known as *linguistic relativity*: different languages divide up human experience in different ways; meanings

Table 4.1 Differing values of 'yes' and 'no'

English	French	Japanese
yes	oui	hai
	si	
no	non	ue
		hai

are structured differently in different languages. The most commonly quoted examples of this principle are the numerous words present in Eskimo languages for snow and in Vietnamese for rice, contrasted with English and French which possess only one word for each of these concepts. Another oft-quoted example is that of colour terms. The colour spectrum offers a continuum with no natural breaks, so we should not be surprised if different languages divide it up in different ways. You may have experienced problems caused by this even between two closely related languages like English and French. Take for instance, the words for brown and purple in the two languages. *The Oxford English Dictionary* offers the following definitions of the relevant colours:

brown	=	'orange and black'
maroon	=	'brownish crimson'
red	=	'a range from bright scarlet or crimson to reddish yellow or brown'
crimson	=	'deep red inclining towards purple'
purple	=	'mixtures of red and blue in various proportions'
violet	=	'a purplish blue'

The *Petit Robert* dictionary gives the following definitions for the French terms:

brun	=	'entre le roux et le noir'
marron	=	'rouge brun'
roux	=	'jaune orangé, rouge orangé, brun-rouge'
rouge	=	'extrémité du spectre solaire'
cramoisi	=	'rouge foncé tirant sur le violet'
pourpre	=	'rouge foncé tirant sur le violet' (sic)
violet	=	'mélange du bleu et du rouge'

If we plot these definitions on to a figure, we can visualise the differences between the two languages (according to these lexicographers at any rate), see Fig. 4.3.

ORANGE   RED   VIOLET

English	brown		maroon	red	crimson	purple	violet
French	brun	roux	marron	rouge	pourpre		violet

ORANGE   ROUGE   VIOLET

Fig. 4.3

The primary colours of the spectrum merge into one another in the following way: yellow > orange > red > violet > indigo > blue > green. In Figure 4.3 we have left *cramoisi* out of account because *Petit Robert* gives it an identical definition to *pourpre*.

We can see from this example that no one colour term in French has its exact equivalent in English: the value of each of the terms is closely bound up with the place it occupies within the overall scheme operating within its language. It is hard to grasp the meaning of one of the terms without taking the value of neighbouring terms into consideration. We need to be able to see its relationship with the other words in the 'paradigm'.

What sorts of patterns can be detected among the words covering a particular semantic field? Linguists have identified three types of paradigmatic relationship underpinning the lexical structures we have in our minds: hyponymy, antonymy and synonymy. Let us take each of these in turn.

4.3.3   Hyponymy

An essential function of human languages is to classify our experiences, grouping together related concepts under more general headings. Thus, a particular semantic field, say 'trees', is identified and under the general heading *arbre* the language places the names for the various types of tree, e.g. *chêne, platane, hêtre, cerisier*, etc., see Fig. 4.4. Likewise, under the general heading *fruit* we would place the names for the various types of fruit, e.g. *pomme, poire, abricot, orange*, etc.

This relationship is known as hyponymy ('naming beneath') and is one of inclusion: the more specific term (the 'hyponym') is felt to be included in

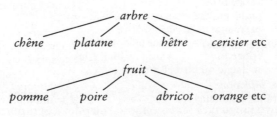

Fig. 4.4

the more general term above (the 'superordinate'). The superordinate term is somehow felt to 'contain' the idea of all the hyponyms: all apples are fruits, but not all fruits are apples.

The examples quoted here are all very obvious and straightforward. Where hyponymy becomes interesting is when we discover that the lexical classifications of experience which are made by natural languages are not necessarily logical or systematic and that as a result they differ significantly as we pass from one language to another. For instance, French has a general (superordinate) term to refer to harvests of all kinds and a long list of more specific terms (hyponyms) referring to the harvests of particular crops, see Fig. 4.5. Thus:

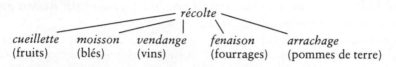

récolte				
cueillette	moisson	vendange	fenaison	arrachage
(fruits)	(blés)	(vins)	(fourrages)	(pommes de terre)

Fig. 4.5

If you wish to translate these terms into English, you will find it difficult to find a single-word equivalent for any of them apart from *récolte*. The lexical grid of French classifies this semantic field in a finer way than English. Another example can be found when we consider the words for different sorts of smell which are available in French and English. In Figure 4.6 the definitions are taken from the *Petit Robert* dictionary:

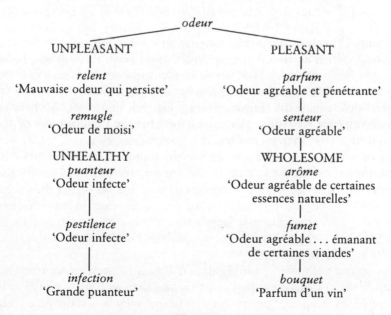

Fig. 4.6

If, now, we attempt to translate these items into English with a single word for each, we are likely in most cases to be disappointed, for English analyses this semantic field in a different way.

4.3.4 *Antonymy*

While hyponymy is a relationship of inclusion, antonymy is a relationship of exclusion or incompatibility, involving oppositeness of meaning. It is possible for words to belong to the same semantic field and yet to be 'opposite' in meaning. Semanticists have distinguished three types of oppositeness:

- complementary opposites
- converse opposites
- true antonyms

'Complementary opposites' of the type *mâle ~ femelle, célibataire ~ marié, vivant ~ mort* have the property that denial of one implies assertion of the other, and assertion of one implies denial of the other. Thus, if a person is not male, then she must be female, and so on. 'Converse opposites' of the type *mari ~ femme, acheter ~ vendre* and *emprunter ~ prêter* suppose reciprocal activities whereby if one exists or occurs, the other must of necessity exist or occur too. 'True antonyms' of the type *grand ~ petit, froid ~ chaud, long ~ court, près ~ loin* behave rather differently. These pairs are all adjectives or adverbs and are not absolutes: they can only be understood in relation to the thing they are describing. For example, at 10°C the weather may be felt to be *froid* in summer, but rather *chaud* in the depths of winter. A 20-mile journey might be considered *long* if it is being undertaken on foot, but quite *court* if we are travelling by car. 'True antonyms' are merely lexical devices for grading and they all imply comparison with some conventionally accepted norm. Someone who declares that politically speaking they are not *de droite* is not auto-matically asserting that they are *de gauche*. There is a multiplicity of points between the two extremes. Denial of one does not necessarily imply assertion of the other, as was the case with complementary opposites: if we say *Notre maison n'est pas grande*, we are not necessarily claiming that it is *petite*. We could be merely pointing out that it is no bigger than what is considered to be the normal size of house in our society. 'Converse opposites' and 'complementary opposites' may not vary substantially from language to language, but there is considerable cross-cultural variation with 'true antonyms'.

The central point about antonyms is that they illustrate a tendency in the human brain to structure things in pairs, and that with these words at least it is impossible to grasp the meaning of of one member of the pair without understanding the meaning of its opposite as well.

4.3.5 Synonymy

The third and perhaps most important relationship which exists between words belonging to a particular semantic field is *synonymy*: lexical items which have the same meanings are synonyms. It is theoretically possible to distinguish between two classes of synonym: complete synonyms and partial synonyms. However, in reality, complete synonyms are extremely rare: they involve words which are completely interchangeable (a) with no change of meaning and (b) in all contexts. Examples of this are hard to find, for, as duplicates, they waste the language's resources. One could, at a pinch, cite as examples the linguistic terms *terminaison* and *désinence,* which both refer to 'word-endings' with little to choose between them as regards meaning and potential contexts. Partial synonymy on the other hand is a very widespread phenomenon. It involves (a) subtle differences of meaning and/or (b) differences in the contexts in which the words concerned may occur.

In what ways are the meanings of synonyms subtly differentiated to leave us with synonyms which are only 'partial'? Here we need to distinguish between denotative meaning and connotative meaning. Denotation covers the relationship between a word and the 'things' to which it refers. *Fleuve* and *rivière* are not complete synonyms because they each have a slightly different denotation: the former refers to a large river which flows into the sea, while the latter refers to a smaller river which is the tributary of a larger one. Criminal slang in French has a large number of 'synonyms' for 'thief', but given the professional need to distinguish between different types of thief, each of the 'synonyms' is allocated a slightly different denotation. The following example is a quotation from Guiraud (1973: 37):

- le *cambrioleur* est le voleur de chambre; la *cambriole* étant en dialecte picard, puis en argot, une petite chambre;
- le *camelot* est un marchand ambulant, survivant de l'ancien *Coesmelot,* formé sur *coesme* qui signifie à la fois mendiant et mercier ambulant;
- l'*escarpe* est un voleur d'après la forme provençale d'écharper (= 'rip up');
- *gouape* est emprunté à l'argot espagnol: *guapo* (un coupe-jarret).'

Clearly there is a link between synonymy and hyponymy – all of the above are hyponyms of *voleur* – but whereas hyponymy is concerned primarily with the relationship between the hyponyms and the superordinate term, synonymy is concerned with relationships between the hyponyms (which are at the same time partial synonyms).

Connotation refers to the emotional associations which may form part of the meaning of a word. Two words may possess the same denotation but have very different connotations. For instance French *la buvette* refers to more or less the same 'thing' as *le snack-bar.* However, the emotional associations of the two words in French are very different, with the former triggering associations with the traditional French *fête champêtre,* with *saucisson, camembert* and red wine, and the latter evoking juke-boxes and

Coca Cola. A major preoccupation of trend-setters, be they in marketing or in teenage clubs, is to demonstrate that they are always ahead of the game. This involves them in the constant production of new synonyms with more 'with it' connotations. An example of a 'série synonymique' in French slang would be the numerous words for 'head'. The 'head' can be likened to a round fruit, so slang words for 'head' have proliferated as follows (taken from Guiraud 1973: 56):

(9)   *tête = pomme > cassis > fraise > citron > tomate > patate* etc.

So, partial synonyms may be distinguished by connotation. They may also be differentated by stylistic level. The words *chef, tête, figure, bobine, gueule*, etc. which we quoted on p. 28, all refer to 'head', but they belong to different levels of formality. Formal style words seek to enhance the dignity of the thing referred to, whereas informal words do the opposite, tending towards disparagement and pejoration, normally in a jocular way. *Véhicule* and *bagnole* both have the same denotation, indeed, they may both be referring to the same glistening Jaguar parked in the drive, but whereas the former takes the car seriously, the latter does not and implies that it is an old wreck. This sort of synonym has a vitally important part to play in the generation of new French slang, whose principal function is give coded emotional signals about the speaker and their relationship with their interlocutors.

Partial synonyms where the words involved have very similar but not completely overlapping meanings are then extremely common, and they perform an indispensable communicative role in expressing subtle differences of denotational or connotative meaning. However, this not to say that in certain contexts two or more words cannot have exactly the same meaning. In the context of a walk in the country the two words *brook* and *stream* would be interchangeable with no change of meaning for most British speakers of English at least. In the following French example *pas* and *marche* are interchangeable:

(10)   L'élève s'avançait d'un *pas*/d'une *marche* hésitant(e).

However, these pairs of words are not interchangeable in all contexts: literary critics write about '*stream* of consciousness novels', but they would not allow 'brook' to figure in this expression. *Pas* cannot be substituted for *marche* in the following sentence:

(11)   La musique jouait une *marche* militaire.

From these examples we can see that synonymy is to a great extent context-dependent, and relations of context are to be the subject of our next section.

In this section we have looked at the ways in which the vocabulary of a language may be structured in speakers' minds. We have seen how the meaning and value of a word cannot be worked out by treating the word as an isolated entity: words belong in structures and derive their value from the place they occupy in their structure. Meaning implies choice, and the meaning of a word is geared to the range of items available in that language from which the item in question is selected. It would appear to be the case that the lexical choices available in different languages are usually not identical.

The suggestion that each language has its own structure, peculiar to it, and that there is no limit to the structural diversity of languages, has been given the label *linguistic relativity*. This idea leads in turn to another question: that of the relationship between language and thought. Do the lexical structures peculiar to our language force us to *think* along certain lines? Does our language determine our thought-processes (*linguistic determinism*)? The idea that it does was pursued by two American linguists and has been named after them as the *Sapir-Whorf hypothesis* (see Yule 1985: 195–98 and Lyons 1981: 301–12). According to this hypothesis, we dissect nature on lines laid down by our native language, and each language thereby imposes a distinct world-view upon its speakers. Philosophically this hypothesis is extremely interesting, and has been taken up by non-linguists for their own purposes. Feminists, for instance, have taken it up to demonstrate how women have traditionally been led to accept a subordinate social role by the imposition of lexical structures reflecting a male-dominated view of the world.

However, linguists now believe that in its strong form the Sapir-Whorf hypothesis is not tenable, and that we are not ultimately the prisoners of our language. Just because Language A possesses a word to denote a particular feature of experience, which is absent from Language B, does not mean that a speaker of Language B cannot grasp the concept in question. English may not have single words for differentiating different types of snow, but phrases like 'slushy snow' and 'powdery snow' enable us to distinguish between them when we need to. Possession of a particular vocabulary undoubtedly enhances our ability to perceive and recall particular ideas, but this does not prevent speakers of other languages with different structures from sharing them. Whatever can be expressed in one language can also be expressed in any other. Provided we allow for a certain amount of 'translation loss' (see Higgins and Hervey 1992), translation from one language to another, no matter how distant their structures are from one another, is always possible. A distinction has been made between the surface structure of language which varies substantially from language to language and a deeper substructure which reflects universal modes of thought. Participation in the latter allows access, with training and experience, to the former. (For a wholesale demolition of the Sapir-Whorf hypothesis see Pinker 1995: 55–58.)

4.4 Words and 'syntagmas'

In section 4.3 we looked at ways in which words are associated with other words 'in our minds' (paradigmatic relations). Now we shall turn to the relationships a word contracts when it is combined with other words in utterances (syntagmatic relations). The key term in this discussion is going to be the word 'context'.

The word 'context' can be used in a wide range of senses and will be taken up again in Chapter 9. Here we shall focus on just two of them: it can refer either to the non-linguistic situation in which an utterance is pronounced, and it can refer to the sequence of linguistic items in which the item we are concerned with occurs. To avoid ambiguity, in what follows we will use the word 'context' to refer to the former and 'co-text' to refer to the latter.

4.4.1 Situational context

Every speech act takes place in a specific physical context, between specific people and to serve a specific function or purpose. In order to make sense of the speech act in question we need to have precise information about each of these things. The following utterance is well-formed grammatically and lexically:

(12) *Je viendrai te voir ici demain.*

However, it is not possible to understand it fully unless we have a good deal of situational knowledge: who are *je* and *te*? What are the date and place referred to? Words like *je*, *le*, *ici* and *demain* are known as **deictic** expressions for they 'point to' various features of the situational (non-linguistic) context as part of their meaning. A dictionary can only provide part of the meaning of such words and we need a lot of non-linguistic information as well.

There is a whole branch of linguistics devoted to examining the relationship between linguistic utterances and the real-world situations in which they are used. It is known as **pragmatics** and we will look at it in Chapter 9. In the rest of this chapter, therefore, we will use the word 'context' not in the sense of 'situation in time and space', but in that of linguistic 'co-text'.

4.4.2 Linguistic context (or 'co-text')

Traditional ideas about word meaning assumed that words were the basic building-blocks of language and that they were quite capable of expressing meaning 'on their own', independently of context. Words were thought to be semantically autonomous. Structural ideas about word meaning, as you might now be in a position to appreciate, reject this idea and stress the importance of a word's belonging to larger groupings of words. When a word is used in speech, it does not normally occur on its own. One-word utterances are rare, and even when they do occur, they are usually part of a conversation where the speaker is reacting to the words of the other partici-pant(s). We will be looking at turn-taking and conversation analysis in Chapter 10, so here we will limit our remarks to a word's relations with its immediate linguistic context, the phrase and the sentence. We will be looking for answers to two basic questions:

1 What factors limit our freedom to place one word next to another?
2 What is the contribution of the 'co-text' to our understanding of a word in use?

4.4.3   *Selectional restrictions*

There are many factors which limit our freedom to select any word and place it next to any other in any order. Some of these restrictions are grammatical: *Je mon père aime** and *Bruns cheveux les** represent combi-nations of words which contravene the grammatical rules of French. Other combinations are impossible not for reasons of grammar but for reasons of logical incompatibility. Chomsky's famous sentence *Colorless green ideas sleep furiously* illustrates this point very neatly.

However, these factors are not the only ones to be borne in mind when we examine the workings of the vocabularies of natural languages. It is possible for chains of words to be grammatically acceptable and logically compatible, but still to be rejected by native-speakers as not being what any of them would normally say. For instance, French speakers normally do not say *recevoir un salaire**, but *toucher* or *percevoir un salaire*. There is nothing grammatically or logically wrong with *recevoir* in this context, the problem is that French people tend not to say it. The same would go for *demander une question**, *donner un discours** and *rencontrer un échec**, which French people do not say, and *poser une question*, *prononcer un discours* and *essuyer un échec* which they do. It is tradition, convention which has fixed these pairings of words in rather arbitrary fashion.

The term used to denote this phenomenon is *collocation*. The collo-cations of a word are its 'habitual neighbours'. Some words have a very narrow range of collocation (i.e. not many habitual neighbours) – *aquilin* can only go with *nez*, *ballants* can only go with *bras*, *diluvienne* can only go with *pluie*. Others have a very wide range and can co-occur with a large number of words, e.g. *faire*, *prendre*, *mettre*. Collocations then are lin-guistically predictable to a greater or lesser extent, depending on the word. The important point they raise, however, is that the selection of one word rather than another to fit a particular context may depend not on its conceptual meaning, but upon a purely lexical convention – which words traditionally go alongside which other words.

French possesses a number of pairs of synonyms like *an ~ année*, *jour ~ journée* and *lieu ~ endroit*, and it is tempting to try to see subtle differences of meaning between each member of the pair. However, such enquiries produce rather meagre results. If, on the other hand, we compare each word with its alternant as regards the types of context in which it is likely to occur, a more useful set of guidelines may result. *Lieu,* for instance, is a very old word inherited from Latin, and it tends to occur in fossilised expressions like *avoir lieu, lieu de naissance, lieux du crime, se rendre sur les lieux. Endroit,* on the other hand, is a more recent creation and, while it cannot occur in the expressions we have just listed, it possesses a much wider range of collocation. When we say that someone speaks French very idiomatically, we usually mean that the person has a sufficiently detailed knowledge of the language to get not only the grammar right, but the collocations right as well.

We have seen how the collocations of a word are to a greater or lesser extent predictable, and this leads us into the question of *idioms* and *clichés,* for these too can be seen as words placed in predictable sequences. Examples of idioms are: *It's raining cats and dogs, Il pleut des cordes, Se mettre sur son trente et un* (= *se parer de ses plus beaux habits*), and a useful dictionary of such expressions in French is by Rat (1968). Idioms are ready-made utterances (in French 'locutions toutes faites'), that is sequences of lexical items thrust together by tradition, which (a) cannot be modified (e.g. by changing one of the words or by introducing an extra one), and which (b) have a global meaning which cannot be inferred from the normal meanings of the component words (the origins of idioms are normally metaphors whose literal meaning has now been lost). Since an idiomatic expression functions as a single semantic unit, which loses its meaning if any part of it is tampered with, it has to be learnt and used as a block. It is generally impossible to produce a word-for-word translation of an idiom into another language: 'To put oneself on to one's thirty-one' makes no sense at all to English speakers.

Clichés are also predictable sequences of linguistic items: stereotyped expressions, commonplace phrases. However, in so far as the term 'cliché' implies disapproval, it is a judgemental, normative one, not a linguistic one. Clichés are to be found on two levels of language use. At the higher level – that of a global speech situation – a cliché would be a whole utterance in a sequence of utterances. As such it is a banal, highly predictable utterance, whose form and content are heavily conditioned by the situational context and require minimal selectivity and choice on the part of the speaker. An example might be the 'Do you come here often?' from one stranger to another on a dance-floor. It requires less effort to repeat an utterance frequently heard in that situation before than to think up something original for oneself. On the function of such semi-ritualised utterances in conversations, see Chapter 10. At the lower level – that of an individual utterance – a cliché is a sequence of words put together by the speaker not as a result of his own individual choice, but by dint of their hearing that sequence frequently on the lips of other speakers. Most English speakers could complete the following utterances in the same way and without difficulty:

She's as blind as a . . .
At this moment in . . .
Let's get down to the . . .

Clichés differ from idioms essentially on the question of modifiability. In the latter the sequence of lexical items belong together as a block which the speaker is not free to modify. In the former, the items in sequence are less closely bound together, and the speaker can choose to modify the sequence in some way without producing nonsense. It is precisely the failure to avoid the most predictable sequence which exposes the speaker to criticism from normative observers and attracts the disparaging label 'cliché'.

4.4.4 Polysemy and contextual meaning

We saw earlier that one-word utterances are extremely rare, and this is hardly surprising, for how much meaning does a word convey outside a particular linguistic context? If we toss out a word in isolation, e.g.:

(13)   *garçon*
(14)   *vert*
(15)   *tirer*

how much meaning does it convey? The answer might be 'Too much meaning', for, in isolation from a context, each of these words has a string of potential meanings. It is the combination with a specific context which singles out the one required. Thus the different meanings of *garçon* become clear in:

(16)   *J'ai perdu mon petit garçon*
                        and
(17)   *Il est devenu garçon de café*

We are confronted here with a widespread feature of the lexicon: *polysemy* or multiple meaning. You could say that polysemy is language's way of economising on signs, for it needs fewer signs if each has several meanings 'disambiguated' by the context.

Examples of polysemy are not difficult to find: *tirer* means 'to take out' and 'to shoot', *poser* means 'to pose', 'to put down' and 'to ask (a question)', *entendre* means 'to hear' and 'to understand'. The Littré dictionary distinguishes 39 meanings for *aller*, 49 for *mettre*, 80 for *prendre* and 82 for *faire*! (Ullman 1969: 200.) In fact, no dictionary can mirror exactly the detail and complexity of the language it is recording, and ultimately every occurrence of a word takes place in new and unique circumstances, inviting an extension of the word's meaning. For instance, every concrete word is capable of metaphorical use, and if a sufficient number of people imitate it, the new use will add a second meaning to the first, making it 'polysemic'.

This is how *bouche* has come to mean 'estuary' and *pied* 'foothills'. Polysemy is, then, a normal condition for a large proportion of a language's vocabulary. If we wish to avoid the dangers of ambiguity implicit in polysemy, without relying on the context, we have to take special steps by way of specialised terms and definitions. This is precisely what happens in the development of scientific terminology.

Many words, then, do not have a fixed core of meaning which remains constant in all contexts. Certain ones are like putty and are moulded into whatever shape the speaker wants to suit the context. This at least is the message to be gained from Williams' (1976) *Keywords* which examines the diverse interpretations which can be put on such terms as *bourgeois*, *culture, nature* and *democracy*.

Whereas *polysemy* involves one form having more than one related meaning, *homonymy* involves one form having more than one *unrelated* meaning, e.g. *air* (= air) and *air* (= tune). A theoretical problem for linguists is then to distinguish between homonymy and polysemy, for both involve one form with multiple meanings. There can be no objective solution to this problem: if speakers feel that there is a conceptual link between the various meanings of a particular form, they are likely to consider the case as one of polysemy. If there is no easily recognised link between them, they will regard the case as one of homonymy.

A phenomenon closely related to polysemy and homonymy is *homophony*. Here we are confronted not with one word which has several meanings, but with several words which have the same pronunciation. For historical phonetics reasons, this phenomenon is relatively widespread in French, e.g.

(18)   /sɛ̃/   –   *saint, ceint, sein*
(19)   /sɑ̃/   –   *sans, sang, cent, sent*
(20)   /vɛR/   –   *vers, ver, verre, vert*

These provide the basis for numerous jokes and puns like Napoleon's exclamation *Ma sacrée toux!* (= 'My bloody cough!') which a dim-witted companion interpreted as *Massacrez tout!* Extended homophony is the key to the following:

(21)   *Gal, amant de la Reine, alla, tour magnanime,*
         Galamment de l'Arène à la Tour Magne à Nîmes

Polysemy, homonymy and homophony all have the effect of increasing the dependency of a word on its context, that is to say that they diminish the semantic autonomy of the individual lexical item. Awareness of the importance of context in word meaning led to the emergence early in the twentieth century of a school of linguistic philosophers known as 'Contextualists'. Their slogan was 'Don't give me the meaning of a word, give me its use!' Now, the Contextualists were surely right to affirm the importance of context in word meaning, but they were surely wrong to suggest that words are totally dependent on context for their meaning. If a word's meaning depends entirely on the particular context in which it is being used, then it brings no new information which cannot be already inferred from the context and is redundant. We saw earlier that if a word is entirely predictable in context and the speaker has no choice about it, the word contributes no new meaning. This is the problem with clichés.

Conclusion

In a sense, word meaning is all about predictability in context: the less a word is predictable in a given context, the more meaning it contributes. The more choice we have about which word to use in a given context, the more meaning the word will bring. In this way we can see that the two sorts of structural relationship we have discussed in this chapter – paradigmatic relations and syntagmatic relations – work conjointly and not separately in allowing words to have meaning. We *choose* from the sets of words stored in our heads the appropriate word required to fill a particular slot in the ongoing *chain* of speech.

What makes learning a second language so difficult and yet so interesting is that each language offers speakers a different set of lexical choices (paradigms) and a different range of combination possibilities (syntagmas) for all of its words. This goes some way to showing why it is so difficult to find words in one language which, on both axes, have their exact equivalent in the other.

Seminar exercises

1.   What factors seem to operate to make lexical dissymmetry between languages so widespread?

2.   What is the difference between 'paradigmatic' and 'syntagmatic' relations?

3.   How do you understand the expression 'meaning implies choice'?

4.   If complete synonymy is so rare, what is the value of the term 'synonymy'?

5.   What is the 'Sapir-Whorf hypothesis'? To what degree are you prepared to subscribe to it?

5

Describing French speech sounds

Phonetics is the study of the sounds of speech. In order to understand this subject adequately, you will need to master a certain amount of new, technical terminology, along with a new alphabet. In the early stages, this may seem unnecessarily abstract and difficult, leading you to ask: 'why do I need to learn this anyway?' The study of the phonetics of French has an obvious practical application – it will help you improve your pronunciation of French by giving you a clearer idea of how the sounds of the language are produced. More importantly, however, it has an intellectual justification, for in studying phonetics you will be exploring the structure of the language. This involves looking for patterns which are not immediately obvious: the sounds of a language are structured systematically; that is, they differ from each other in an organised way. They are not arranged on a random basis, as the lay-person might surmise: if they were, children acquiring their mother tongue would be unable to learn them as quickly and easily as they in fact do.

But why all the technical jargon? The use of a certain amount of terminology is necessary for the accurate description of speech sounds. Lay-persons commonly use such terms as 'guttural', 'harsh', 'flat', 'sloppy' to describe individual sounds or even whole languages, but although terms like these may convey a sort of meaning on an intuitive or impressionistic level, they are entirely inadequate for the purposes of rigorous description (and in fact, as we saw in Chapter 1, they are usually thinly disguised social judgements on the speaker whose accent or language is in question). What is needed, therefore, is a terminology which is as objective as possible; one which refers to actual entities which can be readily verified.

5.1 The description of speech sounds

There are two main approaches to the description of speech sounds: the 'acoustic' and the 'articulatory'. Let us look briefly at each in turn. The *acoustic approach*: it is possible to use instruments such as electrographs and palatographs to establish extremely precise, scientific descriptions of speech sounds. Thus, for example, the properties of vowels can be described in terms of the principal groups of sound frequencies of which they are composed (known as *formants*). However, this approach relies heavily on sophisticated instrumentation, and its results are often open to multiple interpretation.

The *articulatory approach*: this viewpoint establishes descriptions of speech sounds on the basis of the way they are produced by the speaker. The term *articulation* literally means joining or bringing together, and we may understand it in two senses as it applies to the production of speech. On the one hand, the 'articulation' of speech joins sounds together in a continuous stream so as to produce intelligible sequences of sounds. In a further sense, when we speak, we articulate, or bring parts of the vocal tract into contact with one another, or close together, in order to produce our speech sounds. The 'articulatory' mode of description is expressed in terms of the manner and place in which speech sounds are articulated, as air leaves the mouth and nose via the various parts of the vocal tract. It is this articulatory viewpoint which we shall adopt in the present chapter.

For further reading on articulatory and acoustic phonetics, see Ladefoged (1994), Chapters 1, 7, 8; Price (1991), Chapters 1 and 2; Tranel (1987), Chapter 2.

Figure 5.1 shows the parts of the vocal tract which are most involved in the production of speech. This diagram is a so-called 'mid-sagittal' view of the vocal tract, representing an imaginary cut through the middle of the head. Because it is two-dimensional, this view does not capture all of the information necessary for a description of consonants, as we shall see below.

Broadly, certain parts of the vocal tract (tongue, lips, palate, etc.) are moved in relation to one another as air issues through them from the lungs. The vocal tract is essentially a tube, and we can draw an analogy here with the sounds produced by tubular musical instruments (e.g. the trombone, the flute, the clarinet), where different notes are produced by adjusting the length of the tube or otherwise modifying the column of air as it passes through. The processes which take place in the vocal tract are a good deal more complex than what takes place in a flute; but the essential similarity remains: air issues from the lungs, passes through the vocal cords and resonates (vibrates), and the quality of the vibrating air is then modified by various movements of the speech organs.

The numbers in Figure 5.1 refer to the following parts of the vocal tract. In brackets are the adjectives which correspond to some of these parts, and which are used in the description of speech sounds; thus French 't' is a dental sound, 'k' is velar, and so forth.

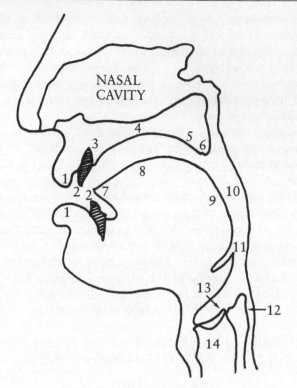

Fig. 5.1 The speech organs

1 Lips (labial)
2 Teeth (dental)
3 Alveolus, or alveolar ridge (alveolar)
4 Hard palate (palatal)
5 Soft palate or velum (velar)
6 Uvula (uvular)
7 Tip of tongue
8 Blade of tongue
9 Back of tongue
10 Pharynx (pharyngeal)
11 Epiglottis
12 Oesophagus
13 Vocal cords (glottal)
14 Larynx (laryngeal)

5.1.1   Criteria for classifying speech sounds

A preliminary distinction which is an easy one for non-specialists to grasp is that between *consonants* (*t, d, f*, etc.) and *vowels* (*a, e, i, o, u*). In phonetic terms, the difference between consonants and vowels is the degree of constriction used to produce each type of sound. When we produce consonants we generally bring the articulators (parts of the vocal tract involved in producing speech) either into contact with each other or into close proximity. In this way the airflow passing through them is constricted or narrowed, so that audible friction is produced. In the production of vowels, less constriction is used, and audible friction is not usually produced, although a sound is of course heard as air vibrates in the vocal tract. This distinction between the different ways in which consonants and vowels are produced means that different sets of criteria are needed to describe them. For both consonants and vowels, one important criterion refers to the place of articulation (i.e. the position of the tongue in relation to the other organs of speech; or the relative position of other organs of speech). However, when describing consonants, we need additional criteria referring to the manner in which they are produced.

5.2 Classifying consonants

We can classify the French consonants according to: (1) place of articulation; (2) manner of articulation; (3) presence or absence of voice. These criteria are explained in turn below.

5.2.1 *The place of articulation*

Three criteria are commonly used in the description of consonants. The first of these is the place of articulation, or the point in the vocal tract where the tongue is brought more or less closely into contact with one of the articulators. Using the terms listed in Figure 5.1, we can now classify the places of articulation which are relevant to the sounds of French. As is customary, we will start from the front with the lips and work backwards.

- *Bilabial* This term derives from the Latin *labia* and means literally 'two lips'. Examples of French (and of course English) bilabial sounds are 'p', 'b' and 'm'. It is easy to sense that both lips are involved in the production of these sounds.
- *Labio-dental* Literally, involving 'lip-tooth'. In these sounds the lower lip and top teeth are brought into play. Examples are French and English 'f' and 'v'.
- *Dental* Involving the back of the teeth and the tip or front of the tongue. The sounds 't', 'd' and 'n' generally have dental realisation (i.e. pronunciation) in French, and sometimes in English.
- *Dental-alveolar* As the term suggests, articulation of consonants at these places involves simultaneously the back of the top teeth, the

alveolar ridge and the tip or blade of the tongue. The sounds 't', 'd' and 'n' can have dental-alveolar realisation in French and English. Individual speakers may vary in the place at which they produce these sounds.

- *Alveolar* The ridge behind the top teeth and the tip or blade of the tongue are involved in alveolar sounds. Examples are French 's', 'z' and 'l' which have alveolar realisation; French 't', 'd' and 'n' are produced further forward than their English equivalents, and are therefore dental rather than alveolar. See dental and dental-alveolar above.

- *Palato-alveolar* These sounds are produced using contact between the tongue blade and the back of the alveolar ridge. Examples are the 'sh' sound in French *chien* and the consonant at the beginning of French *je*.

- *Palatal* The front of the tongue and the hard palate are involved in the production of palatal consonants. Palatal consonants in French are the sound at the beginning of French *yeux*, (or English *you*), and the consonant in the middle of *agneau*. In producing these sounds, the front of the tongue is raised towards the hard palate.

- *Velar* The velum (Latin for 'veil') or soft palate is a muscular flap at the back of the mouth that can be raised and pressed against the pharynx to close off the nasal cavity, thus preventing air from flowing through it. Velar consonants are produced by the action of the back of the tongue and the velum. Examples are French and English 'k', 'g', and the 'ng' sound in English (and French) *parking*.

- *Uvular* The uvula (Latin for 'little grape') is the small fleshy protuberance suspended from the back of the soft palate over the back of the tongue. Uvular consonants are articulated by the back of the tongue and the uvula. French 'r' is a uvular consonant.

- *Glottal* The glottis is the aperture between the *vocal cords* (the action of the vocal cords will be discussed in more detail below). The 'glottal stop' is a very salient feature of some dialects of English, most notably Cockney (e.g. in their pronunciation of the word *bottle*), where it alternates with 't'. The glottal stop is a good deal less common in French, but may be heard in some contexts, between vowels for example, as in *en haut*.

You will probably have noticed that some types of consonants have been given double-barrelled labels, e.g. palato-alveolar, labio-dental. This reflects the various ways in which consonants are articulated. We produce a consonant by bringing the tongue into contact or near contact with one of the passive articulators (those parts of the vocal tract which are capable of little or no movement). Since the tongue is involved in the production of most consonants and moves about while the passive articulators remain static, it is the latter which normally provide the definition of the place of articulation involved. Other movable elements, however, are the lips and the teeth: a bilabial sound is produced using both lips (e.g. the consonant 'p'), and a labio-dental sound is produced using contact between teeth and lips (e.g. the consonant 'f').

5.2.2 The manner of articulation

Two manners of articulation have already been distinguished: *friction* and *plosion*. Consonants produced by friction and plosion are known respectively as *fricatives* and *plosives*. These are described more fully below, along with the other manners of articulation which are relevant to French.

- *Plosives* Plosive consonants are sometimes referred to as 'stops', for they are produced by stopping very briefly the airflow which is issuing through the vocal tract, and then releasing it in such a way that an audible (ex)plosion of sound is heard. We will use the term 'plosive' here. The plosives in English and French are 'p' and 'b'; 't' and 'd'; 'k' and 'g'.
- *Rolls or trills* These consonants are produced by the rapid tapping of one articulator against another. Some dialects of Scots English, and of French, have a trilled alveolar 'r', and one way of producing French 'r' is as a uvular trill, where the back of the tongue and the uvula come into contact in this way.
- *Fricatives* Fricative consonants are produced by bringing two articulators close enough together so that audible friction is produced. The French fricatives, also found in English, are 'f' and 'v'; 's' and 'z'; the 'sh' sound in English *shoe* or French *chien*; and the sound at the end of French *garage*. French 'r' is often produced as a uvular fricative.
- *Nasals* Nasal consonants are produced by directing the airflow passing through the vocal tract into the nasal cavity. This is done by lowering the velum, so that air passes through the nasal cavity, and blocking the air-flow through the mouth at some point. Examples are French and English 'm', 'n', and the 'ng' sound at the end of English (and French) *parking*. A further example is the consonant found in the middle of the French words *agneau* and *oignon*.
- *Approximants (or frictionless continuants)* These consonants are produced by bringing one articulator close to another, but not so close as to produce the type of clearly audible, hissing friction characteristic of fricative consonants. Examples of approximants are the sound at the beginning of English *yacht* or French *yeux,* and the two different sounds at the beginning of French *oui* and *huile.* The fact that these approximant sounds share some of the characteristics both of consonants and vowels is reflected in their often being referred to as 'semi-vowels' or 'semi-consonants'. These three French sounds will be discussed in more detail below.
- *Laterals* Lateral consonants are so called because when they are produced, air passes between the hard palate and one or both sides of the

tongue (Latin *latus* means 'side'). The consonant 'l' in English and French is a lateral. The way in which 'l' is articulated can be quite easily sensed, by making an 'l' sound, holding the position of the tongue, and then breathing in. You should be able to feel cold air on the side(s) of the tongue that are not in contact with the hard palate.

5.2.3   *The presence or absence of voice*

Sounds produced when the vocal cords are vibrating are referred to as *voiced* sounds; correspondingly, sounds produced when the vocal cords are not vibrating are said to be *voiceless*. The vocal cords, which are not in fact cords but muscular folds (some phoneticians refer to them as the *vocal folds*), are located in the upper part of the windpipe (or trachea) known as the *larynx*. The larynx can easily be located, because the thyroid cartilage, a part of the larynx, forms a prominent protrusion in the neck commonly known as the 'Adam's apple'. The presence or absence of voice can be sensed by producing a voiced fricative consonant such as 'z', while placing one's fingers against the Adam's apple. The vibration of the vocal cords can then be clearly felt. If you then produce the corresponding voiceless alveolar fricative 's', you will feel no vibration. Presence or absence of voice distinguishes several sets of French consonants: 'p' and 'b'; 't' and 'd'; 'f' and 'v'; 's' and 'z'. Compare, for instance the pronunciation of the French words *chatte* and *jatte*. The 'ch' sound in *chatte* is voiceless, while the initial consonant in *jatte* is voiced.

5.2.4   *Consonants and their phonetic symbols*

The example of the initial consonants in *chatte* and *jatte* illustrates the problem of representing consonants in a consistent way. French spelling, like English, is less than ideal for this purpose. The English sequence of letters 'ough', for instance, can represent several very different sounds (*cough, through, bough, dough*). George Bernard Shaw produced the classic illustration of the quirks of English spelling by showing that logically, *fish* can be spelt 'ghoti', using 'gh' (= 'f' from 'cough'), 'o' (= 'i' from 'women') and 'ti' (= 'sh' from 'nation'). Similarly, in French the same sound can be spelt in several different ways: the consonant at the beginning of *jatte* can be represented in ordinary spelling, not only by the letter 'j', but also by the sequence 'ge' (as in *geôle*) and by 'g' (as in *marginal*). Therefore, from now on we will use the symbols of the International Phonetic Alphabet (IPA), which represent sounds consistently. The following list shows the IPA symbols for the French consonants, with examples of words which contain them. The letters in the examples which represent each sound are in bold type. Note that IPA symbols are conventionally indicated in square brackets.

The French consonants

IPA symbol	example
[p]	prendre
[b]	bout
[t]	tout
[d]	dans
[k]	carte
[g]	goût
[f]	fou
[v]	ville
[s]	sous
[z]	aisé
[ʃ]	chou
[ʒ]	jour
[R]	rouge
[m]	maison
[n]	nous
[ɲ]	signe
[ŋ]	parking
[l]	long

French semi-consonants

[j]	yeux
[ɥ]	huile
[w]	ouest

In Table 5.1 we can summarise the phonetic properties of the French consonants using the three criteria discussed above.

Table 5.1 Phonetic properties of the French consonants

Place \ Manner	Bilabial	Labio-dental	Dental	Alveolar	Palato-alveolar	Palatal	Velar	Uvular
Plosive	p b		t d				k g	
Roll/Trill				(r)				R
Fricative		f v		s z	ʃ ʒ			
Nasal	m		n			ɲ	ŋ	
Approximant	ɥ w					ɥ j	w	
Lateral				l				

Table 5.1 shows the French consonants classified vertically by manner of articulation, and horizontally by place. Where consonants are shown in pairs, voiceless consonants are shown on the left, voiced on the right.

Three consonants are indicated in two or more cells in the table. In the case of [R], this reflects the fact that this consonant varies in the way in which speakers produce it; although the 'standard' or prescribed pronunciation is as a uvular trill or roll, it is often realised as a fricative or approximant. Some older, rural speakers (and speakers of Canadian French) still pronounce 'r' as a alveolar trill, although this pronunciation is probably dying out.

In the case of the frictionless continuants [w] and [ɥ], they are shown in two places because the configuration of the lips is an important feature of their articulation. When the sound [w] is produced, the back of the tongue is close to the velum; and at the same time, the lips are rounded. In the case of [ɥ], the lips are also rounded, while the tongue approaches the hard palate. We shall see below that lip configuration is one of the criteria used to classify vowels. The fact that this phonetic feature is also used to classify the frictionless continuants [w] and [ɥ] reflects their intermediate status between consonants and vowels. This uneasy status is in turn reflected in the multiplicity of terms used to describe them: semi-vowels, semi-consonants, glides or 'voiced non-syllabic vocoids', as one linguist has termed them.

For further reading on the production of French consonants, see Price (1991), Chapters 5, 6, 13–18; Tranel (1987), Chapters 7–10.

Now do the exercises 2–5 on pp. 90–91.

5.3   Classifying French vowels

We saw in the discussion of French consonants that, because consonants and vowels are produced in different ways, different criteria are required to describe them. This is perhaps best illustrated by the fact that the voice criterion, which distinguishes several sets of French consonants, is simply irrelevant to the description of vowels, since, with a few minor exceptions, all vowels are voiced.

In classifying vowels, perhaps the most important criterion to be used is the position of the tongue in relation to the other organs of speech. Unlike what happens with consonants, the tongue does not touch the other articulators when vowels are produced. This means that it is not helpful to describe the position of the tongue in relation to the other articulators in the mouth as we did with consonants. So, its position is described (1) in terms of *frontness* and *backness* of the tip of the tongue in the mouth, and (2) in terms of *tongue height*. In addition to these two criteria, two others are used to classify French vowels: (3) shape of lips and (4) orality/nasality. The first three of these criteria (front versus back, high versus low and shape of lips) are so closely interlinked that we will have to discuss them together. The oral/nasal distinction gives rise to a separate set of nasal vowels which will be described separately later.

5.3.1   *Oral vowels*

We can classify the French oral vowels according to: (1) frontness/backness of the tongue, (2) tongue height, and (3) shape of lips. Figure 5.2 shows the so-called 'vowel space' which represents the positions of the tongue in relation to various points in the mouth while vowels are being pronounced.

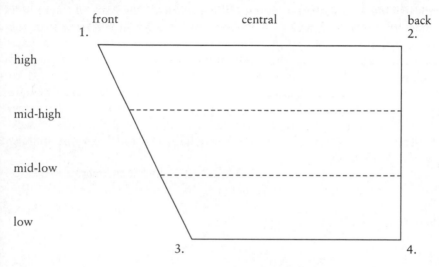

Fig. 5.2 The vowel space

At Point 1 when the tongue is high and front, the blade of the tongue is close to the hard palate, and a 'high front' vowel is produced; as in French *qui*. At Point 2, the back of the tongue is high, close to the velum, and a 'high back' vowel is produced; as in French *bout*. At Point 3, the tip of the tongue is brought forward and low, touching the back of the bottom teeth, and the back of the tongue has been brought forward also. Here, a 'low front' vowel is produced, as in French *ta*. At Point 4, the back of the tongue is retracted towards the pharynx. Here, a 'low back' vowel is produced. This vowel is increasingly rare in French, but can quite often be heard in the negative particle *pas*.

    The four extreme points of this figure show approximately the furthest points in the mouth which the tongue can reach without making contact with the inside of the mouth and producing friction, and hence consonants. French vowels are produced at each of these four points, and also of course at other intermediate points. These intermediate points too are indicated in Figure 5.2. The points situated between the extremes of 'high' and 'low' are described as 'mid-high' and 'mid-low'. However, these terms suggest a precision which is in fact spurious, for 'mid-high' designates a place of articulation somewhere between 'high' and the half-way point between 'high' and 'low'; correspondingly, 'mid-low' refers to a place of articulation some-where between 'low' and the half-way point between 'high' and 'low'. Before leaving the issue of tongue position it is worth pointing out that some textbooks use the terms 'open' and 'close' for 'low' and 'high' respectively.

We have not yet represented the oral vowels which are produced at these four points, because a further criterion is required to classify them: *shape of lips*, that is whether or not the lips are rounded. Figure 5.3 shows the *rounded* French oral vowels, also classified by the front-back and high-low criteria and Figure 5.4 shows the *unrounded* French oral vowels.

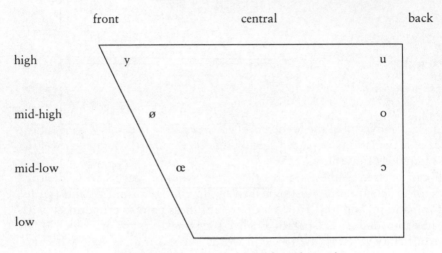

Fig. 5.3 The rounded French oral vowels

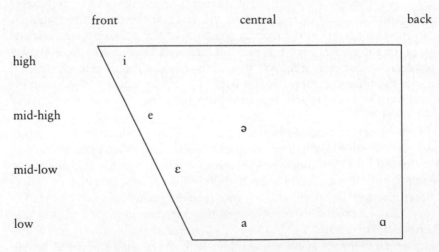

Fig. 5.4 The unrounded French oral vowels

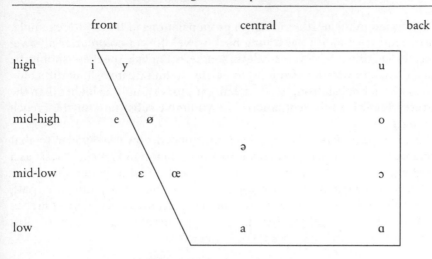

Fig. 5.5 The French oral vowels

Figure 5.5 shows all of the French oral vowels; pairs of vowels with identical place of articulation are placed side by side on the chart, rounded vowels to the right, as is conventional.

It can be seen in these figures that three pairs of vowels with identical place of articulation are distinguished by lip configuration: [i] and [y]; [e] and [ø]; and [ɛ] and [œ]. The first of each of these pairs is pronounced with the lips unrounded, or spread. English-speaking learners of French often have difficulty with [y], the vowel in words like *rue* and *du*, simply because the vowel does not exist in most accents of English. But if one is aware that [i] and [y] are identical except for lip configuration, it is possible to produce an [i], with spread lips, then, while keeping the tongue in the front-high position, to produce [y] by rounding the lips. A similar process can also be performed by rounding the lips while articulating [e] to produce [ø] (as in *peu*, *bleu*), a vowel which English speakers tend to pronounce as [œ].

We will now examine the French oral vowels shown in Figures 5.3 and 5.4 in more detail, considering how they differ from their English equivalents, where appropriate. We will discuss them in the following order:

1. The low vowels [a] and [ɑ].
2. The high vowels [i], [y] and [u].
3. The three pairs of 'mid-vowels':
   [e] and [ɛ]; [ø] and [œ]; [o] and [ɔ].
4. 'Mute-e' or 'schwa', as found in *me*, *te*, *le*, etc.

LOW VOWELS

[a] as in *chat*, *ma*. Low front unrounded. Speakers of northern varieties of British English should have no difficulty with this vowel, which is very close

to that found in the northern English pronunciations of 'bath', for example, where southern English has a long back vowel: [ɑ:] (a colon after a vowel indicates lengthening). Nevertheless, southern English speakers should be familiar enough with low front [a] to be able to imitate it without difficulty. The southern English front 'a', found in 'cat', for example, is higher than the northern English equivalent, and is a less suitable substitute for the French low front [a].

[ɑ] as in *pâte, bas*. This low back unrounded vowel is similar to that found in English 'father'. It is now rather uncommon in French, at least as a vowel which serves to distinguish pairs of words, and although dictionary transcriptions distinguish between pairs such as *patte* [pat] and *pâte* [pɑt], these distinctions are not now present in the vowel inventory of most French speakers. However, [ɑ] is often heard in the negative particle *pas*, most stereotypically in the sequence [ʃɛpɑ] 'dunno'.

THE HIGH VOWELS

[i] as in *vie, qui*. The principal difference between this French vowel and its English equivalent is that French [i] is pronounced with the lips spread further apart. This can be verified by comparing the vowel in French *qui* with that in English 'key'. French [i] is also higher than the English counterpart.

[y] as in *sur, une*. This vowel is front, high and rounded. As was mentioned above, English-speaking learners of French often have difficulty with this vowel, as it is found in few varieties of English (some Scots dialects possess it). If one produces [i] while rounding the lips, a fair approximation to [y] should result. It is important to master this vowel, as it serves to distinguish word pairs like *roue* and *rue*, *boue* and *bu*. The commonest fault is to pronounce [y] as [u], which fatally undermines any attempt at a convincing French accent.

[u] as in *boue, tout*. This back high rounded vowel is similar to its English equivalent, the most salient difference being the degree of lip-rounding used to produce the French vowel; the lips are more tensely rounded, and also further protruded. Again, this can be verified by comparing the vowel in French *tout* with that in English 'too'.

THE MID-VOWELS

[e] as in *chez, les*. This front mid-high unrounded vowel is found in the first part of the English *diphthong* [ei], as in 'bay'. A diphthong is a vowel whose phonetic quality changes as it is pronounced during a single syllable; other English examples are in 'hear', 'mine', 'mouse'. Diphthongs are common in English, but *not* found in standard French. Thus French vowels are 'pure' in the sense that French speakers maintain a consistent phonetic quality as they pronounce a vowel. English speakers tend to diphthongise French vowels; this is a trait which needs to be corrected if one wishes to achieve an accurate French accent.

[ɛ] as in *fait, chaise*. This front mid-low unrounded vowel is similar to that found in English 'bet', but it is more open. The distribution of the mid-vowels will be discussed in detail below.

[ø] as in *peu, bleu*. This vowel is front, mid-high and rounded. English has no front rounded mid-vowels, and the nearest equivalent is the very frequent 'schwa' (IPA symbol: [ə]), the vowel produced centrally in the vowel space and found in unstressed syllables in English words such as 'sofa', 'photograph'. Clearly, this vowel is not an adequate substitute for the French front mid-high rounded vowel, as schwa is central, not front, and unrounded, at least in English. Neither is the stressed equivalent of schwa, as in 'bird' and represented by the IPA symbol [ɜ:], an appropriate substitute. As with the high front rounded vowel [y], the front rounded mid-vowels can be practised by pronouncing their unrounded equivalents [e] and [ɛ], and then rounding the lips.

[œ] as in *peur, neuf*. This vowel is front, mid-low and rounded. It may be practised as described immediately above: by articulating [ɛ], and then rounding the lips.

[o] as in *beau, drôle*. This vowel is back, mid-high, rounded. As with French [e], the problem for speakers of southern English is that the nearest equivalent to [o] is a diphthong; for example, English 'droll' is pronounced [drəul]. Therefore French [o] must be practised as a pure vowel (i.e. not diphthongised), and with the lips much more rounded than for the nearest English equivalent.

[ɔ] as in *folle, bol*. This vowel is back, mid-low, rounded. The nearest English equivalent to this vowel is that found in 'not' or 'dog', for example. Again, the principal difference is the greater degree of lip-rounding used to produce the French vowel.

There is a tendency in French for the high mid-vowels and the low mid-vowels to occur in different types of syllable. Syllables are of two types: open and closed. Open syllables are those which end in a vowel (*thé, peu, beau*) while closed syllables end in a consonant (*bête, oeuf, botte*). You can remember this tendency by opposing 'close' and 'open' as follows:

- mid-high (= mid-*close*) vowels tend to occur in *open* syllables;
- mid-low (= mid-*open*) vowels tend to occur in *closed* syllables.

Thus in the case of the front rounded mid-vowels, singular *œuf* has the front rounded mid-open vowel in a closed syllable: [œf], while plural *œufs* has the front rounded mid-close vowel in an open syllable: [ø]. An example of the front unrounded mid-vowels alternating in this way is the pair *blé* [ble] and *blette* [blɛt]. The two back rounded mid-vowels also often alternate in this way, as for example between singular *os* [ɔs] and plural *os* [o]. As the word 'tendency' implies, this close–open pattern admits of exceptions. Thus the front unrounded mid-vowels are found in both open and closed syllables, as in the pairs of words *gai* [ge] versus *guet* [gɛ]; *fée* [fe] versus *fait* [fɛ]. Nevertheless, the tendency is a strong one, and is a reasonably accurate guide where one is uncertain as to which mid-vowel should be pronounced in a given word.

MUTE-E

The final oral French vowel to be discussed is so-called 'mute-e', as in the monosyllabic words *me*, *te*, *le*, *ce*, etc. This vowel, referred to variously as 'schwa', 'mute-e' ('e muet'), 'e féminin', 'e caduc' (literally 'deciduous' or 'falling e') and represented in the IPA as [ə], is the only central vowel in French. The term 'schwa' relates to the phonetic description of the vowel; it is neither high nor low, front nor back. It differs from English schwa mentioned above principally in that the French vowel is more rounded; indeed, many French speakers produce mute-e as the rounded front mid-low vowel [ø]. The other labels ('mute-e', etc.) refer to the vowel's rather idiosyncratic behaviour in French (and in English and other languages). Probably 'e caduc' is the most suitable label, as it reflects the fact that the vowel is sometimes pronounced and sometimes 'drops', i.e. is not pronounced. Thus for example, the phrase *la remise* may sometimes be pronounced [laRəmiz] and sometimes [laRmiz], depending on several factors, both linguistic and non-linguistic. The factors which favour the elision (non-pronunciation) of mute-e will be discussed in more detail in Chapter 6.

5.3.2   The nasal vowels

So far we have considered the twelve oral vowels of French; those which are articulated with the velum raised to close off the nasal cavity, and allowing the whole of the airflow from the lungs to pass through the mouth. We will now examine the four nasalised vowels. These vowels are articulated with the velum lowered, so that the airflow issues wholly or partially through the nasal cavity. It will be seen that these four vowels correspond more or less closely to their oral equivalents.

[ɛ̃] as in *pain*, *vin*. Nasalised vowels are indicated in the IPA alphabet by placing a tilde (~) over the oral equivalent of the vowel. Thus [ɛ̃] is a front mid-low unrounded nasal vowel. This vowel is in fact rather more open than its oral counterpart.

[œ̃] as in *aucun*, *brun*, *lundi*. Front mid-low rounded nasal. This vowel is also more open than its oral counterpart. The distinction between this vowel and the previous one is absent for many French speakers, who pronounce identically pairs of words such as *brin* [bRɛ̃] and *brun* ([bRœ̃] in standard pronunciation). These speakers produce a vowel which has some of the characteristics of both [ɛ̃] and [œ̃], so that instead of distinguishing between these two vowels, they produce a vowel which is more like an unrounded [œ̃], or like a [ɛ̃] with the lips neutral rather than spread. There is no reason why this pronunciation should not be imitated, since it is a change in progress in French which seems likely to result in only three nasal vowels in the future, and since there are very few pairs of words like 'brin' and 'brun' where a difference of meaning depends on which vowel is used. However, these observations are not true of the other pair of nasal vowels described immediately below, which *must* be clearly distinguished.

[ã] as in *blanc*, *France*. Back low unrounded nasal. The difficulties which English learners of French experience relate not to the pronunciation of this vowel, but, as indicated above, rather to distinguishing between it and the other back nasal vowel. This other vowel will now be described.

[õ] as in *blond*, *fond*. Back mid-low rounded nasal. As was mentioned above, whereas the blurred distinction between the two front nasal vowels can safely be imitated, as it is a distinction which many French speakers ignore, English speakers of French need to observe the distinction between the back nasal vowels. This distinction is principally one of lip-rounding, as the two vowels are otherwise fairly close together in their place of articulation. These two vowels distinguish numerous pairs of words, and confusion is possible if the vowels are not articulated so as to make them distinct from each other. Failure to produce a rounded vowel can radically alter the meaning of the following phrase: *Est-ce qu'il y a beaucoup de concerts dans la région?* An insufficiently rounded vowel in *concerts* may lead the listener to interpret the question as: 'Is there a lot of cancer in the region?' At best, failure to round the vowel in words like *blond* will mark out the speaker as having an unconvincing French accent.

5.3.3   Vowels and their phonetic symbols

The following list shows the IPA symbols for the French vowels, with examples of words which contain them.

The French vowels

IPA symbol	example
[a]	là
[ɑ]	pâte
[i]	île
[y]	vu
[u]	où
[e]	thé
[ɛ]	chaise
[ø]	peu
[œ]	peur
[o]	drôle
[ɔ]	folle
[ə]	me
[ɛ̃]	pain
[œ̃]	brun
[ã]	blanc
[õ]	on

For further reading on the production of French vowels, see Battye and Hintze (1992: 95–122); Price (1991), Chapters 4, 10–12; Tranel (1987), Chapters 3–6.

Now do exercises 6–9 on pp. 91–92.

5.4   Pronunciation in context

We have chosen so far to consider French sounds as if they were pronounced in isolation. While this approach is convenient for purposes of exposition, it is inadequate to the extent that it ignores the important fact that when people speak, they produce speech sounds in a continuous chain. There are no pauses between groups of sounds or words as speakers produce them, a fact which is easy to overlook under the influence of the written word. The fact that sounds occur before and after other sounds in the chain of speech causes them to influence each other – a sound may take on some or all of the phonetic properties of a neighbouring one. Thus for example, the manner in which French [R] is articulated is influenced by the phonetic nature of the sounds which precede and/or follow it: between vowels, as in the word *Paris*, [R] is likely to be articulated 'weakly', i.e. as an approximant, because of the relative lack of constriction with which vowels are produced. By contrast, a preceding voiceless plosive consonant (as in *être*) will cause [R] to be articulated as a trill or fricative, since voiceless plosives are the consonants which are articulated with the greatest degree of force. A following [R] will therefore be influenced by the greater force associated with the plosive. Another example from French is vowel length. French vowels lengthen when followed by the (long) fricative consonants; thus [ɛ] in *fait* is short: [fɛt], but long in *faire*: [fɛ:R].

5.5   From phonetics to phonology

In theory, and increasingly nowadays in practice too as scientific instruments for measuring speech become more sophisticated, we can continue refining our description of the speech sounds of a particular language *ad infinitum*: after all, every speaker of the language has his own distinctive 'voice', pronouncing every vowel and consonant in the language in a way personal to him/herself. However, there comes a point when linguists have to ask themselves how far they want to go in terms of phonetic detail.

5.5.1   Levels of phonetic detail

So far in this chapter, where this seemed necessary for producing French sounds in an authentic way, we have been prepared to go into a certain amount of phonetic detail, specifying, for example, that French [t] is dental as opposed to the English [t] which is alveolar. Relatively fine detail of this nature can be represented in the IPA by adding various diacritical marks; so a dental [t] is represented thus: [t̪]. Nevertheless, in a large number of other cases the student may be forgiven for asking how many of the details of phonetic differences between French and English are worth bothering about. Many differences are in fact so subtle that they may safely be ignored for the purposes of achieving a satisfactory French accent. Phoneticians are entirely sympathetic to this attitude, and in their own work they commonly exercise a distinction between a *narrow* and a *broad* transcription of speech, a narrow transcription being relatively detailed and a broad one less so. Let us consider two examples.

English word-initial plosives (e.g. [p] in 'pit') are *aspirated*, i.e. followed by a brief [h] sound. The fact of the aspiration of the plosives [p, t, k] at the beginning of words in English can be verified if you pronounce a word beginning with one, holding your hand, or a piece of paper, immediately in front of your mouth. The effect of the aspiration, in the form of the puff of breath which follows the stop, can clearly be felt or seen. It will even blow out a lighted match! Initial plosives in French on the other hand, if pronounced authentically, will not produce this effect, as they are unaspirated. A narrow transcription would indicate the aspiration in the English word by placing a small superscript [h] after the IPA symbol; thus English 'pit' would be transcribed [pʰit]. A broad transcription would omit this detail.

Another example is to be found in the transcription of English [l]. This consonant is pronounced differently according to whether it is found at the beginning or at the end of a syllable. Syllable-initial [l] is pronounced as an alveolar lateral, as described in the IPA chart, with the front of the tongue high and front, and the back of the tongue relatively low. In contrast, syllable-final [l] is a 'velarised' [l], with the back of the tongue bunched towards the velum. The difference in the acoustic quality of these two variants can be appreciated if we compare the pronunciation of [l] in the words 'lip' and 'pill'. Syllable-final or velar [l] has a more 'vocalic' acoustic quality, and indeed this variant of [l] may be pronounced as a back vowel such as [u] in some varieties of English, notably Cockney, as in 'a fu*ll* bott*le* of mi*l*k'. Velar [l] is indicated in a narrow phonetic transcription with a tilde through it, thus: [ɫ]. Again, in a broad transcription such a detail could be ignored, depending on the purpose of the transcription.

These examples illustrate the relatively fine phonetic detail which we may or may not take into account, depending on the level of analysis we are interested in. If we are interested in the relatively fine details of difference between two varieties of the same language, for example between Midi French and Alsatian French, a narrow phonetic transcription will be called for. On the other hand, if we are concerned to describe only those sounds of French which serve to distinguish meaning, much phonetic detail can be ignored, and the relevant sounds can be represented in a broad transcription.

5.5.2   Allophones and phonemes

Differences in sound which are not used to differentiate meaning in a particular language are said to be *allophonic*. This is the case with the two sorts of [p] and [l] we have just looked at in English. Differences in sound which are used to differentiate meaning in a particular language are said to be *phonemic*. This is the case with the two sounds [p] and [d] in French, as we can tell from the following examples: *pont ~ dont*. If we are only concerned to isolate those sounds of a language which contrast with other sounds to produce differences of meaning, we can exclude much phonetic detail from our categorisation. We can test whether or not a distinction of sound falls into the phonemic category by finding pairs of words which are phonetically identical in all respects other than the sounds we are interested in. Pairs of words which contrast on the level of meaning in this way are known as minimal pairs. Thus the initial consonants of the French minimal pair *pas* [pa] and *rat* [Ra] are said to be phonemes of French because they are contrastive; i.e. they are instrumental in signalling a difference in meaning between the two words. /p/ and /R/ are therefore phonemes of French.

Thus we can distinguish two levels at which speech sounds may be analysed – the concrete *phonetic* level where many or all distinctions of sound are relevant, and the more abstract *phonemic* level where only distinctions of sound which differentiate meaning are of interest. Conventionally, phonetic units or '*phones*' are enclosed in square brackets (e.g. [p], [l]) and phonemes are enclosed in slashes (e.g. /p/, /l/). A phonetic transcription is therefore enclosed in square brackets and shows a relatively large amount of phonetic detail, depending on the purpose of the transcription. A phonemic transcription is enclosed in slashes, and shows only so much phonetic detail as is necessary to indicate the meaningful contrasts which the phonemes of the language establish.

5.5.3   Complementary distribution

We saw above that sounds vary in their articulation according to the surrounding phonetic context. The influence exerted on a sound which results in variation in its articulation is referred to as *phonetic conditioning*. This conditioning is highly predictable; for example, we have seen that English front or 'clear' /l/ is always syllable-initial, and velar or 'dark' /l/ always syllable-final in most varieties of English. Some English speakers have front /l/ syllable-finally, just as many speakers of American English have dark /l/ syllable-initially; but these are regional features which do not interfere with the communication of conceptual meaning. Thus on the phonemic level we ignore the distinction between English clear and dark /l/, since the difference between the two allophones of /l/ does not serve to contrast meaning in

English. This is logical, because two phonemes must be capable of occurring in the same phonetic context if they are to serve to contrast meaning. But the two allophones of English /l/ are never found in the same phonetic context; each is found in contexts where the other is not. This state of affairs is referred to as *complementary distribution*.

Another example of allophones occurring in complementary distribution is provided by Spanish, where the /s/ phoneme is conditioned by phonetic context. Spanish /s/ is pronounced as a voiceless alveolar fricative when followed by voiceless /p/, as in the following example:

(1)   *esperar* 'to hope' [ɛsperar]

Before a voiced bilabial consonant (a fricative in the following example), Spanish /s/ acquires voicing and is realised as the voiced alveolar fricative [z], as follows:

(2)   *esbozo* 'sketch' [ɛzβoθo]

Pairs of sounds may be allophones in one language, but phonemes in another. Aspirated and unaspirated stops in English occur in complementary distribution. Word-initial voiceless stops have aspiration, as in 'pot' [pʰɔt], 'tot' [tʰɔt] and 'cot' [kʰɔt], but are unaspirated when they occur after /s/, as in 'spot' [spɔt] etc., or at the end of a word. In Quechua, a South American Indian language, both aspirated and unaspirated stops occur word-initially and provide contrasts in meaning, as in the following pair:

(3)   *khacha* [kʰatʃa] 'dirt'
(4)   *kacha* [katʃa] 'messenger'

To summarise: phonemes are the minimal sound units of a language which provide meaningful contrast. At this level, a good deal of fine phonetic detail is irrelevant, and indeed the relatively coarse-grained phonetic criteria which we have used previously to define the French consonants and vowels are sufficient to define the phonemes of French. But each phoneme may have several variant sounds or allophones. These allophones are usually similar phonetically, and they occur in complementary distribution; i.e. each allophone occurs in phonetic contexts where the other does not. A narrow phonetic transcription will include finer allophonic detail. To illustrate the difference, we can contrast a phonemic and a phonetic transcription of the word *France*: phonemic: /fRãs/; phonetic: [fʁɑ̃ːs]. Allophones are also often used to varying degrees by groups of speakers who are differentiated by age, sex, social class, regional origin, etc.

For further reading on pronunciation in context, allophones and phonemes, see Price (1991), Chapter 1; Yule (1985), Chapter 6; and Lass (1984), Chapter 2.

Now do exercise 10 on p. 92.

Seminar exercises

1. Learn the phonetic symbols commonly used for French consonants as given on p. 77. Practise saying the keywords aloud.

2. Below is a list of the consonants and semi-consonants of French. Opposite each consonant, write down the criteria used to describe it: place of articulation (dental, velar, etc.); manner of articulation (plosive, fricative, etc.) and whether or not the vocal cords are vibrating (voiced or voiceless). As a guide, the criteria for the first consonant have been given.

	VOCAL CORDS	PLACE	MANNER
[p]	voiceless	bilabial	plosive
[ɲ]			
[R]			
[ʃ]			
[v]			
[k]			
[d]			
[m]			
[l]			
[s]			
[g]			
[z]			
[b]			
[n]			
[ʒ]			
[f]			
[t]			
[ŋ]			
[j]			
[ɥ]			
[w]			

3. Transcribe your pronunciation of the consonant groups **in bold** in the following words, and then check the correct pronunciation in a dictionary. Some groups are voiced, while others are voiceless. Can you see a pattern or rule which explains this fact?

    e**x**amen, e**x**plication, e**x**ercise, e**x**act, e**x**traordinaire, e**x**quisité

4. We saw that the words *chatte* and *jatte* are distinguished by the presence or absence of voice in the initial consonant.

(a) Find pairs of words which also differ according to this phonetic feature in the other pairs of French consonants which are distinguished by the *voice* criterion (e.g. t/d and f/v).
(b) Find pairs of words whose initial consonants are distinguished by their *place* of articulation.
(c) Find pairs of words whose initial consonants are distinguished by their *manner* of articulation.

5. *Without consulting the tables given earlier in this chapter*, write down the IPA symbols for the following French consonants:

(a) Voiceless dental plosive
(b) Voiced bilabial nasal
(c) Voiced uvular fricative
(d) Voiceless velar plosive
(e) Voiced bilabial-velar approximant
(f) Voiced velar nasal.

6. Below is a list of the vowels of French. They are not listed in any particular order; thus for example, the mid-vowels are not grouped together. Opposite each vowel, write down the criteria used to describe it: tongue position (front, back or central); tongue height (high, low, mid-high, mid-low); lip configuration (rounded, spread, neutral); velum raised or lowered.

	TONGUE POSITION	TONGUE HEIGHT	LIP POSITION	VELUM
[ə]				
[u]				
[a]				
[i]				
[ɛ]				
[ɑ]				
[ø]				
[e]				
[y]				
[ɛ̃]				
[ɔ]				
[œ̃]				
[o]				
[œ]				
[ɑ̃]				
[ɔ̃]				

7. Practise pronouncing out loud the following pairs of vowels, making sure you can make clear the distinction between them:

[e] and [ɛ]; [ø] and [œ]; [o] and [ɔ]; [a] and [ɑ]; [ɛ̃] and [œ̃]; [ɔ̃] and [ɑ̃].

What phonetic features distinguish each pair?

8. Spot the errors in the following transcriptions:

(a) [ʒətRuvləguidRidikyl]
(b) [sɛfaciladiR]
(c) [ilnoufoœ̃nuvoʃɛf]
(d) [lədimanʃʒəsɥilibR]
(e) [sɛmwakɥipɛj]
(f) [lɑ̃pRɔʃɑ̃ilRɑntR]
(g) [avɛklui ɔ̃napadəpRɔblɛm]
(h) [iljalətelefonkison].

9.   Transcribe your pronunciation of the following words, and then check the correct pronunciation in a dictionary. Try to identify the pronunciation feature in each word which is anomalous in relation to the word's spelling, or which may cause problems for English learners of French:

seau,	ingéniosité,
quinzième,	envers,
sculpteur,	bouillon,
sot,	adéquat,
yaourt,	agenda,
donnent,	pronostic,
inattendu,	bilinguisme,
archevêque,	aspect,
compter,	août,
chaos,	tabac,
archéologie,	linguistique,
inimaginable,	immoral,
sceau,	impatient,
inquiet,	habileté,
saut,	aéroport

10.   Below are 16 examples of French words which contain /t/ and /d/. Canadian French /t/ and /d/ undergo 'affrication' (are followed by a fricative) in a certain phonetic context, as shown in the examples below. Which context favours affrication? Can you see a motivation for this process in articulatory terms? Can you see why affrication is not favoured in the other phonetic contexts?

tRavaj	dabɔR
kɔt	statˢy
evidɑ	stil
dwav	paRtˢiR
desy	ɔd
dˢiR	sɥit
dø	adˢylt
dusmɑ	stypid

6
Pronunciation beyond the individual sound

In Chapter 5 we looked at the phonetic characteristics of individual French sounds (or 'segments', as they are sometimes called), and we concluded with a brief discussion of the role they play in the phonological structure of French; that is, how they relate to each other in terms of similarities and meaningful contrasts. Now we will look at French pronunciation beyond the level of individual sounds, for sounds obviously combine together to form larger units of pronunciation (syllables, words, etc.). In Chapter 4 (4.2) we saw how structural linguists distinguish between paradigmatic relations and syntagmatic relations. There the units in question were words (or 'lexical items'). Now we shall see that analogous relations hold between the phonemes of a language: phonemes enter paradigmatic relationships with one another by belonging to a system of oppositions and contrasts which ensures that each phoneme in the language is different from every other; they enter syntagmatic relationships with one another when they combine together to form higher units (syllables, words, etc.). In this chapter, then, we will first examine combinations and interactions (syntagmatic relations) between French speech sounds; we will then look at some aspects of how sounds behave in connected speech: elision, liaison and assimilation; we will conclude with a short section on 'suprasegmental' features of French, namely stress and intonation.

6.1   The syllable

Intermediate between the single sound and the word is the *syllable*. The syllable is a unit of pronunciation which all speakers seem to understand intuitively, and this is reflected in phrases such as: 'Shall I spell it out in words of one syllable?' Many early writing systems were syllabic (e.g. Sumerian, Egyptian and Phoenician), the symbols representing syllables rather than 'individual sounds' (see Yule 1985: 11–12). This fact too seems to confirm that the syllable is a unit which is real for the native-speakers of a language. However, it is surprisingly difficult to define the syllable in a rigorous way. Leaving aside jocular definitions such as: 'a syllable is what the word *syllable* has three of', perhaps the best description that linguists have produced is based on its phonetic properties: 'a syllable is composed of an *obligatory* vowel (or vowel-like sound such as syllabic /l/ or /n/), with *optional* consonants or semi-consonants on either side (on its *margins*)'. Expressing this in another way we can say that a syllable is a nucleus formed of a vowel, with or without consonantal margins. In French (and English) a syllable can consist of a vowel on its own, as in the following French words: *eu*; *a*; *euh*; *hé*; *ait*; *au*; *ou*; *y*; *en*; *on*; *un*; *hein*. It can also consist of a vowel preceded and/or followed by a consonant as in *bu*; *nul*; *brûlé* and so forth.

The rules of syllabification (syllable division) in French are relatively simple. In the transcriptions given below, a full stop indicates a syllable boundary. Monosyllabic words obviously pose no problems, and with poly-syllabic words the guiding principle is that a syllable division occurs before a consonant, if there is one. Thus, when two vowels in a polysyllabic word are separated by a single consonant, the consonant attaches to the second vowel, as in example (1):

(1)   *unanimité* /y.na.ni.mi.te./

In the case of vowels separated by two consonants, the consonant cluster splits, the first consonant closing the first syllable and the second consonant beginning the second, as in example (2):

(2)   *abside* /ap.sid./

The exception to this is consonant clusters whose second consonant is /l/ or /r/. In these cases, both consonants are attached to the beginning of the syllable, as in examples (3) and (4):

(3)   *abrutir* /a.bry.tir./

(4)   *boucler* /bu.kle./

These rules run into potential problems only with the French 'semi-consonants' or 'semi-vowels' (/j/, /w/ and /ɥ/) in such words as *pied*, *soir* and *puis*. Are these sounds to be treated as vowels or as consonants for the purposes of syllabification? The answer is that these sounds behave like consonants rather than vowels. Although they are close to their equivalent full vowels /i/, /u/ and /y/ in their phonetic properties, being articulated in a very similar way, the semi-consonants are only found at the margins of syllables, and do not form the nucleus of a syllable as do vowels. This is illustrated by the pairs of words in the list below. The words in the right-hand column contain a semi-consonant and are monosyllabic, while those in the left-hand column contain two vowels and are bisyllabic:

(5) *pays* /pe.i./   *paye* /pɛj./

(6) *haï* /a.i./   *ail* /aj./

(7) *abbaye* /a.be.i./   *abeille* /a.bɛj./

6.1.1   The structure of French syllables

We saw above that a syllable essentially consists of a vowel, with optional consonants on either side. In French, syllables are of two types: open (e.g. *bu*) and closed (e.g. *nul*). Syllables which end in a vowel are open and those which end in a consonant are closed. In spoken French there is a tendency towards a succession of open syllables, each formed of the sequence: consonant + vowel. We can represent this succession as follows (where C stands for consonant, and V for vowel): CV.CV.CV., etc. For example,

(8) | Je | m'en | vais | ce | matin |
     |----|------|------|----|-------|
     | CV. | CV. | CV. | CV. | CV.CV |

One linguist who examined a corpus of spoken French calculated that 67 per cent of syllables were open ones, with the structure CV or CCV.

This tendency to open syllables is further enhanced by the phenomenon known as *enchaînement* or linking. *Enchaînement* is the attachment of a consonant pronounced at the end of a word to a vowel at the beginning of the next word. This has the effect of creating open syllables. Gadet (1989: 64) quotes the following example:

(9) *Je compte agir en honnête homme*
     /ʒə. kɔ̃. ta. ʒi. Rɑ̃. nɔ. nɛ. tɔm./

In this example, the word-final consonants of *compte*, *agir*, *en* and *honnête* are linked in speech to the vowels which follow. French spelling is clearly an unreliable guide to the way in which syllable divisions are made in speech across words.

6.2   Liaison

Let us now consider another aspect of how French sounds behave in connected speech, namely the phenomenon known as liaison. Whereas *enchaînement* involves word-final consonants *which are pronounced in all phonetic contexts*, liaison is the pronunciation before a following vowel of certain word-final consonants *which are silent in other phonetic contexts*, i.e. before a consonant or a pause. Thus, for example, the French liaison consonant /z/ is silent in the plural definite article *les* before a word beginning with a consonant, as in *les livres* /lelivR/ or before a pause, as in *donne-les* /dɔnle/, but pronounced before a vowel, as in *les églises* /lezegliz/. The only exception to this pattern is the case of words beginning with so-called *h aspiré*, for example *hall, haricot, héros*. Words in this set are not in fact aspirated, and the three examples cited are pronounced [ol], [aRiko], [eRo]. However, the *h aspiré* set of words behave as if they had the initial 'aspirate' consonant [h]. One consequence is that liaison does not occur before the words in the *h aspiré* set. Thus in the singular, *un hall, un haricot, un héros* are pronounced: [œ̃ol], [œ̃aRiko], [œ̃eRo], not [œ̃nol], [œ̃naRiko], [œ̃neRo]. In the plural, *les halls, les haricots, les héros* are pronounced: [leol], [leaRiko], [leeRo], not [lezol], [lezaRiko], [lezeRo]. It is important to be aware at least of the more frequent words in the *h aspiré* set, such *haut* and *hors*. Good dictionaries indicate *h aspiré* words in their transcriptions; for example, the *Petit Robert* transcribes them with an initial apostrophe: *hall* as ['ol]. See Byrne and Churchill (1993: 3–4), or Grevisse (1986: section 49) for further information on *h aspiré*.

To return to regular liaison, the phenomenon is not unique to French. Liaison is also found in English, which in its standard British variety has the liaison consonant /r/ in a word like *hear*, which is silent before a consonant or pause, but pronounced before a vowel. Thus in the sequences: 'I can't hear the noise' or 'I can't hear', no /r/ is pronounced, whereas in 'I can't hear a noise' /r/ reappears.

The liaison consonants found in French are the following, in italic in the examples:

/z/ as in nous *a*vons, allez-*y*, deu*x* ans;
/t/ as in c'es*t* impossible, gran*d* écran;
/n/ as in o*n* est à trois, u*n* ennemi;
/p/ as in beaucou*p* aimé, tro*p* aimable;
/r/ as in dernie*r* acte, premie*r* avril;
/k/ as in san*g* impur (from the Marseillaise).

It can be seen that various orthographic letters represent the six liaison consonants. The first three, /z/, /t/ and /n/, are common in everyday speech, while the second three are rather rare; /k/ especially is seldom heard, and even the *sang impur* in the Marseillaise may be pronounced [sɑ̃ɛ̃pyR] nowadays.

6.2.1   Liaison with and without enchaînement

When a liaison consonant is pronounced it usually also undergoes *enchaînement* or linking to the following vowel. Thus the phrase 'les églises' will syllabify as follows: /le.ze.gliz./. This is known as *la liaison avec enchaînement*. In some cases *enchaînement* and *liaison avec enchaînement* are phonetically identical, as in examples (10) and (11):

(10)   petite amie   /pə.ti.ta.mi./

(11)   petit ami   /pə.ti.ta.mi./

In example (10), the second /t/ in *petite* links to the /a/ in the following word. This /t/ would of course always be pronounced, as it marks the gender of *amie*. Therefore this phrase illustrates *enchaînement* but not liaison. In example (11), because final /t/ is not normally pronounced, there is liaison as well as *enchaînement*.

Liaison normally occurs with *enchaînement* (e.g. *petit ami*), but it occasionally occurs without. One example given by Pierre Encrevé (1987: 32–35), a linguist who has studied the phenomenon, is the sentence: 'J'avais un rêve', where instead of the sequence of open syllables resulting from *enchaînement* – [ʒa. vɛ. zœ̃. Rɛv.] – the liaison consonant /z/ in 'avais' is attached to the preceding vowel – [ʒa. vɛz. œ̃. Rɛv.]. The liaison consonant may also be followed by a glottal stop: [ʒa. vɛz. ʔœ̃. Rɛv.]. This usage need not be imitated by the learner of French, but is interesting to people concerned with the way the French language is used. It is characteristically used by public figures such as politicians and broadcast journalists. An amusing example of liaison without *enchaînement* being used to provide a meaningful contrast is shown in example (12), where a politician, interviewed on the radio, was commenting on the numerous ministerial posts held by François Mitterrand during the Fourth Republic:

(12)　*et quand Monsieur Mitterrand était ministre, et Dieu sait qu'il l'a*
　　　[bo.ku.pe.te.], *pardon* [bo.kup.ʔe.te.]

6.2.2　Liaison categories: invariable, hypercorrect and variable

INVARIABLE LIAISON

Liaison forms of the type: article + noun beginning with a vowel (e.g. *les amis, un an*) are made invariably by all French speakers; any failure to make such a liaison would be a so-called 'performance error', a slip of the tongue resulting from a momentary loss of concentration, tiredness, drunkenness, etc. Invariable liaison forms appear to be built in to French speakers' mental grammars. Traditional prescriptive grammarians refer to this type of liaison as 'obligatory', but it is preferable to use the neutral term 'invariable', since as linguists we are concerned, not to prescribe usage, but to describe it. By no means do all liaison forms fall into the invariable category. Encrevé has estimated that invariable liaison accounts for some 48 per cent of all liaisons made in everyday speech, although this figure would of course depend on the number of variable liaisons made by individual speakers.

HYPERCORRECT LIAISON

In contrast to liaisons which all speakers make, irrespective of socio-linguistic factors such as social class, age, sex, speech style, etc., a further liaison category is labelled by prescriptive grammarians as '*interdite*'. Encrevé calls this category '*erratique*', reflecting the fact that liaisons of this type are regarded as errors of grammar. However, it may be more accurate to call this type of liaison 'hypercorrect', since such errors are likely to be made by speakers who are unsure of the rules governing liaison, and who are led by the influence of spelling into making a liaison where the standard language requires none, believing (wrongly) that such a form is in fact correct. Examples of hypercorrect liaison are pronouncing the liaison consonant /t/ in *et*, and the liaison consonant in a singular noun before a vowel-initial verb, as in *le soldat est parti*.

VARIABLE LIAISON

Between the liaison forms which are always pronounced and those which should never be, lies a large area of variation consisting of those liaisons which prescriptivists call 'optional' ('*facultatives*'). The more neutral term used by Encrevé is simply 'variable', reflecting the fact that speakers sometimes produce such liaison forms and sometimes do not. In contrast to invariable liaison, variable liaison is conditioned by the sociolinguistic factors mentioned above, as well as by purely linguistic factors such as the closeness of the syntactic link between the two units involved, and the phonetic properties of the liaison consonant. Common examples of variable liaisons are:

- Between a verb (generally a frequent one such as *aller* or *être*) and a complement, that is a word or phrase which 'completes' the sense of the verb. Thus, one may hear *c'est un village* pronounced either [sɛtœ̃vilaʒ] or [sɛœ̃vilaʒ].
- After invariable words (typically conjunctions, adverbs and pronouns, such as *depuis*, *pendant*, *toujours*, *quand*). Thus, *quand il arrive* may be pronounced [kɑ̃tilaRiv] or [kɑ̃ilaRiv].

But how do we know when these variable liaisons are likely to be made? To answer this we must now examine briefly the sociolinguistic and linguistic factors involved.

6.2.3   Sociolinguistic factors

Variable liaison is a prestige feature of French pronunciation. This means that it is found most frequently in the more formal styles of speech of educated speakers, when they are paying most attention to their speech production. Relatively few speakers control it fully and it appears to be dependent on a high level of education and literacy. Thus politicians' public speeches often contain much variable liaison. Newsreaders, who are often reading from an autocue even though their speech may appear spontaneous, also produce a large number of variable liaison forms.

Table 6.1 Classification of liaison forms

	Invariable	Variable	'Hypercorrect'
NOUN PHRASE	(1) determiner + noun, pronoun, adjective *vos_enfants* *deux_autres* *un_ancien ami*	(2) plural noun + adjective, verb *des soldats_anglais* *ses plans_ont réussi*	(3) singular noun + adjective, verb *un soldat_anglais* *son plan_a réussi*
VERB GROUP	(4) pronoun + verb *ils_ont compris* *nous en_avons* verb + pronoun *allons-y* *ont-ils compris*	(5) verb + complement *je vais_essayer* *j'avais_entendu* *vous êtes_invité* *il commençait_à lire* *c'est_un village* *il est_impossible* *on est_obligé*	(6)
UNINFLECTED WORDS	(7)	(8) invariable monosyllabic words *en_une journée* *très_intéressant* invariable polysyllabic words *pendant_un jour* *toujours_utile*	(9) *et* + whatever follows *et_on l'a fait*
SPECIAL CASES	(10) set phrases *comment_allez-vous?* *les_États-Unis* *de temps_en temps* *tout_à coup*	(11)	(12) aspirate 'h' *des_héros* *en_haut* article etc. + relevant numerals *cent_huitième* *en_onze jours* *le_un*

Source: Adapted from Encrevé (1987: 47)

LINGUISTIC FACTORS

We can divide the linguistic factors which influence the occurrence of variable liaison into two kinds: phonetic and syntactic.

Phonetic factors
At least one researcher has found that those variable liaison consonants which are articulated with less force are pronounced more often, other things (syntactic factors) being equal. This means that /t/ (a voiceless plosive and hence the type of consonant which requires the greatest amount of articulatory effort) is the *least* likely of the three main liaison consonants to be realised (= pronounced). Of the other two, /n/ requires less force in its articulation than /z/, and is correspondingly more frequently pronounced.

Syntactic factors
Invariable liaisons are made generally between words which are closely tied together syntactically. This is the case, for example, between articles and nouns, e.g. *les enfants*. French is a language which by and large cannot omit definite and indefinite articles. Articles and nouns are therefore closely tied together within the same syntactic unit or phrase, in this case a noun phrase consisting of article + noun. By contrast, liaison between phrases is variable. Many more combinatory possibilities exist across phrases, as between for example a verb phrase and its complement, e.g. *j'aimerais aller en Suisse*. The syntactic link between the verb phrase *aimerais* and its complement *aller* is weaker than that between article and noun. Thus, liaison within phrases tends to be invariable and liaison across phrases variable.

Table 6.1 provides a summary description of the three types of liaison discussed above, and of the four grammatical categories into which each of the three types fall. Examples are given in italics. Some grammatical terms may be unfamiliar. A *determiner* is a word that indicates or determines the status of a following word; examples of determiners are articles, possessive adjectives (*vos*, *mes*), quantifiers such as numerals, and demonstratives (*ces*). The 'uninflected' row refers to words like *très* and *pendant*, whose form does not change, in contrast to nouns and verbs, which carry inflection according to gender and/or number. The 'special cases' row refers to idiosyncratic cases such as set phrases (*de temps en temps* etc.) and *h aspiré*.

For further reading on liaison, see Battye and Hintze (1992: 136–41); Gadet (1989), Chapter 5; Price (1991), Chapter 19.

6.3 Elision

Elision is the dropping or non-pronunciation of certain sounds in connected speech, as for example in English where 'cup of tea' is frequently reduced to 'cuppa tea'. A fairly spectacular but by no means unusual example taken from French is *il me semble*, which in informal style reduces to [imsã(b)], four or even five out of nine phonetic segments being elided. This phrase exemplifies several elision processes which will be discussed more fully below. An examination of the elision processes which take place in rapid speech makes the comprehension difficulties that learners experience understandable. Some spoken forms are far indeed from the pronunciation suggested by their representation in spelling.

In French we need to make an initial distinction between *standard* and *non-standard* elision. Certain elisions form part of the standard language; particularly those involving mute-e in the monosyllabic words *le, je, me, ce, que*, etc. before a vowel, as in *si j'en ai assez, il m'a dit*, and so forth. Similarly, /i/ in *si* elides before a vowel, as in *s'il vous plaît*. The rule here is quite simply that in certain contexts (frequent words such as the examples just shown), when two vowels come into contact the first vowel elides. The exception to this rule is again the set of *h aspiré* words. We saw above that liaison is not possible before words in the *h aspiré* set. Before *h aspiré* words, elision also is impossible. This exception of the *h aspiré* set applies to words whose vowels normally elide before vowel-initial words; again, those given above (*le, je, me, ce, que*, etc.). Thus to consider again the *h aspiré* words given in 6.2, mute-e in the definite article *le* before *hall, haricot* and *héros* does not elide; *le hall, le haricot, le héros* are therefore pronounced: [ləol], [ləaRiko], [ləeRo], not [lol], [laRiko], [leRo]. The vowel in the feminine definite article is of course also affected by the exception which the *h aspiré* set of words provides; thus *la halle* is pronounced [laal], not [lal].

In contrast to standard elision, less socially prestigious speech and more casual speech styles show elisions in contexts where they would not be acceptable in the standard variety. Examples of this are to be found in the tendency of some speakers to reduce consonant groups in words like *expliquer* to *espliquer*; or to elide /i/ in the subject relative pronoun *qui*, as in *l'homme qu'est là-bas*. Stylistic and social variation in speech are linked in that formal ('standard') speech is generally socially prestigious, i.e. characteristic of the upper or middle classes. Conversely, casual ('non-standard') speech is closer to the *populaire*. On this point see above Chapter 2, 2.1.2.

Formal speech, which is nearer to the written form with all its redundancy (on this term see Chapter 2, 2.2.1), contrasts with casual speech in that the latter is marked by more elision or dropping of sounds. In informal style the learner of French needs to master a considerable set of elided forms in order to produce a convincing approximation to a native-speaker's pronunciation. To take an example we have already considered in a previous section involving mute-e, a speaker may say either *la remise* [laRəmiz] or *la r'mise* [laRmiz] according to the context, i.e. the social status of the addressee, the relationship between the speakers, the formality of the situation, etc.

To associate elided forms with informal speech seems to imply that the adoption of casual style always entails reduction and only reduction. The addition of *extra* sounds in casual style is indeed rarer than their reduction. However, the insertion of a mute-e to avoid the need to pronounce certain consonant clusters is encountered fairly often, as in *ours-e blanc* [uRsəblã], *film-e danois* [filmədanwa], *carte bleue* [kaRtəblø]. A mute-e may be inserted in this way, whether it is present in the spelling or not. It may be remarked that French speakers do not seem to frown upon this phenomenon as much as do English speakers when confronted with non-standard 'filum', where again a schwa is inserted, again apparently to break up a consonant group.

6.3.1 Elision of consonants

Elision affects some consonants more than others, but lexical frequency (i.e. how often the word containing the consonant in question occurs in speech) is no doubt a factor: the elision of /l/ from the articles and pronouns is a ready illustration of this. Well-known examples of elision are the reduction of *ils arrivent* [ilzaRiv] to [izaRiv] or even [iaRiv], or of *ils vont* [ilvɔ̃] to [ivɔ̃]. The following examples may be less familiar: reduction of *j'les ai vus* [ʒlezevy] to [ʒezevy], or of *elle nous a dit* [ɛlnuzadi] to [ɛnuzadi]; or of *elle est bien* [ɛlɛbjɛ̃] to [ɛːbjɛ̃], or of *dans la cave* [dãlakav] to [dãakav]. The process operating here is generally the simplification of groups of two or more consonants, although a single consonant may also be elided, as in the last example, or in the very common reduction of *il y a* [ilja] to [ija].

The consonants /R/ and /l/ are particularly susceptible to this process, being both phonetically weak (i.e. articulated with relatively little force) and frequently occurring. The /R/ of northern French, for example, is articulated with little friction, and the muscular effort required to realise it is small in comparison with that required to articulate a fricative such as /s/, say. This can be verified by comparing the amount of effort required, and of audible friction produced, when French /R/ and /s/ are produced in *Paris* as against *Passy*. /R/ is the most frequent consonant in French, at least in the citation forms provided in dictionaries. The tendency to simplify word-final consonant groups results in such reductions as *chambre* [ʃãbR] to [ʃãb] (where mute-e has been previously elided). Other examples are reduction of *parle* to [paːl], and of *bonjour* to [bɔ̃ʒuː]. Frequency of occurrence is also an important factor in the elision of /l/ (and mute-e) from *quelque chose* [kɛlkəʃoz] to [kɛkʃoz] or from *je sais plus* [ʒəsɛply] to [ʃsɛpy]. This latter sequence also features an example of assimilation, which will be discussed in detail below.

Word-final consonant groups of the type exemplified by *chambre* occur frequently in spoken French. Along with all the infinitive verbs which share this phonetic feature (*être, prendre*, etc.) there are many nouns and some adverbs, of varying frequency of occurrence. In more formal speech, words of this type tend to be pronounced in their full form, i.e. the mute-e in *autre* [otRə] will be pronounced more often than in less formal style, while *autr'* [otR] is in turn more characteristic of formal style than *aut'* [ot].

6.3.2   Elision of vowels

The French vowel most subject to elision is mute-e, a fact recognised in dictionaries like *Le Petit Robert* which place the vowel in brackets in the citation form of words where elision is judged to be likely. Sociolinguistic factors such as age, sex, regional origin, social class of speaker and (in)formality of speech style also exert a significant influence. However, the likelihood of mute-e elision is governed mostly by linguistic factors, specifically the number of consonants which will come together if the vowel is elided. We can distinguish at least four phonetic contexts which influence the likelihood of mute-e elision:

1   Mute-e elides very often between two consonants, as in *la semaine, délit de fuite*, whether the two consonants are within a word or not. Another linguistic factor influencing mute-e elision in this context is the frequency of the word concerned; thus in the relatively rare *cheminée*, the vowel will be likely to be retained.

2   Mute-e tends to be retained between three or more consonants, as in *sur le trottoir, une fenêtre*. The crucial factor here is the number of consonants *preceding* the mute-e; if there are two or more, the vowel tends to be retained. Exceptions are frequent, however; again, the influence of lexis, i.e. of frequency of occurrence, is observable in the case of *une semaine* for example, which may reduce to [ynsmɛn], with three consonants coming together as a result of mute-e elision. This elision is quite likely to occur in rapid speech.

The case of mute-e in *autrement* illustrates how the phonetic properties of the surrounding consonants may come into play: this context is claimed by grammarians and indeed by non-prescriptive linguists to be favourable to 100 per cent retention of mute-e, but speakers have in fact the possibility of lengthening the /r/ to produce [otR:mã], or indeed simply of omitting the vowel to produce [otRmã]. The fact that /r/ is a fricative means that the consonant can be lengthened to replace the vowel. Compare the case of *appartement* reducing to [apaRtmã], where a comparable lengthening of the plosive /t/ is unlikely, and where the word must lose a syllable following elision of mute-e.

3   As was mentioned above, the frequent word-final context exemplified by *autre, chambre, ronfle*, etc., is very favourable to mute-e elision, as well as to subsequent elision of word-final /l/ and /R/.

4   When mute-e is found in a series of two or more in adjacent syllables, the vowels elide in one of two regular patterns. Thus in the sequence *je me le*

demande [ʒəmələdəmãd], the conventional rule on mute-e elision is that the vowel will fall after one consonant and be retained after two, to give alternate groups of two consonants, each separated by a mute-e. The elision of the vowels will be governed by the treatment of the first in the series. Thus the foregoing example could be elided to: [ʒəmlədmãd] or [ʒməldəmãd]. The first pattern is reported by one linguist (Gadet 1989: 82) to be regarded by prescriptivists as more pleasing, the second *populaire*. These patterns are no doubt respected in relatively careful speech, but more casual, rapid speech styles may produce fairly impressive consonant clusters resulting from mute-e elision in this context: *parce que je me demande* reduced to [pskʒmdmãd], for example.

6.4   Assimilation

In addition to elision and often consequent upon it, *assimilation* is the other major phonological feature of connected speech that a learner of spoken French needs to be aware of. Assimilation, which means 'becoming similar', involves a consonant (occasionally a vowel) taking on one or more of the phonetic features of a neighbouring one. Thus in *je pense*, for example, mute-e will very often drop and bring into contact the /ʒ/ of *je*, a voiced palatal fricative, and the /p/ of *pense*, an unvoiced bilabial plosive. When /ʒ/ and /p/ come into contact, /ʒ/ becomes *devoiced* under the influence of the following voiceless consonant. One sometimes sees this fact described in novels and *bandes dessinées*, where an attempt is made to represent dialogue in informal style; the usual rendering is *ch'pense*. Similar attempts are made with transcriptions such as *ch'crois, ch'ais pas*, etc.

A distinction needs to be made at this stage between *regressive* and *progressive* assimilation. The former is more common than the latter in French (and in English and indeed most languages), and the foregoing example of *je pense* illustrates the process. In regressive assimilation, a preceding consonant takes on some (sometimes all) of the phonetic properties of the following one. This type of assimilation may result in the devoicing of a preceding voiced consonant, as we have seen; other examples are: *Hauts de Seine*, where [odsɛn] becomes [otsɛn]; and *chemin de fer* where [ʃ(ə)mɛ̃dfɛR] becomes [ʃ(ə)mɛ̃tfɛR]. The inverse process, voicing assimilation, can also occur and results in the voicing of a voiceless consonant in anticipation of what is to follow. Examples of this include *chaque jour*, where [ʃakʒuR] becomes [ʃagʒuR]; *espèce de crétin*, where [ɛspɛsdəkRetɛ̃] becomes [ɛspɛzdəkRetɛ̃] and *on se voit*, where [ɔ̃svwa] becomes [ɔ̃zvwa]. The comparative rarity in English of regressive voicing assimilation makes it more difficult for the Anglophone learner to adopt.

As we remarked above, progressive assimilation is rarer than regressive, in French and across languages generally. This is understandable if we consider the motivation behind assimilation. We have already seen in

Chapter 5 that one sound may influence another in the chain of speech ('phonetic conditioning'). This is not surprising given that sounds follow so rapidly in connected speech; when they are talking, speakers are constantly planning ahead and anticipating what is to come, on all the linguistic levels, phonetic, syntactic and lexical. Thus, for example, when a speaker is about to say *je t'invite*, he or she knows intuitively that the first /t/ in *t'invite* is voiceless, and anticipates this absence of voice by 'switching off' the voice in the /ʒ/ of *je*. The result is [ʃtɛ̃vit].

Occasionally, however, a preceding sound will influence a following one, as in examples (13) and (14):

(13)   *traitement de texte*: [tRɛtmɑ̃dtɛkst] > [tRɛtmɑ̃ntɛkst]

Here, under the influence of the nasal vowel /a/, the following dental plosive /d/ assimilates to the dental nasal /n/. Another example:

(14)   *ça me dérange pas*: [samdeRɑ̃ʒpa] > [samneRɑ̃ʒpa]

Here again, a preceding nasal, /m/ in this case, causes a dental plosive to assimilate to a dental nasal. Notwithstanding the relative rarity of progressive assimilation, we can say that in French, whenever /m/ in *me* precedes a /d/ (following elision of the mute-e in *me*), this particular assimilation is likely.

The examples given above demonstrate assimilation of manner of articulation. We can classify assimilation in French according to three phonetic criteria:

- assimilation of *voice*;
- assimilation of *place* of articulation;
- assimilation of *manner* of articulation.

6.4.1   Voicing assimilation

All the examples so far quoted except the last two illustrate assimilation of voice, for they involve a consonant either acquiring or losing voice. These processes are common in French.

6.4.2   Place of articulation

Assimilation involving the place of articulation is common in English, as in examples such as 'tem pence' and 'hambag', where 'n' has in both cases been 'labialised' under the influence of the following bilabial consonant. These speech processes are incidentally of the type that one notices and condemns when other people use them, even though we frequently use them ourselves. Occasionally such assimilations may be *total*, when a consonant becomes identical with an adjacent one, as in 'ten mice' > 'tem mice' or 'cut-price' >

'cup-price'. But assimilation is usually partial. Place-of-articulation assimilation seems rather uncommon in French, or has at least been little commented on. One example cited in the literature involves 'le weekend prochain', where the influence of the /p/ on the preceding /n/ in 'weekend' (following elision of the /d/) results in the following chain of elision plus assimilation:

(15)   [wikɛndpRoʃɛ̃] > [wikɛnpRoʃɛ̃] > [wikɛmpRoʃɛ̃]

6.4.3   Manner of articulation

Manner-of-articulation assimilation is common in French. Elision of the mute-e of *de* in frequently occurring words and phrases often brings the residual /d/ into contact with a neighbouring nasalised vowel, with the result that the dental plosive /d/ becomes the dental nasal /n/: thus *on demande* may undergo the following process:

(16)   [ɔ̃dəmɑ̃d] > [ɔ̃dmɑ̃d] > [ɔ̃nmɑ̃d]

Here again, the assimilation is regressive and conforms to the general rule. Perhaps more familiar examples of assimilation of dental plosive to dental nasal are *pendant*, where [pɑ̃dɑ̃] becomes [pɑ̃nɑ̃] and an example which may be less familiar is *là-dedans*, where elision of mute-e is again followed by nasalisation of /d/:

(17)   [ladədɑ̃] > [laddɑ̃] > [lannɑ̃]

The frequency of occurrence of the monosyllabic words *de* and *me*, or of the words and phrases in which the prefix *de* occurs, obviously plays a part in influencing the likelihood of assimilation: it can be seen from Table 6.2 that this word or prefix occurs in four out of the seven examples given.

Table 6.2 Types of assimilation in French

Assimilation	Regressive	Progressive
Voice	+ *chaque jour* *chemin de fer*	
Place	− *weekend prochain*	
Manner	+ *là-dedans* *demi-kilo*	− *traitement de texte* *ça me dérange pas*

A final, more straightforward example is *ah bon*, where the bilabial plosive /b/, under the influence of the following nasal vowel, may become a bilabial nasal:

(18)   [abɔ̃] > [amɔ̃]

We can summarise the situation regarding assimilation in French in tabular form, as shown in Table 6.2, where a plus sign indicates that assimilation is frequent or likely, and a minus sign the reverse.

6.4.4   Assimilation of vowels

Assimilation or 'harmony' as it affects vowels in contiguous syllables is an interesting phenomenon, although seemingly rather rare. Examples are *secrétariat* [səkRetaRia] pronounced *sécrétariat* [sekRetaRia]; *maman* [mamã] pronounced [mãmã]; and *surtout* [syRtu]) pronounced [suRtu]. In these cases, a vowel appears to influence another one in an adjacent syllable.

For further reading on elision and assimilation, see Armstrong (1982: 168–85); Gadet (1989), Chapters 6–8; Price (1991), Chapters 11, 18.

6.5   Stress and intonation

These features of pronunciation are often referred to as occurring at the 'suprasegmental' level: the levels of the syllable, word and phrase, as opposed to the level of the individual sound (segment). The whole of this chapter so far has been devoted to examining features of French pronunciation at the suprasegmental level, looking at how sounds interact with each other when combined in the chain of speech. The difference between a connected-speech feature such as liaison and suprasegmental features such as a stress or intonation pattern is that the latter may extend over a sequence of many individual segments or sounds, while liaison and assimilation and elision are concerned with what occurs at the juncture of two sounds. Stress and intonation dictate the musical quality of our speech, providing changes in volume and in the tune or melodic line.

6.5.1   Stress

Stress can be defined as the degree of force which a speaker uses to produce a syllable, *relative to neighbouring syllables*. The degree of force may find expression in pitch, length or loudness. Thus a stressed syllable is more highly pitched, longer, or louder than neighbouring syllables. However, it should be emphasised that the stressed syllable is not highly pitched, etc. in any absolute sense: a speaker with a quiet voice may stress a syllable by using a degree of loudness which would seem relatively quiet for someone with a loud voice. But this does not matter. All that matters is that the stressed syllable should be louder, etc. than the surrounding syllables which the individual speaker produces.

The functioning of the stress system is very different in French and English. English puts stress to a variety of uses to which French does not. First, English makes use of stress to distinguish between the grammatical function of many pairs of words whose spelling is identical: for example, between "increase' (noun) and 'in'crease' (verb) (the symbol ' is placed before a syllable to indicate it is stressed). Second, stress is used in English to indicate contrasts beyond the level of individual words: compare "black-bird' and 'black 'bird', for example. Third, many English 'grammatical' words (on this term see Chapter 3, 3.1.4) have both stressed (or strong) and unstressed (or weak) forms: speakers may use a strong rather than a weak form of a word in order to emphasise what they think is the important element of information in an utterance, as in 'I think John and Norma should go' (unstressed 'and', pronounced [ən] or [n]) as opposed to 'I think John 'and Norma should go' (stressed 'and', pronounced [ænd]).

French is often called a 'syllable-timed' language, while English is described as being 'stress-timed'. In syllable-timed languages, the rhythm of speech is measured in syllables of roughly equal weight, whereas in stress-timed languages it is measured in stressed syllables occurring at regular intervals, regardless of the number of unstressed syllables occurring in between. This has important implications for the way in which poetry is written in the two languages. A more day-to-day consequence of this is that, since every French vowel receives more or less equal stress, the vowels do not reduce to schwa as do those of English. Compare, for instance the pronunciation of the vowels in English 'monopoly' and its French equivalent *monopole*.

More significant, however, is the fact that stress in French is relatively fixed, while English has the possibility of displacing stress if need be. This may be illustrated by comparing the following equivalent French and English sentences:

(19) 'Elle 'y 'a 'ache'''té 'un 'nouv'eau 'livre '''hier
      She 'bought a new 'book there 'yesterday

(The symbol ''' indicates the main or 'primary' stress.) Whereas in English the main stress is free to range over the various words in the sentence as emphasis requires, in French the main stress tends to fall rather mechanically on the last syllable of the word group (phrase or sentence). As a phrase is expanded, the stress is displaced to the last syllable. This can be illustrated by comparing the following French phrases:

(20)   *une sou'ris*

(21)   *une chauve-sou'ris*

(22)   *une chauve-souris 'brune*

Stress is therefore more flexible in English than in French, in the sense that English speakers may choose to emphasise a normally unstressed syllable by displacing stress, provided that in the sentence as a whole stresses continue to be timed at approximately regular intervals. French speakers, on the other hand, tend to employ additional lexical items or different grammatical constructions to emphasise elements which they wish to convey as being important in informational terms. Thus, for example, an English speaker may contradict a declarative by using the strong form of a word, as shown in example (23).

(23) You're not going tonight!
Yes I 'am going! (Weak form: Yes I'm going)

Contrast this with the way a French speaker would contradict the equivalent declarative:

(24) *Tu iras pas ce soir!*
Si, j'irai! (Unstressed form *Oui, j'irai*)

French uses a different word for 'yes', while English uses a stressed form (see above, p. 57). To look again at the example of John and Norma, while English, as we have seen, uses the strong form of 'and' to highlight what is considered to be the informative element of the sentence, i.e. that both John and Norma should go (and not just John), French would tend to add words:

(25) *Je crois que Jean devrait aller, et Norma aussi*

French does, however, use what we may call contrastive stress to clear up ambiguities, as in example (26):

(26) *J'ai dit "récrire, pas "décrire*

Here the symbol " indicates that a greater degree of stress has been applied to the following syllable than to neighbouring ones.

6.5.2 Intonation

The term intonation refers to the patterns of variation in pitch, or 'tunes', that speakers employ in speech. Whereas stress generally concerns individual syllables at the word level, patterns of intonation apply to larger units (often several words long) referred to as 'tone groups'. A tone group is a clause or sentence to which a speaker applies a particular intonation pattern. English and French each have their own intonation patterns, and we need be able to reproduce the characteristic French patterns in order to sound authentically French. It is important to emphasise here that intonation is a complex area of language, and has been little investigated in comparison with phonology, syntax and semantics. A detailed description of the intonational system of French is therefore beyond the scope of this book. We shall confine ourselves here to examining a few of the more salient similarities and differences between French and English intonation. Further reading on stress and intonation is given at the end of the chapter.

FUNCTIONS OF INTONATION

Speech varies constantly in pitch. Although intonation patterns were referred to above as tunes, intonation differs from singing in that notes are not held for any length of time in speech, speakers gliding very rapidly from pitch to pitch. We are so accustomed to intonation in speech that we immediately notice speech which is monotonous: literally, all on one tone. Monotonous speech is viewed unfavourably, as conveying lack of interest, warmth, and other positive human qualities. It is significant that 'robot speech' in science fiction, such as that used by the Daleks and Androids, is portrayed as monotonous.

Speakers use intonation to convey various types of meaning, intention and information. In this section we will consider intonation from two viewpoints: first, intonation at the grammatical level, within phrases or sentences; and second, the function of intonation at the larger-scale discourse level, where phrases and sentences interact.

GRAMMATICAL USE OF INTONATION; OR INTONATION AS PUNCTUATION

To speak of 'intonation as punctuation' is of course to get things the wrong way round, since punctuation can be regarded as an attempt to reproduce intonation, which came first historically. Nevertheless, we can think of intonation as functioning in speech in rather the same way that punctuation functions in writing. Very often, intonation (like punctuation) has a grammatical function, and intonation rather than syntax may be used to convey the 'speech function' of an utterance. The formulation of questions in French illustrates this function of intonation.

Asking questions using intonation
In both English and French, a '*yes–no* question', i.e. one which expects either 'yes' or 'no' as an answer, may be expressed in more than one way. In English, a 'declarative' sentence (a statement) is transformed syntactically into an 'interrrogative' or question in one of two ways, depending on the verb concerned. With the verb 'to be', the transformation is simple: subject and verb are inverted:

(27)	You're wearing red socks (declarative)

(28)	> Are you wearing red socks? (interrogative)

In addition to the syntactic transformation, the declarative and interrogative each have their own intonation patterns. The declarative has a so-called falling pattern, which means that the pitch of the speaker's voice falls during the last section of the utterance: 'socks' in this case. In contrast, interrogatives characteristically have a rising intonation towards the end of the utterance. These patterns are similar in English and French.

Instead of inverting subject and verb, speakers can also use the declarative structure with a rising intonation to convey to a listener that a question is intended. This is true to a much greater extent in French than in English: one researcher (Coveney 1990: 127) found that in a corpus of spoken French, speakers used the declarative structure in 77 per cent of instances to produce *yes–no* questions; thus French speakers prefer to say for example:

(29)   *Vous voulez la tisane?*

rather than:

(30)   *Est-ce que vous voulez la tisane?*

Incidentally, this second structure accounted for the other 23 per cent of instances of *yes–no* questions in the corpus mentioned above. Thus no examples of the most formal structure, *Voulez-vous la tisane?*, were noted. This structure is now appropriate only for the more formal varieties of spoken French.

The use of intonation to ask a *yes–no* question is therefore highly characteristic of French. Note that this use of intonation is rarer in English; the enquiry regarding red socks could be formulated as follows, with rising intonation:

(31)   You're wearing red socks?

However, a question formulated in this way in English would be probably be a request for confirmation of an assumption, rather than for new information. Commoner in English is the use of the affirmative structure with a 'rise–fall' intonation pattern conveying shock or incredulity: 'You're wearing red socks!'

Intonation used to indicate syntactic boundaries

Any textbook on punctuation will mention the difference between the use of a comma to distinguish between 'restrictive' and 'appositive' relative clauses, as illustrated by the following examples:

(32)   My brother who's a pilot . . .

(33)   My brother, who's a pilot . . .

In example (32), the absence of a comma after 'brother' indicates that the speaker has more than one brother, and that one of them is a pilot. The relative clause is distinguishing or defining the brother in question. In example (33), the comma indicates that the speaker has only one brother, and is providing further information or commenting on him. These differences in punctuation parallel the different intonation patterns which characterise the two types of clause. In both French and English, no pause would be made between the noun and relative pronoun 'who' in example (32). In example (33), English would have a rise–fall on 'brother', to indicate a syntactic break, while in the equivalent French utterance (*Mon frère, qui est pilote ...) frère* would carry a rising tone rather than a rise–fall. Thus English and French each have their characteristic intonation patterns, but both languages mark an important syntactic boundary by using intonation.

DISCOURSAL USE OF INTONATION

As well as marking the grammatical function of an utterance which can usefully be considered in isolation from the utterances surrounding it, speakers also use intonation to express a relationship between an utterance and the wider context of a piece of discourse. The term 'relationship' is a very general one which covers several functions. We will mention only two here.

Expressive use of intonation

The example given above concerning red socks illustrates how speakers may use intonation to convey their attitude to what has been said. Again, characteristic intonation patterns are used to do this, and French patterns are different from English ones. The red-socks example illustrates a pattern where French and English differ sharply. This pattern is the so-called 'echo-exclamation', where a speaker repeats or echoes what has just been said, generally to express incredulity; as indicated above, English employs a rise–fall pattern. The French pattern is more complex and very distinctive; it takes the form of a fall–rise–fall pattern on the word or phrase which is echoed. Try eliciting this pattern from a French native-speaker by claiming something improbable, such as the following:

(34)   *Je porte toujours des chaussettes rouges au lit*

Use of intonation to indicate continuation

A final example of intonation used to express the relationship of a phrase to the surrounding discourse is the signalling of continuation: that the utterance is not yet finished. Here again French and English intonation patterns differ. Consider the simple declarative 'Then she left'. In English this would carry a falling intonation, as would the French equivalent *Puis elle est partie*. But if a speaker wished to indicate that there was more to come ('Then she left ...'), in English the last word of the statement would be lengthened, and a fall–rise (or rise–fall–rise) tune would be applied to the word. In the French equivalent, the second syllable of *partie* would similarly be lengthened, but in contrast to English, would carry a 'high level' tune.

We have considered here only a few of the ways in which French and English speakers use intonation to mark the grammatical or discoursal function of a clause or sentence. As indicated above, space does not permit an exhaustive treatment of this subject. But we have seen that declaratives in both languages have falling intonation, while *yes–no* interrogatives show a rising pattern. This is in fact true across many languages and is an important generalisation, since declaratives and interrogatives are two very frequent sentence types. We have also seen that both languages use intonation to indicate grammatical and discoursal boundaries. Thus it is probably true to say that the major functions of intonation are similar in French and English (and many other languages), while each language has its own characteristic intonational melodies.

For further reading on French (and English) stress and intonation, see Armstrong (1982: 131–49); Price (1991), Chapters 9, 20; Tranel (1987), Chapter 12.

Seminar exercises

1.   Indicate the syllable divisions in the following words and phrases. Make sure you use the conventional notation, i.e. phonemic transcription and full stops to indicate syllable boundaries.

(a) *Elle part en avion.*
(b) *Je vais m'inscrire en faculté de médecine.*
(c) *Tu en veux un autre?*
(d) *Un autre avion a été perdu.*
(e) *Le professeur de math a annulé son cours de dix heures.*
(f) *Il m'a dit qu'il voulait travailler en Groenland.*

2.   Indicate which processes of elision and/or assimilation are likely in the following sequences. Transcribe your answers in IPA notation. Identify each type of assimilation: progressive of voice, regressive of manner of articulation, etc.

(a) *Le temps passe vite.* → [Lə tɑ̃ paz vit] regressive of voice
(b) *C'est une longue marche.*
(c) *J'en voudrais un demi-kilo.*
(d) *Il arrive maintenant.*
(e) *Je te le dirai plus tard.*
(f) *Le nouveau chef va nous parler.*

3.   Classify the following sets of examples of liaison according to Table 6.1 on p. 100, i.e. according to liaison category (invariable, variable, hypercorrect) and grammatical category. For convenience each box in the table is numbered, to help you assign each set of liaisons to a box. Each set, arranged under a letter from (a) to (n), belongs to the same liaison category. Then, make sure you can pronounce each example both with and without liaison, where appropriate. Finally, find one more example of (non) liaison to add to those grouped under each letter below.

(a) *vais aller; avez entendu; êtes invité; commençait à pleurer.*
(b) *de temps à autre; accent aigu; vis-à-vis; Champs-Elysées.*

(c) *les arbres; vos enfants; deux autres; un ancien ami.*

(d) *soldat algérien; son projet a réussi; gouvernement américain.*

(e) *en haut; des héros; un homard; des haricots.*

(f) *sont-elles; vas-y.*

(g) *ils ont; nous en avons; je les ai.*

(h) *en une journée; chez Alain; très intéressant; moins aisé;*
     dont il a; quand elle est; pas encore; je n'ai plus écouté.

(i) *et on l'a fait; des pommes et abricots.*

(j) *avant huit jours; la cent onzième.*

(k) *assez intéressant; pendant un jour; toujours utile;*
     absolument impossible; jamais allé.

(l) *des soldats anglais; ses projets ont réussi.*

(m) *aller en ville; accéder à l'indépendance.*

(n) *est intelligente; sont occupés; était entré.*

7

French morphology

We have seen earlier how morphology is concerned with the way words can be decomposed into smaller elements known as 'morphemes', which are the smallest units of meaning or grammatical function existing in a particular language (p. 34). We have also seen that there are two branches to the study of morphology: derivational morphology, which is concerned with the way new words can be produced by the addition of affixes (prefixes and suffixes) to roots, and inflectional morphology, which is concerned with the way one and the same word modifies its form according to the syntactic function it is performing. The ways in which a language generates new words out of pre-existing morphemes and new sentences out of pre-existing words are closely bound up with one another in speakers' linguistic competence, but for expository reasons we are separating them out in this book. We dealt with the first of these issues in Chapter 3. It is now time to look in greater detail at the second.

We will look first in a theoretical way at how a word may modify its morphology (or 'form'). We will then consider the different categories of word ('parts of speech') in French, and will conclude with a discussion of how words in French have their morphology modified according to the different grammatical features which are loaded on to them.

7.1   Different ways in which a word modifies its morphology

7.1.1   *Derivational and inflectional morphemes*

Inflectional morphemes are a rather different kettle of fish from the *derivational morphemes* we considered earlier, for they do a quite different job. If we attach a derivational morpheme like *in-* or *-ation* to a stem, as in *in-utile,* or *excit-ation,* we create a new word, with a different lexical meaning. Attaching an inflectional morpheme to a word does not change the word, rather, it provides additional information about the word. So, if we add tense markers to a verb stem, we do not change the lexical meaning of the verb but rather, we add grammatical information about when the action takes place, e.g. *j'aime, j'aimais, j'aimerai.* Similarly, plural and gender markers do not indicate a change in the lexical meaning of an adjective, but reflect agreement with a plural masculine or feminine noun, e.g. *le petit garçon, la petite fille, les petites filles.*

In French, derivational affixes may occur both as prefixes and as suffixes, but inflectional affixes can only occur as suffixes, i.e. there are no prefixes which modify an existing word by supplying grammatical information *in front of* the word. The addition of a derivational suffix creates a new word with a different meaning from the original and can change its grammatical category (i.e. make a noun into a verb, an adjective into a noun, etc.). French inflectional suffixes never change the category of the word to which they are affixed. They add extra information to the original word, such as number or tense, but do not change the fundamental meaning of a word. If a word were to change grammatical category then, logically, the fundamental meaning of the word must also have changed.

Finally, the interpretation of all inflectional morphemes is constant, unlike that of some derivational morphemes. By this, we mean that speakers will always understand what grammatical information is being supplied when faced with a particular inflectional morpheme. The information does not alter. So, even if the speaker does not know the lexical meaning of a verb, they will recognise the *-ons* ending, for it always indicates 4th person of the verb, just as *-s* on a noun or adjective always indicates plurality. This situation is not always true of derivational morphemes. The prefix *re-,* for example, usually carries a meaning of repetition of an action. However, while in *revoir* the prefix *re-* clearly indicates a repetition of *voir, ressentir* does not mean literally 'to feel again', but means simply 'to feel'. Similarly, the word *racheter* means 'to buy up (a business)', not 'to buy again'. Thus *re-* carries a slightly different meaning with each of these verbs. Inflectional morphology does not present this type of problem to speakers, since the interpretation of inflectional morphemes is always the same in all contexts.

7.1.2   *Identification of morphemes*

We have now established that words vary their form in two ways – derivationally and inflectionally – and in order to explain this we have frequently made use of the term 'morpheme'. But are we sure we can identify French morphemes (i.e. the smallest units of meaning in the language) in the first place? Sometimes this is very easy to do, because the patterns are quite regular and the breakdown into morphemes is uncomplicated. For instance, we can divide *antiraciste* into *anti+rac+iste*, and *traîtreusement* into *traîtr+euse+ment*. Other words, however, do not break down quite so easily. The key to correctly analysing the morphemes in a word lies in the following questions:

- Does the proposed morpheme on its own provide either meaning or grammatical information?
- Does the proposed morpheme occur in other words with the same meaning?
- From this evidence, could a speaker of French (subconsciously) classify it as a morpheme?

Applying these questions to words like *inutilement* produces answers quite easily. We find *in-* elsewhere with the same meaning in words like *insouciant* and *inexplicable*. *Utile* is a free morpheme with a definite meaning and *-ment* is the normal adverbial suffix which transforms an adjective into an adverb. Together, the meaning of word *inutilement* is the composite meanings of *in* + *utile* + *ment*. However, some words pose more serious difficulties. How many separate morphemes should we conclude are present in *violent, conscience* or *amant*? Should we analyse them into the units *viol* + *ent*, *con* + *science* and *am* + *ant* respectively, regarding each of these units as separate morphemes?

We could demonstrate that some of these units are morphemes on the basis of the fact that they exist with the same meaning in other French words: /ɑ̃/ spelt *-ent* or *-ant* in *violent* and *amant* can be found in other adjectives such as *innocent, débilitant* or *menaçant*. The form *science* is a free morpheme (a word which can stand on its own) in French. However, in the case of each of these three words (*violent, conscience, amant*) there is at least one potential morpheme left over which does not fit easily into the pattern of French morphology. Can we easily identify *viol-, con-* or *am-* as morphemes?

We might argue that *viol* is a free morpheme meaning 'rape' and that *-ent* is a adjectival suffix, but can we then say that the meaning of *violent* is the composite of the meaning of *viol* plus the meaning of *-ent*? Linguists' opinions on this are divided: some would argue that *violent* is a single morpheme, while others might want to say that the word contains two morphemes (*viol-* + *-ent*), with the meaning of *viol* changing from 'rape' to something else when it has other morphemes affixed to it. Either is a reasonable account of the word.

Although found in a number of words, *con-* is no longer a productive morpheme in French and *science* now has a more specific meaning than 'knowledge'. It is therefore rather difficult to claim that *conscience* is two morphemes and it would probably be analysed as one.

Although *-ant* could be construed as an adjectival or present participle morpheme, it is not easy to claim the existence of *am-* as a separate morpheme in modern French. It is found in such words as *amour* and *amabilité*, so the link with *amant* is reasonably transparent. However, is the link sufficiently transparent for *am-* to be considered a separate morpheme?

One of the aims of this sort of analysis is to provide a model of the morphological rules which a speaker of French could be supposed to be operating with intuitively. This approach is particularly important to linguists who are trying to establish what it is that native-speakers 'know' when they are said to 'know' a language.

7.1.3   Morphemes, morphs and allomorphs

So far we have painted rather a simple picture of French morphology, implying that it is easy to divide words into their component morphemes. Moreover, up to now, we have used the written forms of words and morphemes in our examples. However, there is often a very big difference between the written form of a morpheme and its spoken counterpart. If we were to conduct an analysis of French morphology based on the spoken word, it would reveal quite a different inventory of morphemes from one based on the written word. The grammar of the spoken language is a very different one from that of writing. In an earlier chapter, we discussed the importance of investigating the spoken word as opposed to the written word, and one of the most important reasons for doing this is that the written word often reflects the language of the past, rather than the language in use today.

A very clear example of this is plural inflection. Its orthographic (written) form is usually *-s* as in *tables, chaises, femmes, chats*, etc. and in Old French this final *-s* was always pronounced. In modern French, however, the facts are quite different. In most instances, the plural morpheme *-s* is simply not pronounced – speakers make no difference between '*chat*' /ʃa/ and '*chats*' /ʃa/. The only time this plural morpheme surfaces in spoken French is in the context of liaison, and then it does so as a voiced fricative /z/. If we look at the question in this way, we have to say that the plural morpheme is generally realised (sounded in speech) as nothing (Ø), except in cases of liaison when it is realised as /z/. From this example alone, it should be clear that the realisation of morphemes in the spoken language is not always what the orthography suggests.

Staying with our example of plural inflection in French, we saw that the plural morpheme is not realised (not pronounced) except in cases of liaison. If we wanted to account for this, we might suggest that there is more than one plural morpheme in French: (Ø) and /z/. Yet, it seems odd to suggest that there are two separate plural morphemes when it is the context in which each one appears which dictates which one is used and not the choice of the actual word it is attached to. Thus /z/ can only ever appear where liaison is possible, never otherwise: it is either one or the other. A neater solution might be to suggest that what we find on the surface in speech is not the whole story, and that morphemes are somewhat more abstract entities than we have hitherto assumed.

Following this line of thought, we could propose that there is a single plural morpheme – /z/ – *underlying* all cases, but whether or not that morpheme is realised (pronounced) depends on the phonological environment it is being asked to appear in. If the next word starts with a vowel, as in *de bons amis,* it will surface with phonetic content (i.e. be pronounced), but, if the next word starts with a consonant making liaison impossible, as in *de bons copains,* it will not surface with phonetic content (i.e. will not be pronounced). What we are suggesting, then, is that we have one underlying morpheme (an abstract entity), and that it comes in two (concrete) phonetic forms, depending on the context.

If morphemes are abstract entities which do not necessarily have a one-to-one relationship with their concrete realisation (there is a one-to-*two* relationship between the morpheme /z/ and its two possible pronunciations Ø or /z/), what are we to call the concrete realisations? We cannot call them morphemes, because they are not, they are *forms of* morphemes. Borrowing from the terminology used in phonology, linguists have labelled the underlying or abstract representation the *morpheme* and its corresponding concrete realisation the *morph,* on a par with the 'phoneme' and the 'phone' (see above, p. 88).

The relationships between morphemes and morphs are many and various:

1 In many cases, e.g. *-age* or *-ment,* the relationship between morpheme and morph is one-to-one, that is to say that in words like *mariage* and *enterrement* the pronunciation of *-age* and *-ment* remains the same, regardless of what comes before or after the words in question, i.e. the morphs corresponding to these morphemes remain constant.
2 In some cases, a single morph can be the concrete realisation of more than one morpheme, particularly in the spoken language, e.g. /e/ can be either the past participle suffix (e.g. *aimé*) or the infinitive marker of verbs (e.g. *aimer*).
3 In some cases a single morph acts as the expression of two morphemes at the same time. If we look at affixes such as *-eur/-euse* in *danseur/danseuse,* we find we can separate the stem *dans-* from the suffixes fairly easily, but the suffixes represent *both* the derivational morpheme meaning 'one who does . . .' *and* the inflectional masculine/feminine morphemes at the same time. When two or more morphemes are realised as one single morph in this way, it is known as *fusion.* As we shall see later in the chapter, fusion is prevalent in verbal morphology in French.
4 In yet other cases, as we have already seen, a single morpheme can be expressed in more than one corresponding morph, e.g. the English past tense marker '-ed' is realised as /d/ after vowels and voiced consonants (e.g. *spied* and *buzzed*), and as /t/ after unvoiced consonants (e.g. *kissed*).

These latter are known as allomorphs (retaining the parallel with
phonemes, phones and allophones, see above pp. 87–88). The distribution of allomorphs (i.e. where each one occurs) depends on the
phonological environment in which they are to be placed. If a morpheme
is not pronounced in a particular environment (i.e. has no concrete
realisation), we refer to it as a zero morph, e.g. the plural marker /z/
realised either as Ø or as /z/.

Allomorphs, just like allophones, are found in two types of distributional
patterns: *complementary distribution* and *free variation*. Complementary
distribution of allomorphs is where the choice of allomorph depends on the
environment, only one of the allomorphs being able to appear in that one
position. Where one can appear, the other cannot, and vice versa. If we now
take the word *inutilement*, it is easy to separate the three morphemes
involved: the prefix *in-*, the stem *utile* and the suffix *-ment*, giving
in+utile+ment. We can also say that /ɛ̃/ is an allomorph in complementary
distribution with /in/ in words like *inconnu*, where the allomorph is
followed by a consonant, rather than by a vowel as in *inutile*. Compare this
example with the prefixes found in *desseller*, and *disparaître*. Here, the
choice between allomorphs /de/ and /dis/ does not depend on the phonological environment. If speakers were to be given the invented word
*congrier**, some would choose to prefix /de/ and others /dis/. These two
allomorphs then, are in free variation because more than one allomorph can
be used in the same environment, just like free variation of allophones.

The relationship between allomorphs of the same morpheme raises other
problems too. If we consider the French prefix *en-*, we can see that it occurs
in speech in two forms: /ɑ̃/ before consonants as in *enlever*, and /ɑ̃n/ before
vowels as in *enivrer*. Here we can see in a transparent way how the single
morpheme *en-* is realised as two allomorphs, depending on the phonological
context. Unfortunately, it is not always possible to see the relationship
between morphs and their underlying morpheme in quite such a clear way.
If we look at the adjective *beau*, we find that its feminine counterpart, *belle*
is phonologically quite different. Trying to propose phonological rules
which would derive /bɛl/ from /bo/ (or even the other way round) would be
very complicated, because it involves a change in phonemes, rather than just
a question of pronunciation or not within certain contexts, as was the case
with *en-*. When the morphological relationship between two morphs is not
transparent, it is known as *suppletion*. Suppletive forms abound in French
and it is these together with fusion which create the irregularities which
cause so much difficulty to the language learner of French.

7.2   Different categories of word

Inflectional morphology is concerned with the way different classes of word
modify their form to suit the grammatical function they are performing.

Thus, a description of the morphology of French relies heavily on being able to identify different groups of words which function in the same way. Elsewhere in the book, we have talked freely of word categories such as nouns, verbs and prepositions without really exploring what we mean when we use the labels. Are they just jargon terms used by people who write grammar books or do they represent real divisions of words into groups that native-speakers of French make use of?

Knowing the meanings of individual words and their internal morphological and phonological structure is not enough to be able to speak and understand a language, as anyone who has tried to read in a foreign language armed only with a dictionary will be able to tell you. When people speak French, they combine words with other words to form larger meaningful units (or phrases), and words and phrases can be combined together to form even larger meaningful units (sentences). Words and phrases cannot be combined together at random. You do not have to be particularly fluent in French to know that (1) is a sentence of French while (2) is not:

(1)   *le chien mange la viande*

(2)   *chien le mange viande la*

Not only would speakers of French be able to tell you that (2) is not a sentence of French, but they would also be able to tell you what is wrong with it: some of the words are not in the right order. On top of that they would probably be able to tell you that the type of word to which *le, la, une* and *son* belong (which grammarians label 'determiners') must precede the type of word to which *chien, viande, fille, lettre* and *ami* belong (which grammarians label 'nouns'). Even a very young speaker of French would be aware of this although, of course, they may not be able to use the same labels as the grammarian.

So, here we have a use for grammatical categories: word order does not depend on individual words, it depends on types, or *categories* of word. This is one of the 'rules' of French syntax. If we assume that French speakers can assign words to categories and, furthermore, store this information tagged to the words in their mental lexicon, then they will be able to obey the 'rules' of French word order without having to worry about the relative orders of every individual word in the French language. In the case of our example sentences, the fact that it is a rule of French that 'determiners precede nouns' automatically means that *le* must precede *chien, une* must precede *fille* and so on.

Further evidence that speakers group their words into grammatical categories is the fact that, without giving it very much thought, they know that, if you want to change a word in a sentence for another word, the choice of replacement word is restricted to words of the same type. For example, speakers of French would all agree that a very large number of words could also appear in place of *livre* in (3):

(3)   *Le petit garçon voit le livre/bâtiment/papier/jardin/verre*, etc.

They would also agree that quite a lot of words could not occur in this context, for example:

(4)   *Le petit garçon voit le* *à* / **vivre* / **rarement* / **que*

Moreover, speakers would be aware that only some nouns could replace *livre*. Feminine nouns like *fille, maison, table,* etc. could not, unless the accompanying determiner also changed. This shows that speakers are not only aware of major types of words (nouns, verbs, adjectives, etc.), but also of subdivisions of words (e.g. masculine and feminine nouns). Again, even very young speakers would be able to manipulate language in this way, long before they meet labels like 'grammatical gender' in the classroom.

It appears, then, that only words belonging to one type can be substituted for the word *livre* and these words belong to the category labelled by grammarians as masculine nouns. The reason why words like *à, vivre, rarement* and *que* cannot replace *livre* is precisely because they are not nouns. The fact that speakers know what can and cannot be substituted shows that they must have a notion of word categorisation. The notion of grammatical category is not simply a convenient invention on the part of writers of grammar books. Speakers themselves use grammatical categories to organise and process their language. Without access to categories, speakers could not process language in the same systematic way.

7.2.1   *Traditional accounts of word categories*

If we wish to describe the French language, then we must be able to describe the word categories that French speakers refer to intuitively when they use their language. Discussion of word categories or word classes in language is not new. Terminology was developed in Antiquity to cope with the grammar of Latin, and in the Middle Ages these terms were applied with greater or lesser success to the description of the 'Modern Languages'. If you look in any 'traditional' grammar book, you will find references to nine principal word categories (or 'parts of speech'):

- nouns, e.g. *femme*
- verbs, e.g, *aimer*
- pronouns of various types,
     personal pronouns: *je, tu, il,* etc.
     demonstrative pronouns: *ça, celle,* etc.
     possessive pronouns: *mien, nôtre,* etc.
     relative pronouns: *qui, que, dont, lequel,* etc.
- adjectives, e.g. *belle*
- adverbs, e.g. *rapidement, cependant*
- articles, *le, une, de,* etc.
- conjunctions, e.g. *et, mais, bien que,* etc.

- prepositions, e.g. *de, jusqu'à*, etc.
- interjections, e.g. *Merde!, Zut alors!*

The names given to these word categories are well established and it would not be helpful for us to propose new and perhaps more appropriate ones here. However, this is not to say that the traditional terminology does not raise serious difficulties for linguists trying to describe a language scientifically. How are we to decide theoretically which words go into which category? Are we to decide on the basis of the sort of *meaning* the word conveys (semantics), or on the basis of its *distribution pattern* and *function* (syntax)? The trouble with the categories you will find in traditional grammars is that they are based on a jumble of all of these criteria.

Traditional accounts of word-class divisions rely heavily on word meanings (semantics) to decide which category a word belongs to. Thus:

- *nouns* denote people, things or places.
- *verbs* denote actions or states.
- *adjectives* denote states or attributes.
- *prepositions* denote location or direction.

It is not hard to see that these definitions are somewhat crude: they would have to be a lot tighter to account for nouns like *démolition* which is an action but is not a verb, or for the prepositions in *obéir à quelqu'un* or *dépendre de quelque chose*, neither of which could reasonably be said to be indicating location or direction. Even if we could provide a detailed enough semantic definition for some word classes, traditional grammars also have to resort to non-semantic criteria for the definition of some of the other categories. Words like *et, mais, si* are known as conjunctions because they are used to conjoin two sentences together, and are categorised according to their function rather than their meaning. Within the major word category of verb, we find several subdivisions which, again, are based on they way they pattern in the language, rather than on any meaning they might convey. Some, like *dormir*, are 'intransitive' (they cannot be followed by an object), while others, like *lire*, are 'transitive' (they tend to be followed by an object).

Meaning, then, is not enough to establish word categories in French; we have to resort to using word function as well. Indeed, we can find convincing evidence that speakers do not use semantic criteria for word classification in the fact that they do not actually need to know the meaning of a word before they can categorise it. The following sentences are perfectly grammatical in French, but the words in bold have all been invented:

(5) *Un* **poulichon** *a* tarité *la grande* **lidore** *que j'ai laissée dans la* **mive**.

(6) *Mes* **gronorats** *étaient très* **nurants** *hier. Ils ont été* **cumbilés** *par Michel*.

Even without knowing the meanings of the words in bold, speakers of French would be reasonably confident that the following sentences were also grammatical:

(7)   *Un* **gronorat** **nurant** *est ici.*

(8)   *Mon frère* **cumbilera** *ce* **gronorat.**

(9)   *Qu'est-ce qu'il a mis dans sa* **mive?**

(10)   *Trois* **lidores** *ont été* **taritées** *par le* **poulichon** *hier.*

Since speakers could not know the meanings of the words in bold, they could not possibly classify them as nouns, adjectives, verbs, etc. according to meaning. Yet, the fact that they would accept the second set of sentences as grammatical shows that they have indeed managed to categorise the words and are treating them as belonging to the following categories:

nouns: *poulichon, gronorat, lidore, mive*
adjectives: *nurant*
verbs: *tariter, cumbiler*

How do speakers know what to do in these circumstances?

7.2.2   A more rigorous way of establishing word categories

If French speakers do not make much use of meaning to categorise words, they must be using information already available within the language to do so. What information could they be using? The most likely answer is that division of words into grammatical categories is done using grammatical information. One way of doing this is to compare a word to other words whose category we already know. If we find that it behaves in a similar way, then we can surmise that it belongs to the same category. To put it in the words of Walter Ruther, 'If it looks like a duck, walks like a duck and quacks like a duck, it's a duck.' There are three main ways to do this: substitution, morphological analysis and distributional analysis. Each method may suffice in itself to categorise a word but, generally, confirmation is needed by applying one of the other methods as well.

Substitution literally means putting a word in the place of another word. If the result is a grammatical sentence (even if the meaning is totally different), then the chances are the two words are in the same category. For example, if we did not know the category of the words *le* and *dort* in the sentence *Le grand garçon dort*, we could try replacing them with words whose categories we *do* know. We find we can replace *le* with other determiners like *ce, un, chaque* but not with words from any other word category, so we conclude that *le* is probably a determiner. *Dort*, on the other hand, can only be replaced by an appropriate form of a verb such as *rire*, *mourir*, and so on, but not by any other word category. Thus we conclude that *dort* is probably a verb.

Substitution is not always a reliable test, however. Two major problems arise with it. First, if test sentences are not chosen carefully, it is possible to replace a word with a word from a different category. In the sentence *Je suis content*, *content* is an adjective, but it could be replaced by *docteur*, a noun, or by the past participle of a verb, such as *arrivé*. The problem here is that we have chosen the wrong sentence as our test sentence: it allows for more than one category of word to appear in a particular position. We must thus choose our test sentences rather more carefully. Second, elements involved in substitution tests must not only belong to the same category, but must also share certain features such as number, gender, tense, and so on. In *Les nouvelles sont intéressantes*, we cannot replace *nouvelles* with, say *garçons* because they do not share the same grammatical gender, nor could we use *navigabilité* here because it is a mass noun which cannot be pluralised. These problems do not mean that substitution is not a valid test, simply that it must be administered carefully with consideration both for the test sentences we choose and for differences between words within the same category.

Another way of determining which category a word might belong to is to see whether or not it conforms to any *morphological pattern* known to apply to various categories. For example, given the word *écrasement*, we see that it is made up of a known verb stem *écrase-* and a known noun suffix *-ment* providing some evidence that *écrasement* is a noun, since the pattern 'Verb + *ment* ⇒ Noun' is found elsewhere, e.g. *étonnement*. Again, although morphology can be a reliable indicator of grammatical category, it does not work very well in isolation for three reasons:

1 Some morphemes can be affixed to more than one category, such as *-eur* which can be affixed to nouns and adjectives or *-é* which can be affixed to nouns, verbs and adjectives.
2 Many words cannot be analysed in this way at all, as we saw earlier in this chapter. This particularly applies to monosyllabic words.
3 Morphological affixation does not occur at all with some categories such as prepositions and conjunctions. Given that many words in other categories are also single morphemes, it is not possible to claim that a word belongs to a particular category just because it has *no* affixation.

By far the most reliable indicator of grammatical category is to see where a word will fit in a structural position. To do this, we take a frame with a gap in it which we know can only be filled by one particular grammatical category. If a word can be used in that gap and the result is a grammatical structure, then that word belongs to that category. This is known as *distributional analysis*. For example, given the following 'frame' (in which the line represents the gap) we find that only verbs can fill the gap:

(11)   *Jean ne — pas*

Similarly, given the frames in examples (12) and (13):

(12)   *La petite — était ici*

(13)   *La — rouge était ici*

we find that only nouns can fill the gaps.

To ensure that we do not fall foul of the problems raised before, namely that certain features like gender, plurality and tense affect which particular words in a category can appear in a frame, we can abstract away slightly from words themselves and provide frames which explicitly mention other categories like the following ones, which could be used to test for nouns:

det[*erminer*] — adj[*ective*]
det adj —

This type of test is only as reliable as its frames. If we use the wrong frame we may find that words of more than one category can fill the gap because two categories share aspects of their distributional pattern. The frame 'adv[*erb*] —' is problematic because both adjectives and adverbs can fill the gap:

(14)   *très content/lentement*

Even if we tighten the frames in such a way as to ensure that only one category can fill the gap, we may still find that two words of that category may not share a whole pattern because of differences between them that do not relate to their membership of the main category. An example of this would be the two adjectives *grand* and *mort*. If we take a set of frames which we know apply to adjectives we find that we cannot put both words into all the frames:

(15)   det n[*oun*] — *L'homme grand/l'homme mort*

(16)   det — n   *Le grand homme/le *mort homme*

(17)   être —   *Il est grand /Il est mort*

(18)   adv —   *très grand / ?? très mort*

To account for these differences, we need to be aware that *grand* is an adjective which can appear both before and after the noun and whose meaning is 'gradable' (i.e. applies to greater or lesser degrees), whereas *mort* can only occur after its noun and its meaning is non-gradable.

These, then, are some of the ways in which speakers of French might use grammatical information to sort out grammatical categories in their language. In what follows, we will look at some of the grammatical categories that exist in French.

7.2.3   *Major and minor categories*

Word categories in French can be loosely divided into two groups: *major* and *minor*. Major categories are those that many of us are already familiar with and consist of nouns such as *table, imagination, foule*, verbs such as *aimer, venir, enchanter*, adjectives such as *content, mal, beau*, adverbs such as *rarement, vite, complètement* and prepositions such as *dans, pour, sans, après*, etc. Major categories contain most of the words we need to produce the essential meaning of a sentence (the content words) and, with the exception of prepositions, are what are known as *open classes*. This means that new words can be freely added to these categories when a new concept enters the French-speaking community.

Minor categories are those which do not so much carry meaning as have a particular function in a sentence, often to restrict the meanings of the words in the major categories. Membership of these categories is highly restricted: you cannot usually add words to these categories, making them what is known as *closed classes*. Examples of minor categories in French are:

- Determiners such as *le, une, ce, mon*, etc. which serve to restrict the reference of the noun they accompany. Note that this word category has one label and includes a number of other traditional word categories such as definite and indefinite articles, demonstrative adjectives, possessive adjectives, and so on. This is because structurally they all behave in a similar fashion: only one of them can accompany a noun, they all occupy the same position in relation to the noun and they must all agree in grammatical gender with the noun. The differences between them depend very largely on semantic and pragmatic differences in terms of reference, a concept which is outside the realms of syntax.
- Auxiliary verbs i.e. *être* and *avoir* and, to a certain extent, *aller* which function as a sort of support to the main verb in terms of tense and aspect;
- Conjunctions such as *mais, et, bien que*, etc. which serve to connect two phrases;
- Proforms which are words such as *le, ce, ils, leur, celui*, etc. which are used instead of a word or phrase and whose interpretation depends on the speaker being able to identify, through discourse, the word or phrase which they represent. These forms are called 'pronouns' in traditional grammars but, because they do in fact represent far more than just nouns, a more appropriate term is 'proform'.

If we play around with the following sentence, we can see why one of the divisions we make is between content (or 'substantive') categories such as nouns and verbs and 'functional' categories such as determiners.

(19)   Une *petite fille* a *vu* le *chien dans* le *parc*

If we remove all the words which are not in italic from this sentence, we are left with a structure which most native-speakers could make some sense of:

(20)   petite fille vu chien dans parc

If, however, we remove all the words in italic, leaving only the others, we are left with a completely uninterpretable structure:

(21)   *Une a le le*

Given the distinction between major and minor categories and their role in carrying the semantic weight of a sentence, it is not perhaps surprising to find that early child language production is typified by the absence of functional categories.

When we look at the word categories we have mentioned so far, it is clear that these are not yet specific enough. Earlier in this chapter, we pointed out that some of the tests for word categories needed to be administered with some caution because not all members of a grammatical category would fit into a pattern. This leads us to conclude that, within the major and minor categories outlined above, there are further sub-categories which a speaker must be aware of to be able to produce and process French structures.

Some of the sub-category distinctions found in grammar books in fact relate to the semantic interpretation of words rather than to their grammatical behaviour. For example, adjectives can be divided into sub-groups such as 'adjectives of colour', 'shape', 'size', 'emotive', and so on which, although quite significant on a semantic level, actually do not have any significance from a structural point of view, because these divisions do not make any difference to where in a sentence an adjective can appear. On the other hand, we might note that adjectives can be divided into pre- and post-nominal, relating to the possible positions they can occupy in a structure. Adjectives like *petit* must appear before a noun, while adjectives such as *mouillé* must appear after a noun. This is a category distinction which has grammatical relevance, as does the distinction between gradable and non-gradable adjectives. Gradable adjectives like *grand* and *intelligent* can be modified by an adverb like *très*. Non-gradable adjectives like *mort* or *carré* cannot. Thus, we conclude that the sub-categories of 'pre-nominal' and 'post-nominal' and 'gradable' and 'non-gradable' are important distinctions we need to make from a grammatical point of view.

We find the same thing with nouns. Distinctions are traditionally made between abstract and concrete nouns and between animate and inanimate nouns. This may reflect the meaning of these nouns, but it does not affect their grammatical behaviour. Other distinctions between different types of noun are structurally more significant: we must make a distinction between, say, masculine and feminine nouns, because this has an effect on what else can appear in the structure (we must give them determiners and adjectives which are of the same gender). We must also distinguish between count nouns (e.g. *voiture*, *pièce*, *métier*) and mass nouns (e.g. *beurre*, *oxygène*, *navigabilité*) because, again, this has a structural effect (mass nouns like *beurre* cannot appear in the plural).

7.3   Grammatical features

In the third section of this chapter we will consider how the forms of words in French come to be modified as additional grammatical features are loaded on to their lexical base – in the case of nouns and adjectives, for instance, this involves the feature of number, in the case of adjectives, it involves the feature of gender, in the case of verbs, it involves the features of person, tense, aspect, voice and modality. We have insufficient space here to offer a detailed description of the morphology of nouns, adjectives and verbs in French. Moreover, it is highly likely that your knowledge of this subject is already quite extensive, so what we will do in the remaining part of this chapter is point to important differences which exist between the morphology of written French and that of spoken French. The French grammar taught in schools is still highly skewed in the direction of the written language. What we hope to do here is show the existence of a rather different set of highly interesting and often surprising patterns in the spoken language (on this topic see Valdman 1976).

7.3.1 French nouns

In the written language the feature number is normally marked on nouns (and adjectives) by the addition of an '-s' to the singular form, the chief exceptions being nouns (and adjectives) ending in '-al' which form their plural in '-aux' (e.g. *cheval* ⇒ *chevaux*). If we look at the spoken language, however, we will observe that the feature number is not normally marked on nouns and adjectives at all, e.g. *femme* /fam/ ⇒ *femmes* /fam/. Final /s/ resurfaces only in liaison forms as a /z/, e.g. *Femmes et enfants d'abord*. The nouns ending in /-al/ provide exceptions to this by marking their plural not in '-ux' as is suggested by the spelling, but in /o/.

This has serious implications for the syntax of spoken French, since the job of marking the feature number is left entirely to the determiner, see example (22):

(22)　Les écoliers détestent les devoirs difficiles
　　　+　　−　　　−　+　　　−　　−

Here we can see quite graphically the large degree of 'redundancy' present in the grammatical markers found in the written language: every word bears a plural marker in the written language, but plural markers occur only on the determiners in speech.

7.3.2 French adjectives

Traditional descriptions of French indicate that the feature gender is normally marked on adjectives by adding an '-e' to the masculine form to form the feminine. Thus: *petit* ⇒ *petite*. This rule is derived entirely from what happens in the written language, for the final schwa represented by '-e' ceased to be pronounced in northern French in the seventeenth century (in most contexts). The rules for gender-marking operating in spoken French are then very different. How can they best be formulated?

If we seek to derive the feminine from the following masculine forms, as happens in traditional grammar, we end up in all sorts of trouble:

(23)   /pti/ (*petit*) ⇒   /ptit/ (*petite*)

(24)   /gRɑ̃/ (*grand*) ⇒   /gRɑ̃d/ (*grande*)

(25)   /afRø/ (*affreux*) ⇒   /afRøz/ (*affreuse*)

We have to stipulate that to form the feminine we add a final consonant to the masculine. However, in the case of these adjectives we need a different consonant for each one. How do we know which adjective takes which consonant? Not a very neat rule. If on the other hand we go against an age-old tradition going back to Adam and Eve (you will recall that *she* was derived from *him*, being created out of one of his spare ribs, Genesis 2.22), we could seek to derive the masculine from the feminine. Life suddenly becomes much simpler:

(26)   /ptit/ (*petite*) ⇒   /pti/ (*petit*)

(27)   /gRɑ̃d/ (*grande*) ⇒   /gRɑ̃/ (*grand*)

(28)   /afRøz/ (*affreuse*) ⇒   /afRø/ (*affreux*)

Here, all we have to do is subtract the final consonant from the feminine form to create the masculine.

With this principle in mind, let us now look at the whole set of adjectives present in spoken French. We can divide them into three broad categories:

1 *Invariables*: these do not differentiate masculine and feminine forms, e.g. *pauvre, vrai(e), seul(e)*.
2 *Subtractives*: here the masculine is derived from the feminine by subtracting the final consonant, e.g. *petit(e), froid(e)*.
3 *Replacives*: here the final consonant alternates between feminine and masculine, /v/ ⇒ /f/, /ʃ/ ⇒ /k/ etc., e.g. *vive – vif, sèche – sec*.

These rules allow us to produce masculine and feminine forms for a majority of adjectives in French, but there remain a number of difficult cases. Among the subtractives there are adjectives of the following type: *moyenne* /mwajɛn/ – *moyen* /mwajɛ̃/, *première* /pRəmjɛR/ – *premier* /pRəmje/. Here, after applying the rule subtracting the final consonant of the feminine form, we need an additional rule modifying the preceding vowel. With so-called 'irregular' adjectives like *belle – beau* and *vieille – vieux*, the modification to the vowel is quite extensive.

Here we have offered a 'structural' analysis of adjective agreement in French. Grammarians working in the 'generative' framework offer a different explanation where both masculine and feminine derive from an abstract, neutral morpheme (see Valdman 1976: 155–63). However, the general point we wish to make is that once we go beyond the patterns visible in the written language, we can uncover lots of new and potentially more inter-esting ones in speech.

7.3.3 French verbs

The following attempts to look at the French verb utilising some of the concepts that have been discussed earlier in this chapter. Let us take as our main example a 'regular' French verb, *fermer*. We know that this is a verb because we can perform all three of the word tests described earlier (see above p. 124). In the sentence *La petite fille ferme la porte*, we can substitute a number of other verbs like *ouvre, touche, voit*, etc. for our form *ferme*. Distributional analysis shows that *ferme* can fit into a frame that is known to apply to verbs: NE — PAS, as in *La petite fille ne ferme pas la porte*. Finally, the morphology which we know applies to verbs applies to *fermer*. We can add the past participle *-é* and create *fermé*, or the nominal suffix *-ature* and create *fermature*.

You might feel that the exercise is rather pointless – we all know *fermer* is a verb, why go to all the trouble of demonstrating this self-evident fact? The reason is that linguists are not prepared to take any feature of language for granted. They try to ensure that every claim they make about language can be scientifically verified.

Establishing *fermer* is a verb is relatively easy. What is more difficult than establishing the word class of this item is identifying its morphology, for French verbs are characterised by a large amount of suppletion and fusion (see pp. 119–20). The verb *fermer* can be analysed as a stem (*ferm-*) to which various inflectional suffixes are added to create the infinitive (*-er*) and various tensed versions of the verb. The present, imperfect, past historic, and present and past participle forms of the verb are all created from the stem plus single morph affixes (as in *je ferm+ais* or *ils ferm+èrent*). The future and conditional verb forms on the other hand are created by combining the stem with the infinitive affix (in this case, *-er*) and an additional morph (as in *je ferm+er+ai* or *nous ferm+er+ions*).

Identifying the stem in a verb like *fermer* does not cause us any particular problems because the stem remains the same throughout the different parts of the verb (e.g. *je ferme – nous fermons*). This is the case for many French verbs. However, a sizeable number have a stem which alternates from person to person, e.g.:

(29) *j'appelle* *– nous appelons*

(30) *je viens* *– nous venons*

(31) *je crains* *– nous craignons*

Verb stems presenting the alternation /ɛ/ – /ə/ belong largely in the 'regular' *-er* conjugation. Verbs presenting the other alternations are usually classed as 'irregular'. Although in each case the different verb stems have a morphological relationship with one another (they are different concrete realisations of the same morpheme, the bound root), this relationship is not always transparent (e.g. /jɛ̃/) – /ə/ and /ɛ̃/ – /ɛ/) and must thus be considered as a case of suppletion (see above p. 120).

If we pass on now from the stem of the verb to its endings, we find a very good example of the differences between the morphology of written and spoken French. When we look at the different written forms indicating person for the verb *fermer*, we find that there are five forms:

	PRESENT		IMPERFECT	
	je/il/elle/on	*ferme*	*je/tu*	*fermais*
	tu	*fermes*	*il/elle/on*	*fermait*
(32)	*nous*	*fermons*	*nous*	*fermions*
	vous	*fermez*	*vous*	*fermiez*
	ils/elles	*ferment*	*ils/elles*	*fermaient*

However, when we look at the spoken forms of the same verb, we find that there are only three different endings:

		PRESENT	IMPERFECT
	je/il/elle/on/tu/ils/elles	/fɛRm/	/fɛRmɛ/
(33)	*nous*	/fɛRmɔ̃/	/fɛRmjɔ̃/
	vous	/fɛRme/	/fɛRmje/

Looking at verb forms from a spoken point of view certainly presents a simpler picture than the written forms would imply.

However, it raises another issue. With the form /fɛRm/ common to the 1st, 2nd, 3rd and 6th persons of the verb, we seem to be confronted with the stem of the verb occurring on its own, without suffixes marking the different persons involved. Yet, since person-marking clearly exists in other verbs (*je suis, tu es, ils sont*, etc), it could seem odd to suggest that there is no inflectional morpheme for the present form for 1st, 2nd and 3rd person singular and 6th person plural here. What we might suggest is that, in the case of *fermer*, the underlying morphemes of person and tense have no corresponding concrete forms in persons 1, 2, 3 and 6, and that this is another example where an underlying morpheme is expressed by a *zero morph*. See above p. 120.

Another aspect of French morphology which is clearly visible in the endings of French verbs is fusion, see above p. 119. The ending *-ais* in *je fermais* represents both the imperfect and the 1st person singular at one and the same time. What we have here is a single morph which is acting as a concrete realisation of two morphemes, tense and person, at the same time. Fusion is also seen in some past participle forms of verbs where the participle and the stem are combined into an indivisible unit, as in *pris* (< *prendre*).

TENSE, ASPECT AND MOOD

You will note that, so far, we have looked mainly at the way verbs mark the different persons. However, French verb morphology also has to mark the features of tense, aspect and mood. *Tense* has much to do with time – past, present and future in relation to the speaker's point of reference. However, time is not the only thing involved with so-called tense-endings. Some of the verbal affixes relate not only to tense (which locates an event in time), but also to *aspect* which describes the state of the event or its duration, for example, whether something is finished or still ongoing at a particular point in time. 'Perfective' aspect involves a point-action or one which has a clear beginning and/or end, the clearest example being the past historic, e.g.:

(34)   *Louis XIV* régna 72 *ans*

'Imperfective' aspect involves a continuous or habitual action, the beginning or end of which is not important, the clearest example being the imperfect, e.g.:

(35)   *Il* faisait *cela, lorsque sa mère entra dans sa chambre*

Aspect and tense are not clearly distinguished from each other in French because of the fusion of verbal suffixes. Those suffixes which are labelled imperfect, for example, can express not only past tense, but also an imperfective aspect where the event in question has no clear starting or finishing point. In the present tense, French verb morphology makes no such distinction of aspect, though English does. For example, English makes use of two verbal constructions to distinguish between present progressive (ongoing actions) and present habitual: I *am reading* the newspaper now/I *read* the newspaper every day. French, on the other hand, only uses one verb form for both aspects: Je *lis* le journal tous les jours/maintenant. If the progressive aspect was to be emphasised, then a phrase such as *être en train de* would generally be used.

Another difference between French and English verbal morphology is that French has different verbal forms to express indicative and subjunctive *moods*. The subjunctive form of a verb is generally to be found in subordinate clauses and is traditionally referred to as expressing the fact that a verbal action is hypothetical rather than real or actual. Whether or not this is the case, and there is much dispute over the exact role/meaning of the subjunctive in French, the fact remains that yet more verbal morphology is at play. Once again, we find suffixes which are the result of fusion between mood and person/number (e.g. *que tu vienes*) and cases of suppletion when the verb stem alters as we find in verbs like *savoir* (*nous savons/sachions*).

Lastly, while English has a range of modal auxiliaries such as *may, might, could, would, will,* etc. to express *modality* (best thought of in terms of 'permission' and 'probability'), French does not. There are two main 'modal' verbs, *devoir* and *pouvoir*, and it is the verbal morphology affixed to these verb stems which typically expresses the modality of the utterance. Thus, in *Il doit le faire* and *Il peut le faire* it is the present verb forms of *devoir* and *pouvoir* which do the work of English *must* and *may* respectively, while the conditional verb forms found in *Il devrait le faire* and *Il pourrait le faire* are comparable to the modal auxiliaries *should* and *might* in English. It should be noted here that it is not only through the use of *devoir* and *pouvoir* that modality can be expressed through French verbal morphology. The conditional forms of other verbs such as *ferait* in *Il le ferait* also carry a probability interpretation expressible in English only by the modal auxiliary *would* as in *He would do it*. Once again, we find that the verbal suffixes are the result of fusion between tense, aspect and modality.

Seminar exercises

1.   Transcribe the following sentences, and then for both the written and spoken forms highlight the markers of plurality (i.e. forms which are distinct from the singular) and encircle the markers of feminine gender (i.e. forms which are distinct from the corresponding masculine forms):

(a) *Vos judicieuses remarques ont été retenues.*
(b) *Certaines veuves sont devenues dévotes.*
(c) *Quelques concierges sont aimables.*
(d) *Les déceptions sentimentales sont douloureuses.*
(e) *Tes filles étaient vexées.*

2.   Write down in IPA the spoken form of the 3rd and 6th persons, present tense of the following verbs:

chanter
coudre
courir
craindre
devoir
fuir
mettre
passer
prendre
rire
tenir

Group the verbs into classes according to the rules required to derive the form of the 3rd person from that of the 6th person.

3.   For each of the following, define the term and provide two examples from French not found in this book.

(a) fusion
(b) suppletion
(c) allomorphs

(i) in complementary distribution
(ii) in free variation

4.   Conjugate the following verbs in the present, future and imperfect tenses:

   chanter   venir   jeter   boire

Indicate the cases of fusion, suppletion, allomorphs, irregularities which you find there.

|8|

French syntax

In the last chapter, we looked at the internal structure of French words and examined some of the rules which govern their morphology. So far, however, we have said nothing much about the way in which these words and word categories may be combined to create larger units (phrases, clauses and ultimately sentences). In this chapter, therefore, we will examine the way words combine together in French and the phrases and sentences which they form, i.e. the *syntax* of the language.

8.1   Phrases

If we take the sentence:

(1)   *Le petit garçon voit le chien*

we intuitively feel that, apart from the fact that it is a string of words drawn from different grammatical categories, some of the words 'belong together' more than others do. In all probability we will cluster the words into two main groups:

(2)   [*Le petit garçon*] + [*voit le chien*]

These groups we will call 'phrases'. On closer inspection we realise that the second of these phrases can be subdivided further:

(3)   [*voit*] + [*le chien*]

Most speakers of French are quite successful at breaking down sentences into their respective phrases. No native-speaker of French, for example, would want to say that the phrase *voit le chien* breaks down into [*voit le*] + [*chien*]. They intuitively 'know' that the article *le* 'belongs to' the noun *chien* more than it belongs to the verb *voit*. All French sentences are made up of different phrases and even very complicated ones can be broken down into relatively simple phrasal units in this way.

We would want to label phrases like *le petit garçon* as *Noun Phrases* (NPs), because the hub of the phrase is the noun, while phrases like *voit le chien* are called *Verb Phrases* (VPs) because the most important part of the phrase is the verb. Other phrasal categories we find in French include *Prepositional Phrases* (PPs) which contain a preposition such as *à, de, dans, sur*, etc. plus a Noun Phrase, e.g. *dans la maison, après vous, à six heures; Adverbial Phrases* (AdvPs) which contain an adverb and any elements which qualify it such as *très lentement, tout bêtement;* and *Adjectival Phrases* (APs) such as *complètement stupide.*

Phrases are not units of any specific length. Depending on the type of phrase, they can be anything from one word long to many words long, such as the two Noun Phrases *Marie*, which consists only of a Proper Noun (PN), and *le type qui m'a demandé de lui donner des sous*, which contains a Noun followed by a Relative Clause, but which is nevertheless still a Noun Phrase as a whole.

A phrase can contain a number of words and, indeed, other phrases: the main word in a phrase (the head) can be *modified* by other elements in the phrase. This is to say that some other element in the phrase can serve to give extra information about, or help identify, the head of the phrase. However, the elements which can appear in different phrases are limited by the category of the phrase in question. Within a Noun Phrase, nouns can be modified by Adjectival Phrases (e.g. *le* **très petit** *garçon*), by Prepositional Phrases (e.g. *les chaussures* **de Marie**) or by a Relative Clause (e.g. *le type* **que j'ai vu hier**). Within a Verb Phrase, verbs can be modified by adverbs, but not by adjectives (e.g. *Il mange* **lentement/***lent**). (Note: we use an asterisk to indicate that a structure or word within a structure is not grammatical in French.) Words or phrases which modify other words and phrases are always optional. Other elements in a phrase are not necessarily optional. Noun Phrases in French, for example, nearly always contain a determiner, and, if the verb in a Verb Phrase requires, say, an object or an indirect object, then this must be present in the phrase itself.

It is particularly important to understand the distinction between the grammatical category of a phrase and its function in a sentence. In the sentence **La maison** *est très petite,* the words in bold belong to a grammatical category which is a Noun Phrase, but this Noun Phrase functions as the subject of the sentence. Similarly, in the sentence *J'ai vu Marie* **au moment prévu** the phrase in bold belongs to the category Prepositional Phrase (because it contains a Preposition and a Noun Phrase) and functions as a time adverbial, giving information about when the action took place.

When it comes to identifying the phrases which make up French sentences, we do not only have to rely on speakers' intuitions as to which words 'belong together', strong as they may be. Just as we could use tests to find out the categories of words (see above pp. 124–26), we can use similar tests to decide on phrasal categories or even whether a string of words constitutes a phrase or not. Recall that substitution and distributional analysis were two ways of seeing if a word belonged to a particular category. We can use the same type of tests for phrases. In the sentence *Jean* **veut aller au cinéma** we can argue that the words in bold constitute a Verb Phrase because we can replace them with other Verb Phrases and still be left with a grammatically acceptable sentence:

(4)

Jean	*veut aller au cinéma*
	dort
	mange la viande
	parle à Marie, etc.

And in the following:

(5)   *Le petit garçon voit le chien*

we can replace the Noun Phrase *le chien*, but not *voit le chien*, with any of the following:

> *Pierre*
> *le petit chat*
> *un livre intéressant*
> *la maison au coin de la rue*
> *l'homme qu'il a vu mardi soir*

Only Noun Phrases can appear in the gaps in the following sentences:

(6)   *Jean envoie — à Paris*
       — est dans la maison

while only Verb Phrases can appear in these gaps:

(7)   *Ne pas — sera stupide*
       Pierre a demandé à Marie de —

Another test is quite useful when it comes to identifying phrases and their categories: *pronominalisation*, that is when a string of words can be replaced by a proform (traditionally referred to as 'pronoun', see above p. 127).

First, a proform can only replace a whole phrase, not part of one. Thus, the proform *il* can replace all of the strings of words in bold in these sentences:

(8)   **Henri** *veut aller voir ce film*

(9)   **Le livre que je lisais hier** *était intéressant*

(10)   **Le beau petit chat gris** *a mangé notre viande*

This tells us that they are all Noun Phrases. However, *il* cannot be substituted for the strings in bold in these sentences:

(11)   **Henri veut aller voir** *ce film*

(12)   **Le livre** *que je lisais hier était intéressant*

(13)   *Le beau petit* **chat gris a mangé** *notre viande*

which means that the words in bold here do not constitute Noun Phrases or, in the case of the sentence (12), are not the whole Noun Phrase.

Second, particular types of phrase can only be replaced by particular types of proform, giving us an indication of what phrasal category we are dealing with. Thus, a phrase containing a Preposition and a plural Noun Phrase, such as *à mes parents*, can be replaced by the proform *leur*:

(14)   *Je vais parler* à mes parents/*Je vais* leur *parler*

This pronominalisation tells us that the phrase in bold is indeed a phrase and that it is prepositional.

In French, then, words belong to a limited number of word categories (nouns, verbs, prepositions, etc.) and combine together in particular ways to make phrases, which in turn belong to a limited number of categories (NP, VP, PP, etc.). These phrases combine together with other words and phrases until we reach the sentence, which is nothing more mysterious than a number of phrases joined together.

8.2   Sentences and clauses

Sentences come in several varieties which are worth looking at now, because the differences between them are important to an understanding of the way that French syntax operates. Sentences (or Main Clauses) fall into one of four different types:

- Declaratives such as: *Jean aime Marie*
  Le gouvernement ne comprend rien
  Pierre a acheté une nouvelle maison
- Interrogatives such as: *Que fais-tu?*
  Est-ce qu'il aime Marie?
  Qui a acheté une nouvelle maison?
- Exclamatives such as: *Qu'elle est belle!*
  Qu'est-ce il peut être méchant!
- Imperatives such as   *Venez voir!*
  Allons au bureau!
  Qu'elle passe à la maison!

The main sentence type we will be concerned with here is declaratives, but this is simply for reasons of space.

Sentences are made up of *clauses*. A clause which can form a sentence completely on its own, without having to be part of a larger phrase or clause, is known as a main clause. Thus, *Ma fille est partie en ville* is a main clause. This in turn calls forth a distinction between Simple sentences (consisting simply of a main clause) and Complex sentences, created either by *co-ordinating* two or more main clauses, e.g.:

(15)   *Elle est en fac/et ça lui plaît*

or by *subordinating* one or more clauses to the main clause, e.g.:

(16)   Quand elle est à la fac, *elle est heureuse comme tout*

(17)   *Le bonhomme* que j'ai vu hier *n'est plus là*

(18)   *Le type a demandé* que Marie vienne là

The clauses which are subordinated to main clauses are then known as subordinate clauses. Subordinate clauses are in fact 'contained within' or embedded in the main clause. This is perhaps better seen if we show it in the following way:

(19)   *Le type a demandé*
             que Marie vienne là

In theory, there is no limit to the amount of embedding that can occur in French sentences, although, of course, in practice we are limited by the amount of time we have to speak! We can embed the sentence *Le type a demandé que Marie vienne là* into another clause:

(20)   Paul dit
             que le type a demandé
                   que Marie vienne là

There exist three broad types of subordinate clause:

1   Adverbial clauses introduced by conjunctions like *quand, puisque, de sorte que, si, pour que*, e.g.:

Quand elle m'a vu, *elle a vite fait de partir*

In traditional grammar books these clauses are subdivided into temporal, causal, conditional, purpose clauses, etc.

2   Noun clauses, or complement clauses, so called because, as the object of a verb, they 'complete' the sense of a verb, e.g.:

Elle a voulu que je vienne manger à la maison

It is worth drawing a distinction at this point between a complement and a modifier (see above p. 137). 'Complement' is the general term for what we more usually think of as direct objects, indirect objects and noun clauses introduced by *que* (= sentential objects), and are essential to the understanding of a phrase. In the case of verbs, complements are usually but not always obligatory. A verb like *mettre*, for example, must have an NP and a PP complement with it, while a verb like *manger* can but does not have to have an NP complement. Nouns and adjectives can also have complements (*la destruction* de la cité, *content* de te voir) but these are always optional. Modifiers, on the other hand, only provide additional information, usually about time, place, manner, etc. and are always optional. It is important not to confuse a modifer with a complement just because it appears in what looks like a complement position, although it must be said that this is not always an easy task. In examples (21)–(24), the phrases in bold in examples

(21) and (23) are complements but the phrases in roman in examples (22) and (24) are modifiers:

(21)   *Elle a pris un mouchoir* dans son sac

(22)   *Elle mange* dans la cuisine

(23)   *Michel va* à Paris

(24)   *Je vais rencontrer Michel* à Paris

3   Relative (or adjectival) clauses, introduced by relative pronouns like *qui, que, lequel, dont, où,* serve to modify an NP, e.g.:

(25)   *Le bonhomme* qui m'a prêté le bouquin *est parti à Paris*

Relative clauses can themselves be divided into two groups: *restrictive relatives* which distinguish the identity of the Noun Phrase from a larger group: in the above example, out of the group of all 'blokes', it is the one who lent me the book who concerns us here; and *appositive relatives* which provide additional information about the Noun Phrase:

(26)   *Il a passé chez sa copine* qui lui a filé 300F

In example (26) we already know the identity of the girlfriend, the relative clause gives us extra information about her. However, just as we suggested that the division into animate and inanimate had little bearing on the syntactic behaviour of nouns (see above p. 128), so we might argue that the interpretation of relative clauses as restrictive or appositive is a semantic or pragmatic issue rather than a syntactic one, since the distinction does not seem to affect grammatical behaviour of relative clauses (see above p. 111).

8.3   Syntax and the combination rules of language

All speakers of French are able to manipulate grammatical categories from a very early stage in the language acquisition. Moreover, they can do so without necessarily ever having any conscious knowledge of what they are doing: French children who learn about 'parts of speech' in school have been using grammatical categories well before they could ever put conventional labels on them. In this and the last chapter, we have identified three different types of category: word, phrase and feature (see above p. 128). We shall now look at the way in which these categories and their various combinations operate in the structure of the French language.

When we look at sentences in French, we find that their interpretation depends not only on the meaning of the individual words and phrases but also on the way they have been combined. To take a simple example, the following sentences all contain exactly the same words, but each sentence has a different meaning from the others:

(27)   *Le petit garçon voit le chien*

(28)   *Le garçon voit le petit chien*

(29)   *Le chien voit le petit garçon*

In (27) and (29) it is the boy who is small, in (28) it is the dog. In (27) and (28) it is the boy who is doing the seeing, the dog is being seen. In (29) the roles are reversed. None of these interpretations could come just from the individual meanings of the words involved, since exactly the same words have been used in all three sentences. The differences in meaning of each sentence come from the fact that, in each one, the words and phrases are in a different position in relation to each other.

In French, as in English, but not to the same extent in all languages, words cannot be combined together at random. There are strict 'rules' about combinations which, when broken, lead to an utterance being ungrammatical. We could not, for example, combine the words in the sentences above in the following way and still have a grammatical sentence of French:

(30)   *Le chien le mange garçon petit*

8.3.1   The boundaries of syntax

Before we go any further, we must define what we mean by 'ungrammatical'. Sentences can be ill-formed according to the rules of French language structure for several reasons, not all of them syntactic. To be able to isolate syntactic criteria for sentence structure we must be able to separate syntax from the rules relating to the morphology, phonology, semantics, pragmatics and discourse. That we can do so is illustrated by the following examples:

(31)   *Jean aimait Marie*

(32)   *Jean Marie aimait*

(33)   *Jean aimons Marie*

Sentence (31) is grammatical, because both the morphology of the verb and its position conform to the rules of French morphology and syntax. Sentence (32), however, is ungrammatical because in French, verbs must normally precede their complements. The fact that the morphology of the verb – third person singular – is grammatical does not save the sentence. Sentence (33) is ungrammatical, despite the fact that the verb is in the appropriate position, because the agreement morphology in *aimons* is inappropriate.

Moreover, as we shall see in the next chapter, syntactic rules are not necessarily the same as those which govern discourse. The following sentences do not seem to be linked to each other in a way that would make a comprehensible discourse.

(34)   *Jean aime Marie. Le petit chat voit la viande. Mon fils s'appelle Daniel.*

However, just because they do not make much sense from a discourse point of view does not mean that each individual sentence is syntactically ill-formed. They are not: each one obeys the rules of French syntax by having a subject, a verb and an object. Thus, odd discourse structure does not necessarily equal syntactic ill-formedness.

We can also separate syntax from pragmatic and semantic rules of French. Pragmatics governs the interpretation of utterances within a particular real-world context. If we take a sentence such as:

(35)   *Ma chaise me parle chaque matin*

most people would agree that this is an odd thing to say, because chairs do not usually talk. It is nevertheless possible to imagine a world, such as in a science-fiction novel, where chairs have the power of speech. This means that the oddity of sentence (35) stems from the oddity of its interpretation in the world as we know it, its pragmatics, and not from the oddity of the syntax.

Semantics governs the propositional meaning of linguistic structures. The sentence:

(36)   *La table carrée est ronde*

is odd from a semantic point of view because something which is round cannot also be square – the two concepts are mutually exclusive, no matter what science-fiction world we try to imagine. However, semantic ill-formedness, such as this, does not mean that the sentence is syntactically ill-formed. We can produce any number of French sentences which consist of a Noun Phrase, a verb and an adjective:

(37)   *La petite fille est intelligente*

(38)   *Jean est gros*

(39)   *La table carrée est belle*

Syntax, then, is the study of the structure of sentences. It can sometimes be rather difficult to decide whether a particular issue is in fact limited to the syntax of the language or whether it relates to other parts, such as, say, morphology or semantics. However, it is important to realise that we can look at French from a syntactic view point quite separately from other issues.

When sentences are 'well-formed', it means that they conform to all the rules of French grammar that govern the production of sentences. If a sentence is 'ill-formed' it means it does not conform to the rules of French grammar in some way. It is important to remember what we said earlier about the various meanings of the word 'grammar' (see above p. 5). We are not referring here to rules set out in grammar books, rather, to the rules internalised in the minds of native-speakers of French. If we are studying the syntax of French, we have to be able to isolate syntactic rules for the formation of sentences from other rules which operate on them. For the rest of this chapter, if we refer to a sentence as being 'ungrammatical' or 'ill-formed', we mean specifically that it does not obey the syntactic rules of French.

The study of syntax is usually limited to the word as the smallest unit and the sentence as the largest unit. To a certain extent, this is an arbitrary division as many linguists consider that phenomena below word level (e.g. pronunciation) and above sentence level (discourse) are relevant to syntax, as we shall see in the next two chapters. For example, the interpretation of pronouns spans more than just the sentence that a pronoun may be in. If we want to know what *il* refers to in the following sentence, we must know what has been previously said:

(40)   *Il voulait voir Michel*

In spite of this, it is generally agreed that discussions of the syntax of a language are more or less limited to the sentence.

8.3.2   The transformational-generative approach to syntax

Among linguists there exist numerous approaches to the study of grammar, but the one adopted here was initiated by the linguist Noam Chomsky (see Ouhalla 1994). His approach and his terminology are radically different from those of traditional grammar, but we believe that they provide exceptionally important insights into the subject. In the Chomskyan approach, the central task of a linguist studying French sentence structure is to provide a hypothetical model of the grammar lodged in the brain of French speakers that they make use of in order to produce French sentences. It is important to note that this sort of grammar starts off by trying to explain basic features of a language which most other grammars take for granted. In what follows, therefore, we will not be looking at rarefied subtleties in French grammar, but rather at very simple and basic structures – in order to investigate the sort of thing which native-speakers of French 'know' intuitively about the language they are using.

We said in the last chapter that an awareness of the different categories of words and of the different types of phrase is essential, if we are to understand how speakers of French organise their language. We saw too that there exists within the language a finite number of word categories and a finite number of phrasal categories. Moreover, when we look at French sentences from the point of view of what categories of words are combined with what, we find that the same patterns keep recurring: we have, in fact, a finite set of combination rules which can produce or generate an infinite set of French sentences. In the Chomskyan perspective, any grammar proposed for the French language must reflect its *generative* nature. One part of the grammarian's task is to suggest a number of rules which will generate the structure of phrases we find in French. Unsurprisingly, the rules of this type which they propose are called *phrase structure rules*. Each speaker has their own set of vocabulary items (their mental lexicon) which they combine in a variety of structures (according to phrase structure rules).

8.3.3   Phrase structure rules

We saw earlier in this chapter that there are four main sentence types in French, Declarative, Imperative, Exclamative and Interrogative. If we look at the most common type that we use, the Declarative, we find a constantly recurring pattern: no matter how long (or short) declarative sentences may be, and regardless of what else they might contain, they always consist of two essential elements – a Noun Phrase (NP) and a Verb Phrase (VP), which perform the grammatical functions of *subject* and *predicate*:

	NP	VP
(41)	*Jean*	*dort*
(42)	*Cette table*	*est petite*
(43)	*Le professeur d'anglais*	*m'a donné une mauvaise note*
(44)	*Il*	*demande à son oncle d'aller à Londres*

We can account for this recurring pattern by means of a simple phrase structure rule which says that 'a sentence consists of a Noun Phrase and a Verb Phrase'. This rule can be expressed formulaically in the following way:

S ⇒ NP + VP

In order to read this formula we take it that 'the element to the left of the arrow consists of the elements to the right of the arrow'. Such use of symbols and formulae takes Arts students a long way from their normal way of describing things. However, linguists find it necessary, if they are to uncover the often complex patterns which underlie the language we use.

If we now turn to the two elements which make up a sentence, the NP and VP, we find we can make up similar phrase structure rules for them as well. Verb Phrases always have a verb in them, but they can also contain other elements, depending on the type of verb. When we group verbs into their different sub-categories, we find that we can make comments on the patterns and write different phrase structure rules to cover them:

VP ⇒ V   when the verb is intransitive as in
              dormir
VP ⇒ V NP   when the verb is transitive, i.e. takes a direct object as in
              manger [*la salade*]
VP ⇒ V PP   when the verb takes an indirect object as in
              parler [*à ma mère*]

VP ⇒ V NP PP   when the verb takes both a direct and an indirect object as in
donner [*le livre*] [*à la fille*]
VP ⇒ V VP   when the verb is followed by an infinitive as in
vouloir [*donner le livre à la fille*]

We can do the same thing with Noun Phrases. To represent the Noun Phrases found in French, we can formulate the phrase structure combinations on the right of the arrow:

NP ⇒ PN   *Jean* (PN stands for 'proper name')
NP ⇒ Det N   *La fille*
NP ⇒ Det Adj N   *La petite fille*
NP ⇒ Det N Adj   *La fille intelligente*
NP ⇒ Det Adj N Adj   *La petite fille intelligente*

When we consider these rules, we might be impressed by their neatness, but we could nevertheless feel that they do not tell us the whole story: first they do not tell us that adjectives are only optional extras in a Noun Phrase; second they do not tell us we can have more then one adjective in succession, as in *la belle petite fille*; and finally, another thing we might notice about them is that the last of these rules 'includes' or contains within it the previous three. We can rewrite the NP formula to incorporate these facts, and to do this the convention is to place brackets around an element to express optionality and to add an asterisk to indicate that we can have one or more of the item in question. (Note: this is an additional use of the asterisk, the more widely occurring convention for its use being the one we observed earlier denoting an ungrammatical sentence.)

NP ⇒ PN
NP ⇒ Det (Adj)* N (Adj)*

Having thus considered Verb Phrases and Noun Phrases, we can treat Prepositional Phrases in the same way:

PP ⇒ P NP as in *avec ma voiture*

Given the phrase structure rules for a sentence, Verb Phrases, Noun Phrases, and Prepositional Phrases, and assuming that, whenever we find a phrasal category (i.e. NP, VP, etc.) to the right of an arrow, we must apply another phrase structure rule (i.e. spell out what NP, VP, etc. consist of) until there are no more to apply, we now have the beginnings of a grammar (i.e. a set of rules) which can generate many different sentences of French.

8.3.4   Tree diagrams

To make this clearer for us on paper, phrase structure rules can be represented in another way, using tree diagrams. Tree diagrams say exactly the same thing as phrase structure rules but use lines to link phrases with their constituent parts instead of arrows. The tree diagram for the rule for sentences would look like Fig. 8.1:

Fig. 8.1

Using the rules proposed, you should be able to see how we can work out the phrase structure and draw the tree diagram for the rest of the sentence:

NP ⇒ PN

accounts for *Jean*, see Fig. 8.2.

Fig. 8.2

VP ⇒ V NP

divides the VP into two, see Fig. 8.3.

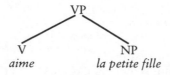

Fig. 8.3

and the NP rule

NP ⇒ Det (Adj)* N (Adj)*

accounts for *la petite fille*, see Fig. 8.4.

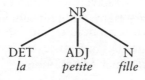

Fig. 8.4

Thus, put together, and once we have filled out the word categories Det, N, V and Adj with actual words of French, we can produce the entire tree diagram for the sentence *Jean aime la petite fille*, see Fig. 8.5.

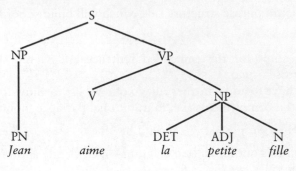

Fig. 8.5

The main advantage of drawing tree diagrams is that, once we can 'read' them we can see at a glance how the phrases in a sentence are put together and what their relationship to each other is.

8.3.5   Subordination or 'embedding'

We noted above (p. 140) that a sentence can have 'embedded' within it one or more 'subordinate' clauses. Sentences like the following can theoretically go on for ever like the 'House that Jack Built' – we only have to add another layer such as *Henri sait que . . .* to lengthen it:

(45)   *Jean remarque*
            que Marie a dit
                  que Pierre croit
                        que Paul est amoureux de Colette

A noticeable thing about sentences like this is that, each time a verb takes a sentential object (i.e. in traditional parlance 'is followed by a subordinate noun clause', see above p. 140), the subordinate sentence is introduced by *que*. Thus we have:

(46)   *Jean remarque* **que** *Marie est ici*

(47)   *Marie dit* **que** *Pierre est stupide*

(48)   *Pierre croit* **que** *Paul aime Colette*

This use of *que* – to introduce a complement clause – has earned it in transformational-generative terminology the label 'complementiser'. The use of a 'complementiser' in these instances in French is obligatory, unlike its English counterpart *that* which is optional:

(49)   Mary says (that) Peter is stupid

In order to produce sentences which have a main clause containing *que* introducing an embedded sentence acting as complement to the main verb, let us assume that as well as the normal rule for declarative sentences:

S ⇒ NP VP

there is an extra phrase structure rule which will build subordinate clauses:

S′ ⇒ Comp S

(where S′ stands for the embedded sentence and Comp stands for the 'complementiser' *que*).

We now have to add a further rule to our VP list to allow for verbs which take sentential complements (i.e. in traditional parlance 'noun clauses'):

VP ⇒ V S′

We can flesh this out into a tree diagram which clearly shows the repetitive nature of the rules, see Fig. 8.6.

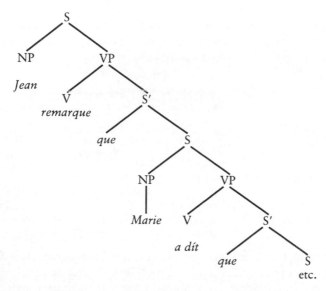

Fig. 8.6

8.3.6   Sub-categorisation frames

We now have a set of phrase structure rules which account for a large number of French sentences and which ensure that the words and phrases are placed in the right order. But we are still faced with a problem. As it stands, our description of French grammar only includes our phrase structure rules accompanied by a lexicon listing all the words in the language labelled to indicate which category (noun, verb, adjective, etc.) each belongs to. How do we account for the ungrammaticality of sentences like the following?

(50)   *Jean dort les enfants**

(51)   *Pierre veut**

(52)   *Le médecin parle les fonctionnaires**

If you look back at the phrase structure rules we proposed for VPs, (see above p. 145), these sentences should be possible, yet they are ungrammatical.

The problem is caused because, as they stand, phrase structure rules are simply filled out by words drawn from the lexicon ('lexical items') and there is nothing to stop us putting any verb in wherever we find the symbol V. Yet what follows a verb in a clause is very much dependent on the type of verb we are dealing with. Verbs like *dormir* do not have an object, verbs like *aimer* take an NP direct object and verbs like *parler* are followed by a PP.

One way of dealing with what is essentially the idiosyncratic behaviour of French verbs is to assume that the information is present in the speaker's mental lexicon attached to each lexical item. In other words, transitive verbs like *voir* will be 'flagged' in speakers' minds as having to appear with an NP complement (a collective word for object, indirect object, etc. See above p. 145); verbs like *obéir* would be flagged as taking a PP complement and verbs like *dormir* would be flagged as taking no complement at all. Since verbs which take different types of complement actually form sub-categories of verbs, we call the flagging *sub-categorisation*.

We can represent this sub-categorisation by adding sub-categorisation frames to our representation of individual words in the mental lexicon in the following way:

dormir – (V) [_Ø]   – takes no NP complement (e.g. *Marie dort*)
laver   – (V) [_NP]   – takes an NP complement (e.g. *Il lave la vaisselle*)
dire   – (V) [_NP(PP)]   – takes an NP complement and optionally a PP
                            complement (e.g. *dire quelque chose à quelqu'un*)

(Remember that the subscript _ in this notation system indicates the slot in the sentence occupied by the item we are talking about, here the Verb (V).)

Some verbs, like *vouloir*, have several frames to account for the different structures they can appear in:

vouloir – (V) [_NP]   e.g. *vouloir quelque chose*
           (V) [_VP]   e.g. *vouloir faire quelque chose*
           (V) [_S']   e.g. *vouloir qu'il fasse quelque chose*

Not only verbs can have sub-categorisation frames, nouns and adjectives can too:

content (Adj)   [_PP]   e.g. *content de faire quelque chose*
                 [_S']   e.g. *content que tu sois là*
destruction (N) [_PP]   e.g. *destruction de la cité*

8.3.7   Related sentences

So far, we have discussed how we can represent the structure of different French sentences and, if we elaborated the phrase structure rules enough, we would probably succeed in producing a grammar that would generate all the possible structures found in the French language. An interesting problem arises, however, when we consider the following pairs of sentences:

(53)   *Mon frère a vendu ma bicyclette*

(54)   *Ma bicyclette a été vendue par mon frère*

(55)   *Il va à Paris*

(56)   *Où va-t-il?*

(57)   *Paul voit Marie*

(58)   *Paul la voit*

Intuitively, we feel that these pairs of sentences are related in some fairly strong way. If we were to ask a speaker of French to describe the relationships, we might well find that they talk about 'replacement' or 'movement' or 'changing words around'. Reflecting speakers' feelings about the links between such structures, some linguists feel that the pairs of sentences are actually related in a way that simply making up phrase structure rules to generate them would not capture. For this reason, we find that it is often assumed that at a subconscious level, speakers are aware that the sentences (53) to (58) actually have two levels of structure, the *surface structure* that we see in the examples and a *deep structure* which is essentially similar to the sentences (53), (55) and (57). The phrase structure rules we have discussed could then be seen as only applying to the deep structure; other rules are assumed to apply to transform the deep structures into the surface structures found in (54), (56) and (58). This type of syntactic model is often referred to as *transformational grammar* precisely because it proposes that some sentences in a language are the result of a transformation of one structure into another.

Without going into any detail about what these transformational rules may look like, it suffices to assume that some mechanism would allow, say, the subject–verb inversion in (56), or the pronominalisation in (58). Whatever this mechanism might be (and it is the subject of much interest in syntactic theory), it could explain why speakers of French intuitively realise that the subject *la bicyclette* in (54) is actually the object of the verb *vendre* and is not a mechanical sales person!

8.4   Syntactic differences between English and French

Although it has a lot in common with other languages, the syntax of French differs in many respects from that of English. Example: in English both a direct object and an indirect object can become the subject of the related passive sentence. Thus:

(59)   Peter gave the book to Paul
            D.O.   I.O.

(60)   The book was given to Paul by Peter

(61)   Paul was given the book by Peter

In French, while

(62)   *Pierre a donné le livre à Paul*

can be transformed into

(63)   *Le livre a été donné à Paul par Pierre*

the following sentence is ungrammatical:

(64)   **Paul a été donné le livre par Pierre*

Example: in English, when an object pronoun replaces a noun, as in:

(65)   John kissed Mary

giving

(66)   John kissed her

the pronoun stays in the position occupied by the noun. In French, however, the pronoun 'moves' to take up a position before the verb, as in:

(67)   *Jean embrassa Marie*

giving

(68)   *Jean l'embrassa*

Example: If we look at the structure of straightforward declarative sentences in French, we also find a number of other differences from English. In French, adverbs can intervene between a verb and its object as in:

(69)   *Jean boit lentement son café*

a position which is not possible for the English counterpart:

(70)   *John drinks slowly his coffee

Example: In French the 'complementiser' *que* in subordinate clauses is obligatory, but its English equivalent *that* is optional in some cases:

(71)   John has said (that) he's seen it

whereas in French:

(72)   *Jean a dit* **qu'***il l'a vu* (*que* cannot be omitted)

Example: In English, the verb *obey* takes an NP complement:

(73)   John obeys **his parents**

while in French, *obéir* takes a PP complement:

(74)   *Jean obéit* **à ses parents**

Conclusion

In this chapter, we have proposed three major syntactic elements that might describe French sentences: phrase structure rules, sub-categorisation and some kind of 'movement' element to 'transform' one structure into another. If we suppose that each of these three elements are at work in all languages, while differing in the details according to the specific requirements of a particular language, it becomes fairly easy to formulate in general terms the ways French differs from English. In the examples relating to the position of adverbs (69–70) and to the obligatory nature of 'complementisers' in French (71–72), we simply have to propose that French phrase structure rules differ in these ways from those applying in English. Since we have assumed that individual words have their own peculiar sub-categorisation frames, then it is easy to see why apparent direct translations like *obey/obéir à* (73–74) are not in fact possible. Finally, if we assume that English, but not French, has a mechanism for changing (or 'moving') an indirect object into the subject of a passive sentence (59–62), we can explain why structures like *Paul a été donné* ... are not grammatical in French. Similarly, we can assume that French has a 'movement-rule' which moves a pronoun to the front of a verb, a rule not operating in English (65–68).

We can employ the same general principles to describe syntactic differences between different dialects of French, between child language and adult language and between different historical stages of the language.

Seminar exercises

1.   Try to separate the following sentences into phrases, giving the category (NP, VP, etc.) of each phrase. Remember that a phrase can contain other phrases as well as words.

(a) *Tous les matins elle passait quelques minutes à regarder la Seine.*
(b) *Ma tante fait toujours une promenade après le dîner.*
(c) *Toutes les peintures représentent des animaux.*
(d) *La prochaine fois je suivrai le chemin que vous m'avez indiqué.*

2.   Identify the subordinate clauses in the following sentences and say what type they are.

(a) *Je suis étonné que vous ne puissiez pas faire d'économies.*
(b) *Comment étaient les voitures qu'ils ont aperçues?*
(c) *Jean, qui est mon frère, a seize ans.*
(d) *Il y a une odeur délicieuse qui vient de la cuisine.*
(e) *On pense que pour tuer les animaux ces hommes utilisaient des armes qu'ils fabriquaient.*

3.   What are the phrase structure rules needed to 'generate' the following set of sentences?

(a) *Pierre veut aller chez ses parents.*
(b) *Mes parents sont vieux.*
(c) *Il a besoin d'un couteau.*
(d) *Il vend sa bicyclette à son ami.*
(e) *C'est une petite rue tranquille.*
(f) *La femme que j'ai vue sait nager.*

4.   Draw labelled tree diagrams for the following sentences:

(a) *Nous devions aller à Paris.*
(b) *Après les mathématiques il a eu un cours d'anglais.*
(c) *Il a trouvé un dessin préhistorique.*
(d) *Le petit chat gris commence à manger la viande.*

5.   State what the sub-categorisation frames for the following verbs would be:

vouloir	*dire*
regarder	*aimer*
manger	*savoir*
pouvoir	*demander*
faire	*mettre*

6.   For each of the following differences between French and English, try to identify which part of the grammar (the lexicon, the phrase structure rules or the movement component) might contain them:

(a) Ask your mother to help me.
     *Demandez à ta mère de m'aider.
(b) *Likes he this cake?
     Aime-t-il ce gâteau?
(c) I don't know who he spoke to.
     *Je ne sais pas qui il a parlé à.
(d) I want John to go to the cinema.
     Je veux que Jean aille au cinéma.
(e) John often goes to the cinema.
     Jean va souvent au cinéma.

7.   In the following phrases, try to identify whether the phrases in bold are complements or modifiers.

(a) *Ils partent* **à la campagne en été.**
(b) *Le taureau de feu faisait peur* **à tout le monde.**
(c) *Ils ont croisé un autre bateau* **dans la brume.**
(d) *Elle a mis un mouchoir* **dans sa poche.**
(e) *Un matin, sa tante est entrée* **dans sa chambre.**
(f) *Elle ramasse ses affaires* **en un clin d'œil.**

9

Doing things with French

So far in this book, we have considered the French language at three different levels of analysis, that is at the phonological, lexical and grammatical levels. This approach has enabled us to focus attention on the patterns (paradigmatic and syntagmatic) in which the sounds, words and sentences of French are organised. On each of these levels, the language has been looked at as a sort of code, with lower level units (phonemes) combining to make higher level ones (morphemes and words) which in turn combine to make higher units still (phrases, clauses and sentences). In so doing we have regarded the 'sentence' as the highest unit of grammatical description and we have treated the language as a system more or less abstracted from the situations in which it is used and from the speakers using it.

In the remaining chapters of this book we are to go beyond this in tackling two general questions: how do French speakers apply the abstract linguistic rules we have been describing in order to do things and to get things done in the real world? Is there linguistic life above the level of the sentence, i.e. can we observe patterns in units of language bigger than sentences? The branches of linguistics concerned with handling these questions are pragmatics for the former and discourse analysis and conversation analysis for the latter. This chapter will be concerned with pragmatics.

9.1   Preliminary notions

We saw in Chapter 2 that sociolinguists looking at French are interested in the variability inherent in the language, enabling it to be spoken by a great variety of users and to be put to a wide range of uses in many different situations. In this chapter we will examine in more detail how human beings tailor their use of language to fit the real-life situations in which they find themselves, in order to get their meanings across.

If we listen to what happens in our own ordinary, everyday interaction, we will notice that when we talk, we do not always explicitly spell out in so many words exactly what we mean. For example, when someone says:

(1)   *qu'il est tard*

the literal meaning of the sentence could be an innocent reflection about the time of day, but in the context of a boring party, the speaker could be using this to mean

(2)   *je veux m'en aller*

Indeed, someone who insists on specifying in words precisely what they mean in conversation or who insists that others do so is seldom sought after for social encounters! Perhaps surprisingly, most of the time we feel that we know what is meant in even the most indirect of exchanges, and we are usually satisfied that we make ourselves understood when we talk. So, in order to function adequately in French we need to know a great deal in addition to the appropriate vocabulary and grammatical constructions. This additional level of linguistic knowledge is the concern of *pragmatics*.

It is neither very easy nor in fact particularly useful to provide a concise and exclusive definition of pragmatics, indeed, among certain linguists this level has been nicknamed the 'waste-basket of linguistics' (Mey 1993: 13). In everyday use, the word 'pragmatic' conveys the idea of 'relating to *practical* concerns rather than to theories'. This level of linguistic analysis brings together the abstract system of language and the concrete world of *context*. Within linguistics, pragmatics is closely linked to semantics as both are concerned with meaning. However, whereas semantics is concerned with word meaning and sentence meaning, pragmatics is concerned with con-textualised meaning.

Pragmaticians who want to study how language is used by real speakers in real situations need a particular set of intellectual tools, that is a theoretical framework and metalanguage, that will enable them to link language and context. In this chapter we will begin by looking at some of the theoretical notions which are central to pragmatics, then we shall move on to consider how we use French to say what we mean and to do what we want to achieve in the real world.

9.1.1   Sentences and utterances

Just as most lay-persons can intuitively recognise words (see Chapter 3, 3.1), many of them also are fairly confident in their ability to identify and construct sentences. However, a sentence is much easier to identify in a written text than it is in a spoken discourse. Indeed, the notion of 'sentence' only became widespread with the development of literacy in the eighteenth and nineteenth centuries, and if we listen to what happens in everyday conversations, we seldom hear what are generally considered to be grammatically complete sentences. Consider, for example (3) to (6) below.

(3)   *salut*

(4)   *rien*

(5)   *eh bien alors*

(6)   *c'est-à-dire*

Each of these expressions is quite likely to occur as someone's turn in a conversation, for they are perfectly adequate contributions, despite the fact that they are not sentences. So, to avoid referring to contributions such as these as 'incomplete sentences', pragmaticians make a distinction between sentences and *utterances*. We can in fact use this distinction to help us set out the domain of pragmatics: whereas syntax and semantics focus on how sentences convey meaning, pragmatics is concerned with how utterances convey meaning.

A sentence is an abstract theoretical unit which is recognised using grammatical criteria, whereas an utterance is an actually occurring stretch of spoken language. An utterance can be a sentence, part of a sentence or something in place of a sentence, such as *mm hmm* in English or *ouais* in French, or even a laugh, produced in a context (see Levinson 1983: 18). When a pragmatician looks at what is traditionally called a 'sentence' (e.g. *Je vais passer te voir en rentrant chez moi*), he sees two sorts of thing – a 'sentence' (= the application of the rules of grammar and vocabulary producing a well-formed and meaningful sequence of words) and an 'utterance' (= the combination of the 'sentence' with a real-world context). As we saw in (1) and (2) above, the interpretation of an utterance is not fully determined by its linguistic properties.

9.1.2   Context

We have already used the term 'context' a number of times in our discussion of the nature of pragmatics, but we will need a more precise idea of what is meant by it if the notion is to be incorporated into a rigorous study of French. Elinor Ochs (1979: 2–5) examines the scope of the notion of context under four headings.

THE SETTING

Aspects of the social and spatial environment of an encounter are classified under this heading, such as the room in which an encounter takes place and the relationship between those taking part in the encounter. It is also important to note that context does not systematically include all aspects of the physical and social world, and that neither the physical nor the social environment are fixed and immutable realities. For example, by using *vous* when meeting a student to discuss a late assignment, a lecturer can establish a formal setting to the encounter, but the setting to that same encounter may be transformed by switching to *tu* to address the student when the topic of discussion moves to an impending staff/student get-together.

THE EXTRA-SITUATIONAL CONTEXT

'Interlocutors have awarenesses of and assumptions about objects, events and states of affairs outside the interactional setting and these affect how language is used and understood' (see Ochs 1979: 5). The context of our cultural knowledge and the expectations we have of real-world situations would thus, for example lead us to respond differently to the utterance *tu m'emmerdes* if it is pronounced by a lecturer during class time, or by a friend in the bar during a social gathering.

THE BEHAVIOURAL ENVIRONMENT

Features of behaviour such as gaze, posture, even passing or pointing, are an important part of the context of an exchange. A considerable amount of research has shown that speakers use these features of behaviour to organise their own talk, and to show their attention to the talk of others. By means of gaze, for example, a speaker may signal an intention to continue speaking, or may indicate that someone else should take the floor.

LANGUAGE

The language of an encounter is also a significant feature of context. Talk is organised sequentially, in that one contribution or turn in a conversation becomes the context to which the following turn is shaped. Indeed, if a speaker wants to make a contribution to the talk which is not related to the previous talk, they usually preface that contribution with something explicit to ensure that the previous talk is not seen as context, such as *attends*, *tiens* or even *qu'est-ce que je voulais te dire* or *mais il faut que je te dise*. Equally importantly, the choices a speaker makes, for example between standard and non-standard varieties of language (see Chapter 2, 2.2.2) can act as 'contextualisation cues' (see Gumperz 1982: 131). Contextualisation cues are signals which help speakers interpret what is meant, using processes of inferencing (see 9.2.2). Imagine, for instance, a lecturer enquiring after the whereabouts of a friend of yours. If the lecturer were to use the more colloquial *pote* rather than the formal *camarade de classe*, this choice might lead you to infer that the enquiry was related to the lecturer's genuine concern for their well-being, rather than an attempt to chase up the student in question for non-attendance in class.

9.1.3   Applying the notion of context

At this point it may be helpful to illustrate how these various aspects of context contribute to our understanding of utterances. The following exchange, cited by L.-J. Calvet in a lecture delivered in Newcastle in 1994, was part of a televised interview with François Mitterrand:

(7)
INTERVIEWER: *on dit que vous êtes chébran*
MITTERRAND: *mais on ne dit plus chébran on dit câblé ou même bléca*

Our knowledge of grammar and of word meaning (see Chapter 4 especially 4.3) takes us part of the way in explaining the linguistic choices made by these speakers. We can thereby account for the interviewing journalist's choice of the impersonal pronoun *on*, rather than associating himself explicitly with the remark he is making by choosing either *je* or *nous* from the paradigmatic set of French pronouns. Note that Mitterrand also chooses to use this potentially ambiguous pronoun. In this instance, however, the *on* enables him to suggest his own inclusion in the set of speakers who use the terms he refers to, rather than *ils*, a choice of pronoun which automatically precludes the speaker. Equally, both speakers choose the verb *dire* from the lexical paradigm which includes all the possible ways to express the act of producing an utterance. Among the items with a similar conceptual content featuring in that particular lexical paradigm we would expect to find *constater*, *déclarer*, *prononcer*, all of which had been rejected in favour of *dire*. And we can also see that the particular form of *dire*, that is *dit*, has been chosen as a result of the syntagmatic relation between the pronoun *on* and the following verb.

But our discussion thus far does not appear to help us understand what is going on between the three adjectives *chébran*, *câblé* and *bléca*, for these are all synonyms meaning 'switched on', 'with it'. Furthermore, all three lexical items are examples of *verlan*, the French backslang which is commonly used by young people, particularly those living in inner cities or those who are considered to be marginal to mainstream society (see Chapter 2, 2.1.3). This means that the use of these words in our exchange has not been determined by considerations of register or by differences in the connotations of the words (see Chapter 4, 4.3.5).

So if we are to understand why Mitterrand takes the unusual step of correcting the journalist's choice of word, or more precisely, carrying out a *repair* to the journalist's utterance, we need to bring to bear on the actual words spoken our knowledge about the various aspects of context of this exchange.

THE SETTING

We need to know that this exchange was part of an extended interview with President Mitterrand which was broadcast on national television and radio.

As with all political or news interviews, the talk is not really produced for the journalist taking part. Indeed, a journalist is generally expected to maintain a neutralistic position in this type of encounter. The talk is really for the benefit of the overhearing audience, in this case, the voting French public (see Heritage and Greatbatch 1991: 107).

THE EXTRA-SITUATIONAL CONTEXT

President Mitterrand was coming to the end of his second term of office when this exchange occurred. French politicians, especially those in the highest positions, were being increasingly criticised for being out of touch with ordinary people in France, and particularly with deprived young people, who form a somewhat problematic sub-group of contemporary French society. Most importantly, immediately prior to the interview, the problems of young marginals had attracted a great deal of public attention. And although President Mitterrand was not running for office he was intending to add the weight of his support to his party's candidate for office, and was keen to end his presidency on a positive note.

THE BEHAVIOURAL ENVIRONMENT

Careful study of a video recording of this exchange would no doubt enable us to see how the two speakers used their gaze and body movements to support and co-ordinate their conversational activities, including showing that they are listening to each other and taking turns at speaking.

LANGUAGE

We can see that the interviewer's utterance forms the context for Mitterrand's utterance, indeed, Mitterrand's contribution can only be seen as a repair if we examine it in respect of the previous talk. The choice of *verlan* as opposed to the standard variety of French we would expect the President and the interviewer to use is also highly significant. As we noted above, *verlan* is the backslang which is used by the young people living in the deprived urban areas of France. It plays a particularly important role in the cultural identity of this marginal social group. The lexicon of *verlan* is constantly being added to and updated, particularly as items lose their special status and pass into everyday usage, as is the case of the term *beur* for example, (see Chapter 2, 2.1.3). Thus, without regular contact with young people living in deprived urban areas, it is very difficult to keep abreast of the terms in current use.

Equipped with this contextual knowledge, we can now clearly see that by making this repair, Mitterrand is showing the interviewing journalist and, more importantly for a politician, the overhearing audience listening to or watching the interview, that he is in touch with young people. By means of the repair, which involved replacing one, out-dated, word of *verlan* with the more up-to-date term, he can effectively make the point without any explicit reference to the potentially damaging criticisms that had been recently voiced.

So these two pragmatic notions, utterance and context, enable us to make sense of what is in strict grammatical and semantic terms a rather strange or even nonsensical exchange. By evoking various aspects of the context we have been able to provide a more comprehensive explanation for the choices of word than could otherwise be given.

9.2   Meaning in context

If we look at the following examples (developed from Grundy 1995) as sentences (i.e. applying the rules of grammar and semantics), we can easily work out their literal meaning:

(8)   *Je viendrai te voir ici demain.*

(9)   *Les Verts ont gagné.*

(10)   *C'est toi que j'aime.*

(11)   *C'est encore moi.*

However, it is only when we can look at them as utterances (i.e. in combination with our knowledge of the particular real-world context in which they are being used) that we are able to make full sense of them. In (8) meaning depends crucially on *deixis* = the persons referred to by *je* and *te* and on the place and date referred to by *ici* and *demain*. In (9) the *implied meaning* could be very positive if the opponents of *les Verts* (here the St Etienne football team, not a group of ecologists) were Paris-Saint Germain (currently top of the league), but pretty negative if the opponents were Sochaux (currently at the bottom of the league). Utterance (10), profferred by a wife to a husband has the same literal meaning as *Je t'aime*, but the *presupposition* upon which it is based is completely different – it could presuppose that she is having an affair with the man next door, but not a very deep one since she protests that it's her husband she really loves. Utterance (11) is on the face of it a completely redundant statement, but it is in fact something people often find themselves saying. The reason for this is that, as a *speech act* it is not a statement at all: it is usually offered as an apology for disturbing someone a second or third time. In what follows we will look briefly at these four notions: deixis, implicatures, presuppositions and speech acts.

9.2.1 Deictics

Consider the following utterance:

(12) *Demain nous allons manger chez sa mère, qui habite assez loin d'ici. Tu peux nous accompagner? Comme je t'ai déjà expliqué, je n'aurai certainement pas le temps d'y aller à pied.*

In order to fully make sense of the utterance in (12), we need to know more about the context in which it occurred, because many of the words are deictics, pointing to some aspect of that context. In this example we can distinguish several different types of deictic which indicate different aspects of the context.

Je, tu, nous and *sa* are deictics which refer to *person*. Note that in our example, *sa*, unlike the English *his* or *her*, gives no information about whose mother is being talked about. In spoken French any problem of ambiguity may be resolved as in (13) and (14) below:

(13) *sa mère à lui*

(14) *sa mère à elle*

In French, unlike English, we can often distinguish between the deictic second person pronoun referring to one or referring to more than one addressee. Thus *vous* in (15) is clearly addressed to more than one person while *tu* in (16) is addressed to a single addressee:

(15) *avez-vous fini vos desserts?*

(16) *veux-tu une pomme?*

We cannot always be sure of the number of addressees, however. The utterance in (17) could either be addressed to more than one person, or to one person with whom the speaker uses a polite or formal form of address:

(17) *vous êtes en retard*

In this example, the pronoun *vous* could be functioning as a *social* deictic rather than a deictic of person. Social deictics point to some aspect of the social relationship between interlocutors. In French, they include the second person pronouns *tu* and *vous* and terms of address such as *Monsieur le docteur* and *Madame le juge*.

So, returning to our discussion of (12) above, while *je, nous* and *sa* are very clearly deictics of person, *tu* is not only a deictic of person but it is also a social deictic which points to a more intimate social relationship between the speaker and the addressee.

Also in (12), *ici* and *y* are deictics of place. They refer to some location which can only be determined from the context of the utterance. In this particular example, we can also consider *assez loin* as a deictic of place because its meaning is context-dependent. Other deictics of place in French include *voici, voilà* and *là-bas*. Here we can also make a distinction between a gestural use of deictics, where the sense of the deictic can only be established by knowing what is being pointed at by the speaker as in (18):

(18)   *le voici*

and a symbolic use, where the linguistic context of the deictic contributes to our understanding of what is being referred to, as in (19):

(19)   *le voilà, en dessous de la chaise*

Non-deictic means for referring to place include units of measurement and precise references that do not depend on the context of the utterance for their meaning, as in (20). Deictics of place are often combined with non-deictic means of perceiving and measuring space:

(20)   *L'école Jules Ferry se trouve à trois cent mètres de l'église qui est au coin de la Place de la République*

Returning to (12) above, *demain* is a deictic of time, the meaning of which depends on when the utterance was produced. Time deixis is also achieved in French by adverbs of time such as *maintenant, plus tard, avant* and *après*, and by the use of references to specific moments or stretches of time which are combined with adverbs, for example *lundi prochain, la semaine dernière* and *d'ici un an*. And, as we can see in (12), verb tense also contributes to time deixis.

9.2.2   *Implicatures and inferencing*

We have already noted that often when we talk we do not explicitly explain in words everything we mean. We express what we want to say in ways which we expect our conversation partner to be able to interpret, given the context of our talk. Our conversation partners expect our talk to be intelligible. They use the context of talk to make sense of what has been said. So each party to the talk relies on the contextual knowledge they share to work out, or *negotiate the meaning* of, what is said.

But not only can we make ourselves understood without detailed explanations, we can even get our message across without any linguistic repesentation of our message at all. That we commonly do so is clear when you consider how unsurprising the examples illustrating this are, in (21) and (22):

(21)   *qu'il fait froid ici*

(22)   *tu trouves pas qu'il fait froid ici?*

Each of these utterances produced in the context of a room with an open window can serve to get the window closed even though there is neither any direct nor even indirect reference made to windows, and there is no mention of the fact that the window was open in the first place. How can this happen?

Using the appropriate aspect of the context of the utterance, in this case the open window, we can *infer* that the speaker wishes to communicate a request to have the window closed. And in producing the utterance, our speaker trusts that we will indeed go beyond what they have said to infer what they meant. As you can see from our examples (21) and (22), the same request can be inferred from the declarative (21) as from the interrogative (22), given the same context of the open window. So we can also conclude that the *inferences* which we make from what is said are not necessarily determined by the syntactic structure of the utterance.

Much of the groundwork for examining how the meaning of an utterance is conveyed was initiated by philosophers. Among them, Grice's ideas about meaning, first presented in 1957, have been the starting-point for much work in pragmatics. Grice proposed a distinction between natural meaning, that is information which is conveyed by means of direct evidence of that information, and non-natural meaning, that is information that is *intentionally* conveyed. An illustration of Grice's distinction could be helpful (see also Chapter 1, 1.2.1).

A student attending a lecture in theoretical pragmatics with black circles round the eyes, incessantly yawning, is clearly tired. The natural meaning of black circles around the eyes and yawning is a state of tiredness. But we cannot say that the student intended to communicate this state of tiredness, we can simply say that the yawning and so on provide direct and natural evidence of the fact that the student is tired.

If, on the other hand, a classmate in that same lecture begins to yawn incessantly at a particularly dry and theoretical part of the talk, perhaps adding to the effect by covering the yawns with some rather dramatised gestures, we can see that the classmate is intending to communicate a response to a rather tedious lecture. We are no longer looking at the natural meaning of a yawn, and we can infer this student's intention to communicate a state of boredom. Of course this student could equally convey the same information by producing an utterance, such as those in (23) and (24):

(23)   *plus intéressant tu meurs*

(24)   *je m'ennuie*

Note that information can be more or less explicitly communicated. So in (23) a state of boredom is communicated by a commonly used idiom, whereas in (24) it is directly referred to in the lexical meaning of the utterance.

Grice went on to suggest that we convey our intended meaning by adhering to pragmatic principles when we communicate. We talk about pragmatic principles rather than rules because these principles are not binding or restrictive in the same sense as grammatical rules are. We can see that this is the case if we think about the consequences of not applying the appropriate rules or principles. If we produce an ungrammatical sentence as in (25), we are simply not understood and communication breaks down:

(25)   *une thé de je tasse vouloir**

If, on the other hand, we get involved in an anomalous or apparently ill-formed exchange, communication continues since participants use the context to make the necessary inferences to find a possible meaning for even the most obscure utterances. To illustrate, the following exchanges are potentially ill-formed, but it is fairly easy to come up with a possible context which would render each of them perfectly coherent:

(26)   A: *t'as vu mes clés?*

(27)   B: *ton sac à main est en dessous de ta chaise*

(28)   A: *à quelle heure veux-tu venir?*

(29)   B: *Sylvie finit son cours à 19h*

Grice called his guidelines for effective communication the *Co-operative Principle*, and proposed four constituent *maxims*. These are the maxim of *quality*, concerned with the truthfulness and accuracy of a speaker's contribution; the maxim of *quantity*, that the contribution conveys enough, that is neither too much nor too little information; the maxim of *relevance*, that the speaker's contribution be relevant to the interaction, and the maxim of *manner*, concerned with the orderliness and the clarity of the contribution.

Grice suggested that even when the maxims do not appear to have been respected, we continue to work on the assumption that our interlocutor has conformed to the maxims in some other, less obvious way. We therefore work to infer the meaning of what has been said, basing our inferences in the assumption of an underlying co-operation.

Theoretically, any number of inferences could be generated by an utterance, but not all these inferences are intentionally communicated. Grice makes a distinction between those inferences that arise as a result of adhering to or of deliberately flouting the co-operative principle, which he terms *conversational implicatures*, and those inferences that arise from culturally specific conventions, which he terms *conventional implicatures*. The latter are fixed by cultural conventions, and would include, for example, the inferences which we make when our conversation partner addresses us as *vous* rather than *tu* or vice versa or those we make when a speaker chooses between standard or non-standard forms of language (see Chapter 2 pp. 22ff). Conversational implicatures, on the other hand, are not necessarily limited by any specific cultural knowledge as they are based on a presumption of rational co-operation in interaction.

Grice's ideas have provoked a considerable amount of debate. Nevertheless, his basic assumption about the efficient and rational nature of conversation remains fundamental to our understanding of meaning in interaction, enabling us to account for how speakers can mean more than they explicitly say and how hearers manage to understand them.

9.2.3 *Presuppositions*

In the previous section we were concerned with how addressees make the necessary inferences to understand what the speaker is trying to say. In this section we will be looking at the same problem the other way round: we will be considering the way speakers design what they are saying in the light of the assumptions they make about the current state of knowledge in their addressee. In example (10) above the wayward wife is presupposing that her husband already knows about her affair with the man next door.

In all acts of communication we are constantly gauging and monitoring how much our interlocutor knows already and how much new information we can safely add. Typically in French the definite article (*le, la, les*) introduces known information – *J'ai vu* la *dame (dont tu me parlais hier)* – and the indefinite and partitive articles new or unknown information – *J'ai vu* un *monsieur ce matin qui* . . . , *Il y a* de la *boue sur la moquette.* Some linguists make a distinction between 'theme' and 'rheme', the former representing known information, the starting-point of an utterance, while the latter represents new or not known information which the speaker is revealing about the 'theme'. A further distinction is often made between conventional (or encyclopaedic) knowledge and conversational knowledge. This also can be illustrated with reference to the use of articles in French. The definite article presents known information, but the information may be known about in one of two ways – it may be known about as a result of what the speaker has just told him (conversational knowledge):

(30)   *je viens de discuter avec* une *vielle dame qui a été interpellée par la police*

(31)   *qu'est-ce qu'elle avait fait,* la *vieille dame?*

It may be known about because members of the speech community in question share that knowledge about their world on an ongoing basis (encyclopaedic knowledge):

(32)   *après dix ans de fiançailles, le couple est enfin passé devant* le *maire*

Everyone in France lives in a *commune*, presided over by a *maire* and it is the *maire de la commune* who conducts civil marriage ceremonies. This 'encyclopaedic' knowledge can be assumed to be known by all French speakers, in metropolitan France at least. Hence the use of the definite article.

9.2.4   Speech acts

It was the philosopher J. L. Austin who first pointed out that when we produce an utterance we are actually doing an action (see Nunan 1993: 65–66). We use an abstract language system to describe the world as we perceive it, as in (33), to respond to the world as we perceive it, as in (34), or to change some aspect of the world, as in (35):

(33)   *elle est partie à la gare*

(34)   *je suis désolé qu'elle est partie*

(35)   *va la chercher à la gare*

Speech acts (actions carried out by means of language) have been categorised in any number of ways, the most familiar being according to the grammatical structure of the utterance: declarative sentences make statements, interrogative sentences ask questions, imperative sentences give orders and exclamative sentences make exclamations. Unfortunately for us, however, real-life language use is rather more subtle and complex than this. We do many more things with language than these four actions just enumerated. We make requests, greetings, complaints, warnings. We give advice. Some speech acts we perform directly and explicitly, some we carry out more indirectly.

Traditionally, linguists have been concerned overwhelmingly with only one type of speech act: making statements. This is the sort of thing which goes on much of the time when we write, and our central concern as readers is to evaluate the truth or falsehood of what we are reading. Such issues are important in the field of 'truth-conditional semantics'. However, a much wider range of speech acts is encountered when we examine the language used in everyday speech, and very often the question of truth or falsehood is superseded by other concerns, such as appropriateness.

Speech acts provide a link between language and action. The following utterances can both be construed as a promise:

(36)   *je vous promets un cours intéressant*

(37)   *ça va t'intéresser mon cours si tu viens*

Now, with promises, the question of truth or falsehood is not really important. What matters is whether the person is really making a promise, and for us to be convinced of this, a number of provisos have to be met. First, the person making it must be in a position to carry it out. So utterances (36) and (37) would only constitute a promise if they were to be pronounced by someone actually involved in the class, a teacher or even a student planning some form of practical joke. That person must also be sincere in making our promise. So producing the utterances with a rather ironical tone, referring to part of a course which is renowned as difficult and dry, would clearly not constitute making that promise. The promise must equally be acknowledged as such by those involved in the interaction. Such necessary provisos are known as *felicity conditions*. They have little to do with language but everything to do with context. *Promettre* is one of a special group of verbs known as *performative* verbs which, when pronounced and of course if all the necessary felicity conditions are satisfied, actually do or perform a specific action or act.

Many of these performative verbs are used in very restricted circumstances by a few, specially authorised speakers.

(38)   *je vous déclare homme et femme unis par les liens du mariage*

So for example, the utterance in (38), produced by a French mayor at the end of a specific ceremony with specific participants, actually marries the couple to whom the utterance is addressed. But of course the same utterance does not perform the same act if it is pronounced by revellers in the course of the stag night set aside for the purpose of *enterrer la vie de garçon* of the future bridegroom.

Although performative verbs make a clear link between producing an utterance and acting in a real context, there are very few such verbs. Austin and his students went on to suggest that in pronouncing any utterance, a speaker is simultaneously producing three different types of act.

The *locutionary act* is the act of actually producing an utterance with specific references and meaning. So in producing (36) or (37) above, the locutionary act would be to match the appropriate linguistic items to definite references in the real world, fixing the sense of the utterance.

The *illocutionary act* is the act of making a promise, a threat, even a statement, by virtue of producing an utterance. So returning again to examples (36) and (37), the conventional illocutionary force of these utterances is to make a promise. Much of the work of speech act theorists has been focused on identifying the illocutionary force of utterances, and classifying different types of illocutionary act.

The *perlocutionary act* is the act of producing an effect on the addressees by producing an utterance. So the aforementioned utterances could excite, warn or even threaten an addressee. The potential effects of any utterance are numerous and very varied, depending on the specific context of a particular utterance. It has, indeed, proved very difficult to delimit the possible perlocutionary effects of an utterance.

These three types of act embrace the linguistic process of producing a stretch of language, the performance of a specific action in a particular context, and the production of a particular effect on our conversation partners. Of the three, the one which is most important for students of French to understand is the second (illocutionary act), for very commonly the speech acts we perform are not what they appear to be on the linguistic surface. The following statements are on the face of it rather pointless:

(39)   *c'est encore moi*

(40)   *c'est encore toi*

However, if you imagine the contexts in which these utterances might be used, you will notice that their illocutionary force is not to make a statement at all, but to make an apology (39) and a complaint (40). The following utterance is ostensibly an exclamation, triggered by the warmth of a room:

(41)   *qu'il fait chaud ici*

However, it is easy to imagine a context where the illocutionary force of this utterance is in fact a request (e.g. to turn the central heating down). The following utterance is ostensibly a question requesting information:

(42)   *qu'est-ce que tu fais ce soir?*

However, it is easy to imagine a context where its illocutionary force is that of an invitation. An utterance can produce more than one speech act, and the process of matching utterances and acts is not always clear-cut. Speech act theory enables us to consider language in terms of action, so that we can see what language users are doing in real-world contexts when they use their language. Much of our conversational behaviour is indirect and requires us to invoke the 'conversational maxims' discussed on p. 165 in order to fully appreciate what is going on. We will return to this theme in the next chapter when we discuss conversation analysis.

Conclusion

In this chapter we have seen how the context of an utterance, the scope of which includes the speaker, the social and physical setting, the actual language used and the wider cultural setting, all contribute very significantly to the meaning of that utterance. We have looked at how we co-operate to make ourselves understood in a particular context, and how we can mean so much more than we explicitly say. We have seen how we use language to do things in a specific context, either directly or indirectly, relying on processes of inference to produce actions.

The ideas introduced here have a number of implications for learners of French as a second language, striving to develop their capacity to use the language in contexts where they do not necessarily share the same expectations about language use as native-speakers. The pragmatic level of linguistic competence is often overlooked in language-teaching programmes, despite the obvious difficulties which it causes for learners. In overcoming these difficulties, language learners can develop a sensitivity to the subtler aspects of communication and improve their communication skills all round.

Seminar exercises

1.   Distinguish between *deictic* and *non-deictic* references in the following extract from Albert Camus' novel *L'Etranger*, and indicate to which grammatical category each deictic belongs:

L'asile de vieillards est à Marengo, à quatre-vingts kilomètres d'Alger. Je prendrai l'autobus à deux heures et j'arriverai dans l'après-midi. Ainsi, je pourrai veiller et je rentrerai demain soir. J'ai demandé deux jours de congé à mon patron et il ne pouvait pas me les refuser avec une excuse pareille. Mais il n'avait pas l'air content. Je lui ai même dit: «Ce n'est pas de ma faute.» En somme, je n'avais pas à m'excuser. C'était plutôt à lui de me présenter ses condoléances. Mais il le fera sans doute après-demain quand il me verra en deuil.

2.   What kind of contextual knowledge do we need to understand what is going on in this headline and summary, from *Le Figaro Économie*, dated 4 September 1995?

Le thé glacé se boit comme du petit-lait
Après les États-Unis, le thé glacé fait l'objet d'un véritable engouement en Europe avec un milliard de litres consommés. Une vogue qui surfe sur celle des boissons plates, peu caloriques, saines et fraîches. Les poids lourds de l'alimentation se ruent vers ce nouvel eldorado.

3.   How can we account for the dialogue below?

A: *je suis allée à la piscine hier soir*
B: *mon cours, c'est lundi*

4.   How could the pragmatic issues we have been discussing in this chapter affect the task of translating texts from French to English? Illustrate your discussion with examples where possible.

10
Analysing discourse and everyday conversation

Pragmatics is not the only branch of linguistics which looks at linguistic communication in terms transcending the traditional notion of 'sentence' (the highest unit of analysis in grammar). At the beginning of the previous chapter we raised the general question: is there linguistic life above the level of the sentence, i.e. can we observe patterns in units of language bigger than sentences? This final chapter will be devoted to showing how linguists approach an answer to this in discourse analysis and conversation analysis.

10.1   Discourse analysis

Discourse analysis is concerned with uncovering regularities in chunks of language larger than individual sentences or utterances. The word 'discourse' features nowadays in many discussions about language, and has come to cover a wide range of meanings. So before we go on to look at discourse analysis, it would be helpful to consider some of the meanings currently given to the word.

In the social sciences, 'discourse' is often used in the following way:

> Different discourses are more or less coherent ways of talking and thinking about a particular set of things such as food or activities such as child rearing. The physical actions associated with 'discourses' are often known as 'practices' or even 'discursive practices'.
>
> (Anderson 1988: 23)

Here the notion of discourse is commonly linked to ideas of relative power, exercised through language. So Anderson discusses the 'discourse of workers' and the 'discourse of management' (1988: 256) in relation to the relative power of the two groups. 'Discourse' refers to a hidden political agenda, to an underlying ideology, to the way in which language is implicitly used to influence an audience. In the field of literary criticism, 'discourse' is often used in a similar way, though for some writers it is little more than a synonym for the traditional term 'style'.

Even among linguists there exists a wide range of approaches (see Schiffrin 1994). What all these approaches have in common is an interest in the organisation of bigger chunks of language than sentences and an overriding preoccupation with language in use (see Stubbs 1983). For a helpful introduction to the basic concepts see Nunan (1993).

10.1.1   Text type and genre

Sentences which are joined together to produce a longer discourse are connected so that the resulting text as a whole makes sense to the recipient, its global meaning being more than the sum of the meanings of its component sentences. But how big are the chunks of language which fall within the purview of discourse analysis? What units of language can be distinguished above the level of sentence? In the written language we can recognise units such as paragraphs, chapters, newspaper articles, poems, novels, etc. In the spoken language we can distinguish monologues of various types (e.g. lectures, sermons) and different sorts of dialogue. We will look at the structure of conversations more closely later on. The chief point to be made here is that each of the different text types which can be distinguished follows certain patterns of linguistic organisation which distinguish them from the others, the recognition of which forms an important part of our communicative competence.

When we produce an extended piece of writing, we do not enjoy unfettered freedom to write what we like, how we like. Setting aside consideration of the *content* of what we write, we are also restricted by conventional expectations born of the *genre* or *text type* of the piece which we are producing. The genre of our piece obliges us to follow a particular overall structure, and imposes on us certain lexical and syntactic choices at strategic places in the text. Thus a fairy-story will normally begin with *Il était une fois* ..., a formal letter will normally end with *Veuillez croire, Cher Monsieur, en l'expression de mes sentiments les plus distingués* ..., and so on. An exercise at the end of this chapter contains a number of texts belonging to different genres. Attempt to identify the formal characteristics which enable you to give them a text type label (e.g. 'bus-ticket', 'personal column advertisement'), without relying too heavily on the 'meaning' of the texts in question. Clearly, this sort of activity comes close to much of what goes on in literary stylistics, investigating an author's particular use of language.

Let us now focus on how language users connect the sentences they produce to form stretches of French which hang together as texts, i.e. discourse which is both *cohesive* and *coherent*.

10.1.2   Cohesion

The smaller, sentential units making up a stretch of discourse are linked together in various ways to give the text a degree of surface 'cohesion'. This is achieved through the use of a series of devices, in particular *connectives*, *anaphora* and *cataphora*.

Connectives include co-ordinating conjunctions such as *et* and *mais*, adverbs such as *cependant, pourtant* and *ensuite*, and subordinating conjunctions such as *avant que, de sorte que*. They express a wide range of relationships between the constituent units of a discourse. In Table 10.1 the vertical columns indicate the sorts of relationship which are made between ideas brought together in a text and the various connectives used to express these relationships. The horizontal divisions express different levels of complexity in the expression of these relationships – level one consisting of simple co-ordinating conjunctions and adverbs, level two consisting of more elaborate adverbial connectors and level three involving subordination and embedding.

Table 10.1 Linking devices in French

	List	Temporal sequence	Logical sequence	Contrast of ideas
I	et	puis	donc	mais
	ou	alors	car	
	aussi	maintenant	ainsi	
II	également	d'abord	aussi	par contre
	en outre	ensuite	(+ inversion)	pourtant
	d'ailleurs	autrefois	c'est pourquoi	en revanche
	de même	de nos jours		
	etc.	etc.	etc.	etc.
III	qui/que	avant que	puisque	alors que
	lequel	pendant que	de sorte que	bien que
	de même que	dès que	attendu que	même si
	etc.	etc.	etc.	etc.

Discourse deictics refer to a previous part of a discourse, to an earlier utterance as in (1) or to a previous part of the current utterance, as in (2).

(1)   cela *me fait rire*

(2)   *c'est un avare, mais* ceci *dit il a un bon cœur*

Anaphora involves a reference to a previously occurring noun, as in:

(3)   *Pierre habite au rez de chaussée.* Sa *mère vient de la Guadeloupe.*

or to a previously occurring nominal group, as in (4):

(4)   *passe-moi le livre rouge écrit par Régine Déforges qui est là-bas sur l'étagère à côté de la fenêtre, je* le *trouve vachement intéressant*

Cataphora involves a reference to a following noun or nominal group:

(5)   son *sac à main* à Solange *est en dessous de son manteau*

(6)   sa *mère* à Florent *est venue nous inviter*

Cataphoric reference is particularly common in spoken French.

References backwards and forwards within a text, written or spoken, are closely related to the notions of *topicalisation* and *focusing* (ideas we have already referred to in the previous chapter in connection with the terms *theme* and *rheme*). The *topic* of an utterance is that element which the speaker assumes the hearer knows already, whereas the *focus* (or *comment*) of an utterance is the new information the speaker wishes to get across. If the speaker is not sure whether the hearer knows precisely what he is about to refer to as topic, he will have to topicalise. If he is satisfied on this score, he is then free to highlight if necessary the particular bit of new information which he wishes to focus on, using various focusing devices.

In English we make ample use of stress for these purposes. Imagine a conversation between a man and wife concerning their relationship with one another. He might utter the words 'I love you' at some point during the conversation, but the utterance will have very different meanings depending on which word receives the stress. French cannot use word-stress in this way and has to resort to syntactic devices for topicalisation and focusing.

In a normal unmarked sentence the grammatical subject tends also to be the topic, with all or part of the rest of the sentence providing the comment. Consider, for instance, the sentence **Le chien** *a mordu le facteur*, where the hearer is assumed to have prior knowledge about the existence of the dog. However, in order to be sure that the hearer hooks the message on to the right part of what he knows already, the speaker may feel the need to draw attention to it, as in the sentence **Le chien**, *il a mordu le facteur*. Grammatical objects can also provide the topic, and they can be topicalised in a similar way, as in the sentence **Sylvie**, *je ne l'ai pas vue de la journée*. Structures such as these, where the noun is recapitulated by its pronoun, are referred to as 'dislocated structures'. They are particularly common in spoken French.

In a similar way, French has to have recourse to syntactic devices if it wishes to highlight the *focus* (or comment) of a sentence. In the case of the dog and the postman, if the speaker wished to focus on the fact that the postman was bitten, he could put the sentence into the passive (*Le facteur* a été mordu *par le chien*). Alternatively he could use a variety of 'clefting devices' like *c'est ... que ...* and *ce qui ... c'est ...*, as in **C'est le facteur qui** *a été mordu par le chien*.

10.1.3   Coherence

The units making up a stretch of discourse are not only interlinked by cohesive devices, but they are arranged together to make sense. That is, they are organised to produce a coherent argument, narrative, description, etc. We order the components of our discourse, both the language and the message we want to convey, according to some sort of logic which draws on our expectations of how the world and how language are organised. We go on to finish our discourse and identify the concluding parts clearly so that our text (whatever its purpose) reaches a satisfying end.

As readers or listeners approaching any written or spoken text, we make a prior assumption that it is coherent, and we make every effort to make sense of the seemingly most incoherent piece of discourse (see Chapter 9, pp. 163–65) e.g.:

> (7)   *Ing. H., 38 a., dyn., bne prés., ch. poste comm., contact client., sit. act., déplac. évent. France, étr. Ecr. 1.670 "Le Monde" Publ.*

On what does the reader base their interpretation of the writer's intended meaning? What is the process of comprehension? We strive to recognise the regularities of discourse structure present in the text. We bring to bear on the text the whole of our resources of sociocultural knowledge. We supply any links missing from the text by making the inferences we consider necessary. The net result is as Yule (1985: 112) says: 'Our understanding of what we read does not directly come from what words and sentences are on the page, but from the interpretation we create, in our minds, of what we read.'

10.2   Conversation analysis

For most of us, by far the most common speech event we are involved in is everyday conversation. Much of what we do in our personal, social and, indeed, our working lives is achieved through ordinary conversation. It is through such talk that we build and maintain our social identities and our relationships with others. And in our conversations we carry out many of the tasks we need to perform in order to maintain our peaceful co-existence in the society in which we live. We socialise our children by means of talk, so that they in turn are equipped to function within our speech community. In order to interact more effectively in French, then, we can see that it would be very useful for us to consider how conversations are put together in closer detail.

Everyday conversation is all too easily dismissed by lay-persons as insignificant chit-chat, or (as the French might say) *de la parlotte*. Conversation is usually spontaneous, and to the lay-person it probably appears that there is little pattern or organisation behind the various contributions. Without ever having been explicitly taught, we all seem to know who can say what, and when and where we can say it. We can, and very often do, converse with complete strangers as well as with people we know, with no prior idea of what we will be discussing, and yet we do not often come away from an encounter (in our own language at any rate) feeling that we could not understand what went on, or that we could not make the contributions that we would have liked to make. Any problems or misunderstandings are usually dealt with so effectively during the course of interaction, that the 'repair work' carried out by participants passes off unnoticed. However, none of this should lull us into the belief that conversations happen purely randomly and that there are no principles underpinning their organisation.

From the point of view of the learner of a foreign language conversation is exceptionally important: as learners of French we feel we must develop the ability to effectively maintain a conversation with native-speakers. Undergraduates following degree courses in French usually set great store by the 'conversation classes' run by the *lecteurs*. From the linguist's viewpoint too, conversation is a rich and exciting area of investigation. The study of conversation is pertinent to several academic disciplines outside linguistics, implying that we can approach the subject from a number of different theoretical viewpoints, depending on the particular aspects of conversation we wish to focus on. In this section, we will draw insights from the fields of anthropology and sociology for they have contributed very significantly to linguists' understanding of how conversations work. In the first part of what follows we will examine speech events, and the general issues of who can say what, when and how. We will then consider the basic ways in which conversations are structured, closing with a discussion of how participants in a conversation position themselves *vis à vis* one another.

10.2.1   Speech situations, speech events, speech acts

As linguists attempt to analyse the phenomenon of speech, they commonly make a distinction between 'speech situations', 'speech events' and 'speech acts'. Speech situations are social occasions which provide the context for speech events. Thus, a *repas* or a *cours de linguistique* are 'situations' which provide the context for particular 'events', such as a conversation, a more formal after-dinner speech or the exchanges during the course of the question-and-answer session at the end of a lecture. Speech events can, in turn, be broken down into their constituent speech acts (see Chapter 9, 9.2.3). So, to illustrate, at a *soirée* (the speech situation), a conversational exchange between two guests (the speech event) can comprise greetings, making offers, accepting offers, and so on (speech acts).

Our knowledge of language and of the way in which it has to be adapted to handle particular speech situations forms a major part of our cultural knowledge: 'discourse (and language in general) is a part of culture: because culture is a framework for acting, believing, and understanding, culture is the framework in which communication (and the use of utterances) becomes meaningful' (Schiffrin 1994: 408). This does not mean that all those from a particular culture share exactly the same cultural knowledge. There are large areas of overlap, but our individual cultural knowledge is to an extent personal to us and not the equivalent to a complete member's guide or handbook. Such knowledge depends, in part at least, on our personal experience of specific features of our environment, on our education, and on our individual make-up (e.g. our ability to use language, or our capacity to learn and adapt to new circumstances).

As our cultural knowledge of the target speech community increases, we become progressively more alert to what sort of linguistic feature belong to particular speech situations. In this way most French speakers could identify the utterances in (8) as forming part of a religious service:

(8)   A: *que la paix du seigneur soit toujours avec vous*
       B: *et avec votre esprit*

They would recognise lexical items such as *paix*, *seigneur* and *esprit*, together with structures such as *que* + subjunctive as items which frequently occur in religious discourse.

Equipped with cultural knowledge of this sort, we build our expectations of how we should act in different speech situations, and how we expect others to act. When we use language in a different cultural context, some of our expectations and our subsequent reactions which are based on these expectations will not match the expectations of native-speakers in those speech situations. But when we come to understand that our expectations of interaction have a cultural perspective, we are better placed to understand how language is used in interaction in both our own and any other culture we encounter.

Who may say what, when and how are determined to an extent by the respective *roles* played by the participants in the speech event. In more formal situations the nature of the various contributions is rigidly fixed according to the role of the participants. Thus, the *prêtre* produces certain prescribed utterances during a religious service, which he is not permitted to modify and which cannot be produced by any other participant (i.e. a member of the congregation). In the same way, it is up to a lecturer to deliver a lecture, and it is not acceptable for a student to assume that role and deliver a lecture himself, unless specifically invited to do so. In less formal situations who may say what, when and how is much less rigidly fixed.

Predetermined contributions to more formal speech situations may have been written down beforehand, as is indeed the case for religious services, and for many lectures. They highlight the differences between *planned* and *unplanned* discourse. When the utterances produced have been planned, the resulting talk tends to be characterised by linguistic features normally associated more with writing than with everyday speech. That is, planned utterances tend to be made up of more complex syntactic constructions than those typically used in spontaneous conversation. There is less reliance on either the contextual features of the event, such as gesture, gaze or other aspects of behaviour, or on inference work by participants at the event. This means that the messages conveyed by the talk and the links between the different contributions making up the event tend to be much more explicit than they have to be in everyday conversation. The vocabulary used in such situations tends to be formal rather than familiar.

Ethnographers of communication (see Saville-Troike 1982) are interested above all in interaction in the most formal or the most exotic speech situations, such as disputations in law courts. But it has been shown that the talk in even the most formal of these settings shows organisational features that are based upon those which help us structure our contributions in ordinary conversation. So it is to the structure of mundane, everyday conversation that we will turn our attention.

10.2.2   *The structure of conversations*

We noted earlier that meaning is something which is jointly negotiated by those taking part in an exchange. In this section, we will see that conversations are jointly constructed by conversational partners along guidelines provided by our shared expectations. This is not to say that we cannot go against conventional expectations when we talk. What it means is more that, if we do make a contribution to a conversation which flouts the expectations of our conversation partners, our behaviour in doing so becomes noticeable and *accountable*. And we are accountable, not to the academic analyst examining the encounter, but to our conversation partners, who can call on us to explain our anomalous behaviour and justify our actions. They may even sanction us in some way for our behaviour.

So, for example, in France it is customary to greet anyone you meet for the first time that day. This applies in most situations, regardless of the level of intimacy between the participants of an encounter. You are expected to greet the strangers you meet in the *boulangerie*, as well as your colleagues when you arrive at work in the morning. These greetings usually take the form of a *Bonjour Messieurs–Dames* addressed to the queue in the *boulangerie*, and a *Bonjour Monsieur (Madame)* addressed to each individual colleague, often accompanied with a handshake. They pass almost unnoticed, they are expected, acknowledged but never usually commented on. On the other hand, if someone arrives without making the expected greeting, the missed greeting is not only noticeable by its absence, it is likely to be commented on, and it will require some kind of explanation, if the person who failed to make it is not to be considered rude, bad-tempered or even antisocial.

TURN-TAKING

We noted in our discussion of the notion of context (see Chapter 9, 9.1.2) that talk in conversation is sequentially organised. The sequential nature of conversation means that the interaction unfolds as contributions are added by participants. We can therefore see what an utterance is doing by the place it occupies in the conversation. In order to illustrate the significance of this sequential organisation, look at the dialogue in (9).

(9) Céline: *ça va?*
Françoise: *ça va*

If you read the dialogue aloud, you will most probably produce Céline's utterance with the rising intonation pattern which typically accompanies a question (see Chapter 6, p. 110). Françoise's utterance, on the other hand, will probably have the falling intonation characteristic of a declarative statement. Although the two utterances have an almost identical form, they can nevertheless be easily distinguished by their position in the exchange: the first utterance forms the context for the second, which is shaped accordingly.

One feature of conversation that is so obvious that we could easily overlook its significance is the fact that conversation is made up of turns by different people. One speaker usually talks at a time, and when that speaker stops talking, another speaker begins talking, often almost immediately the first speaker has stopped talking. Taking turns is fundamental to so many of our activities, a common way of sharing out resources or ensuring access to as many people as possible. Even before they can talk, we teach young babies to take turns in games such as *cou-cou* in French, or *peek-a-boo* in English. In conversation, the resource we take turns in having access to is termed the *floor*. When we are the person doing the talking in a conversation, we are the speaker who is currently 'holding the floor'.

Among the participants at an encounter, we can distinguish between those who are potential next speakers and those who are not entitled to hold the floor, the overhearing audience. The overhearing audience may be ratified participants in the encounter, as in the case of business negotiations conducted by the Managing Director with the Financial Director hovering alongside, or unratified participants, as in the case of someone sitting behind conversation partners in a *café*. Although we tend to think of talk being produced for listeners who are potential next speakers, there are special speech situations in which the talk is produced for the benefit of the overhearing audience, as in television interviews.

We noted that, for most of the time in conversation, only one speaker holds the floor. Another person speaking at the same time runs the risk of being seen as interrupting. Although simultaneous talk can be acceptable, it may be perceived as interruptive behaviour by co-conversationalists. Interruptive behaviour may be considered to be disruptive or even aggressive. Interruptions can therefore be sanctioned, and those who persistently interrupt their conversation partners may be judged to be poor conversation partners. What constitutes an acceptable level of overlapping talk seems to vary between speech communities. So what seems to an upper-class British English speaker to be a rather interruptive and therefore aggressive conversation style may be perfectly normal talk for a family meal in the south of

France. Conversely, what appears to our upper-class British English speaker to be normal turn-taking behaviour may seem to represent a reluctance to participate, showing a certain *froideur* to southern French interlocutors. Of course, we must be careful not to overgeneralise as there are many distinct French- or English-speaking communities with their own normalised expectations. Thus, overlapping speech may be acceptable to English speakers in New York but not to French speakers in Strasbourg. And equally, expectations vary according to other contextual aspects of the talk. So, the amount of overlapping talk acceptable during a formal dinner is not the same as that which is acceptable at a student gathering in a bar.

When we look at transcriptions of conversation, we find certain kinds of turns which regularly overlap the talk of the speaker holding the floor without causing any sanctions or even any apparent disturbance to the conversation. Among these turns we find contributions which are placed during long turns by one speaker, at points when another could possibly take the floor. These turns very seldom convey any specific lexical meaning but signal that the participant is happy for the person currently speaking to carry on holding the floor. Such turns are more supportive than interruptive, contributing to the joint construction of a successful exchange. The particles occurring in this role are known as *continuers*. *Mm hmm* and *uh huh* are common continuers in English, while in French *ouais* and even *d'accord* are often used for this purpose.

If the incidence of overlapping talk may indicate that an exchange is unsuccessful, the same is also true for excessive pauses without talk. Once again, we must be wary of overgeneralising, as the contextual features of the exchange contribute to determining what is an acceptable length for pauses between turns. Some periods of silence or lapses of conversation would be expected during a long train journey, from Paris to Bordeaux, for instance. Indeed, a conversation partner who talked non-stop for the whole journey could be rather tedious. It is equally perfectly acceptable for close friends and families to spend entire evenings in silence together. Nevertheless, during the course of conversations, silences of more than one second tend to be avoided.

Transcriptions of conversation show that little of the talk overlaps and there are few silent pauses between turns. But how do we manage to co-ordinate our turn-taking without overlapping our talk or leaving the sort of pauses which make the conversation stilted and awkward? Sacks, Schegloff and Jefferson (1974) proposed a mechanism by which turn-taking is organised, based on their findings from data recorded from naturally occurring conversation. They found that conversation partners tend not to interrupt each other in mid-utterance. Furthermore, changes in speaker tend to occur at the end of a 'turn construction unit', which consists of syntactic structures such as phrases or clauses. They called these end points *transition relevance places*, which is usually shortened to TRP. TRPs are easy for native-speakers to anticipate for they can usually predict the completion of a syntactic unit, even though they do not yet know exactly what their conversation partner is going to say. Turn construction units are also often linked by supra-segmental intonation patterns (see Chapter 6).

That participants recognise TRPs is shown by the way in which speakers often start speaking together. In most cases, when more than one speaker starts speaking simultaneously, one speaker very quickly takes control of the floor while the others drop out, often until the next TRP. But there are occasions when speakers compete more strongly for the floor. They increase the volume at which they speak, syllable by syllable, until one succeeds in dominating the others. The speaker who gains the floor may recycle the beginning of the turn, or may carry straight on with the turn construction unit underway.

The next speaker may self-select, as shown above, or they may be chosen by the person currently holding the floor. The easiest way of selecting the next speaker is to name them directly, as shown in (10) and (11):

(10)   *t'as eu des nouvelles de ta famille* Jérémie?

(11)   *qu'est-ce que vous en pensez* Monsieur le directeur?

Once the current speaker has selected someone else to speak, they must stop talking at the next TRP so that the person who has been chosen may take the floor.

If the conversation is to be successful, the other participants also have to pay attention to what the speaker is saying so that they know when they should take the floor, or when it is acceptable for them to do so. But because participants are accountable for their actions in the course of their inter-action, they have a vested interest in listening to the turn of the current speaker, in case they are selected as next speaker. To be selected and not to take the floor at the next TRP would be noticeable to all those participating in the conversation.

ADJACENCY PAIRS

We very often expect certain utterances to follow each other in a sequence of talk. In our dialogue in 10.2.2 above, the greeting *ça va* was followed by a second part. We expect an answer in response to a question, an acceptance or even a refusal in response to an invitation. This form of sequential organ-isation is very common in everyday conversation. Paired utterances such as greeting/greeting or question/answer sequences are known as *adjacency pairs*. Once a current speaker has produced the first part of an adjacency pair, that speaker stops speaking at the next TRP, for the next speaker to provide the second part of the pair.

The first part and the second part of the adjacency pair may be made up of the same kind of utterance, as is the case for exchanges of greetings, well-wishing or even insults. The first part may alternatively be followed by some other kind of utterance such as some form of acceptance or refusal, follow-ing an offer, invitation or compliment, for example. The expectation that a second part will follow the first part of an adjacency pair is so strong that any utterance produced by the next speaker will be considered as a second part, regardless of what the particular utterance consists of. And a speaker who withholds the second part to an adjacency pair is at risk of having to account for or being sanctioned for the action.

Certain second parts to utterances such as requests, offers and invitations which will typically require some form of action or undertaking on the part of the addressee can be followed by one of several second parts. Analysts have found that some of these second parts are produced immediately following the first part. This is the case when the addressee accepts the action or undertaking set out in the first part of the pair. These acceptance-type utterances are termed *preferred* second parts. Second parts in which the proposal of the first part of the pair are not accepted are *dispreferred* responses. The latter are generally marked by some form of hesitation or pause before the speaker begins, and may even be prefaced by an account to justify the following negative response.

Adjacency pairs often occur in sequences. So, for example, an invitation to a *soirée* is commonly preceded by a question, *qu'est-ce que tu fais ce soir?* This question prefaces the following invitation, giving the participants the chance to jointly construct the following exchange to their mutual satisfaction. Indeed, if the person invited shows any hesitation before responding to an invitation, this is seen as preceding a dispreferred response, and the speaker making the invitation will often take the floor again to modify the original invitation.

But why do we go to all the bother of producing extended sequences of turns to avoid producing dispreferred responses to the first part of an adjacency pair? In the next section, we will consider one theory as to why conversationalists are prepared to make such efforts to ensure that all parties are satisfied by their interaction.

10.2.3   *Positioning ourselves* vis à vis *our addressee*

A major element in all our conversational interactions is our concern for the listener's reaction to what we are saying. We design our talk to suit our audience (a) with respect to their state of knowledge ('topicalisation') and (b) with respect to the sort of relationship we wish to have with them. Here we are concerned with the latter, and it is possible to characterise our relationships with our co-conversationalists in terms of *proximity* and *distance*. We will look at how this works in French by glancing firstly at address forms (*tu* versus *vous*) and then at politeness theory.

ADDRESS FORMS

In French, as in a wide range of languages, the nature of the relationship between speakers is signalled by pronouns of address, see Table 10.2.

Table 10.2 Pronouns of address in European languages

	Proximity		Distance	
French	*tu*	(T)	*vous*	(V)
Spanish	*tu*	[+ vosotros]	*usted*	[+ ustedes]
Italian	*tu*	[+ voi]	*lei*	[+ Loro]
German	*du*	[+ lhr]	*Sie*	

In French the plural form *vous* is used with singular reference to express distance, whereas *tu* expresses proximity. Standard English has lost this distinction, so that English speakers of French do not select the appropriate T – V form in an effortless way. Moreover, the languages we have just quoted which observe the distinction do not all apply it in an identical way. However, Brown and Gilman (1971) studied this phenomenon across several languages and established two general principles (or 'semantics') which appear to underpin most usages:

- the semantic of *power* (expressed by non-reciprocal use of T – V);
- the semantic of *solidarity* (expressed by reciprocal use of T – V).

Over the past century usage in French seems to have shifted. In earlier times non-reciprocal uses were much more common than today (a speaker gives T and receives V, or vice versa), symbolising unequal power relationships. Nowadays reciprocal uses seem to dominate (a speaker gives and receives T, or V as the case may be). The semantic of power has given way to the semantic of solidarity.

POLITENESS

In English we talk about *saving face*. This notion of face was first given a technical sense by the sociologist Erving Goffman (1963), and has subsequently been adapted by Brown and Levinson (1987), as a central notion in their theory accounting for language usage. All full, adult members of a society have a public self-image, their 'face'. 'Face' in this sense is not permanent like a physical characteristic, it is something that we have to maintain in the course of our dealings with each other, and equally important, something we expect those we come in contact with to respect. And, indeed, they have a vested interest in doing so because they also have their own face to maintain, which they expect us, in turn, to respect.

Brown and Levinson divide face into two distinct varieties which they term *negative face* and *positive face*. Negative face is people's need to be unimpeded in what they do. When we use polite formulae such as those in (12) and (13), we are attending to the negative face needs of our interlocutor, by trying to avoid or at least minimise the imposition we are making on them:

(12)   *excusez-moi de vous déranger, mais est-ce que je peux vous demander l'heure, s'il vous plaît*

(13)   *veuillez prendre rendez-vous pour en parler avec mon secrétaire*

Positive face is people's need for approval, their desire for at least some of their wants to be shared by others, their wish to be treated by others as a friend and confidant. And we can all recognise that we want to be understood, accepted, respected and even liked, and that we would like this appreciation to be reflected in our encounters.

(14)   *tu as bien travaillé*

(15)   *tu es mignonne*

The utterances in (14) and (15) attend to the positive face needs of the person to whom they are addressed.

There is a distinct cautionary note to add, however. Let us take the case of (14). If you have gone for a drink after lectures with an attractive classmate, this may not be the utterance you would hope to hear, to satisfy your positive face wants. Equally, if (15) is uttered by a lecturer presented with a piece of work you have laboured over and are particularly proud of, you could be justified in being less than satisfied. Furthermore, given that face wants are common to us all, the lecturer concerned should be aware of your expectation of some form of positive face work following your endeavours. The withholding of the appropriate face work can therefore trigger any number of inferences, either intentionally or unintentionally. We can therefore conclude that we only expect certain people to attend to certain aspects of our positive face. We also expect people to know which aspects of our positive face they are entitled to attend to and which aspects it would be inappropriate or even totally unacceptable for them to attend to.

When we attend to the positive face wants of someone, we are putting our own face at risk by visibly assuming that we are among those people entitled to attend to that particular face need. Often in encounters, it is preferable not to risk our face, so we tend to stick to more neutral, safer contributions, such as *parler de la pluie et du beau temps*. Moreover, we do not always attend to face wants. If, for example, an eminent professor of French was just about to step out in front of a passing vehicle, we would be unlikely to preface our utterance with any attention to negative face, such as *excusez-moi Monsieur le Professeur* or *veuillez me permettre de vous prévenir ...*, the sort of formulae we would normally use to preface any imposition on the negative face wants of someone of such high status. We wouldn't hesitate to yell *arrête* in a tone of voice we would not usually use to the professor. In this context, the need to convey the danger of the passing vehicle outweighs the need to attend to the face wants of the addressee.

FACE THREATENING ACTS

Very often we produce utterances which upset either the positive face or the negative face of ourselves or of our interlocutor. An example would be asking someone to lend you 100F. Such an action would be termed a *face threatening act* by Brown and Levinson. The degree of threat involved in any face threatening act depends on a number of contextual features of the utterance. For instance, the *relative power* of the participants of the exchange over each other is clearly significant. It is much easier to ask to borrow 100F from a fellow student for Friday night's festivities than it is to ask one's parents, let alone the bank manager, for the same amount. This is because parents, and especially bank managers, are in a position of power relative to your own. Similarly, we can distinguish between participants in terms of *social distance*. It is easier to make the request of a classmate with whom you have already established a reciprocal arrangement for weekend outings, than it is to ask someone who just sits next to you occasionally. We must also consider how society *ranks* the seriousness of the particular face threatening act. Asking for the loan of 10 000F would constitute a greater threat to face than our request for 100F. We can therefore determine the degree of threat involved in terms of the relative power and social distance of the participants, and the rank of the particular act.

According to the degree of threat to face, we can select from a number of strategies which can be used to carry out face threatening acts, requiring varied amounts of work and producing a variety of payoffs. To consider these strategies, it may be useful to have a particular face threatening act in mind. Think of a student who has not completed the work due for submission that day. The student would like to ask to submit the work the following week. If the student asks to hand in the work late they are performing an act which potentially threatens the positive and the negative faces of both the lecturer and the student. The student's request could threaten the lecturer's negative face by impeding the lecturer's marking schedule or messing up arrangements for the return of the work in the following class. It could threaten the lecturer's positive face because the set work is something that the lecturer considers useful and interesting, a view he would like to be shared by the students. The student's positive face could be threatened by the resulting disapproval from the lecturer, their negative face would be threatened if the request were not to be granted.

The student's first choice is whether to actually make the request or not. Deciding against carrying out the face threatening act and saying nothing has the payoff that there is no threat to the lecturer's face at all, but the student cannot get the necessary consent, which puts their own face at risk.

The student can make the request indirectly, off record. We saw earlier that we carry out a great deal of our speech acts in an indirect rather than a direct manner. To understand this point, let us look again at examples we considered earlier:

(16)   *qu'il fait froid ici*

(17)   *tu trouves pas qu'il fait froid ici*

(18)   *ferme la fenêtre*

We saw in Chapter 9 how the first two utterances in (16) and (17) above, if pronounced in a certain context, would be responded to in the same way as the utterance in (18). So why do we go to all the trouble of producing indirect utterances like (16) and (17) that carry implicatures (i.e. shut the window), which we have to hope that our conversation partners will be prepared to puzzle out? Why not simply produce direct utterances like (18) which appear to be more efficient for communicating our meaning? Why be so *indirect* about things? The answer probably lies in *politeness theory* and the saving of face.

The student's request to submit the work late could be made indirectly in the following way:

(19)   *les dates limites sont tellement frustrantes quand on a tant de matériel à exploiter et tant de choses à dire*

The payoff of such indirect strategies is that the student can deny their intention to convey the request if the lecturer retorts *mais est-ce que ça veut dire que tu n'as pas encore fini ton travail?* and there is little threat to the lecturer's negative face. But there is equally no guarantee that the request will be acknowledged let alone granted.

The student may prefer to be more direct and make the face threatening act on record. And although this is more obviously damaging, the student can attempt to limit the damage by taking *redressive action*. Redressive action involves attending to either the positive or the negative face of the addressee by means of positive or negative *politeness strategies*.

If the student opts to use negative politeness strategies, they would typically use some form of self-effacement or restraint in their utterance, or a higher degree of formality than might otherwise be expected, as in (20) or (21):

(20)   *je suis désolé d'avoir à vous ennuyer avec mes problèmes*

(21)   *veuillez excuser mon retard mais je ne me suis pas organisé comme il aurait fallu*

Such negative politeness strategies have the payoff of limiting the threat to the lecturer's negative face.

On the other hand, the student might feel confident of their position to attend to the positive face wants of the lecturer, with positive politeness strategies, such as appealing to something common to both parties, or even making a joke about the request, as illustrated in (22) and (23). Positive politeness strategies involve a certain degree of risk to the student, because they imply that the student is among those entitled to attend to that particular aspect of the lecturer's positive face wants.

(22)   *tu comprends la pression sous laquelle j'ai à travailler*

(23)   *tiens, tu peux avoir un weekend tranquille sans ma copie*

The student also has the option to ask the lecturer straight out, without applying any strategies at all, that is baldly, without redress. This is probably the most effective way of making an unambiguous request. There may also be some payoff in terms of appreciation for directness or *franc-parler* but the damage to face is most significant, and the student must be sure that they can afford to be as blunt as shown in (24):

(24)   *je vais vous rendre mon travail la semaine prochaine*

The fact that we have our face to maintain is common to us all, regardless of the society we live in or the culture we are part of. What differs between when we use English in an English speech community or French in a French speech community is how we go about the task of maintaining our face, and how we expect others to attend to our face. You may feel, for instance, that many of the polite formulae which are used in letter-writing in French are particularly stilted, even pompous, when compared to those used in English letter-writing (see Adamson *et al.* 1986: 210–20). But expressions such as that in (25) are commonly used in official correspondence to minimise the imposition of a following request.

(25)   *J'ai l'honneur de solliciter de votre haute bienveillance de . . .*

In order to minimise our imposition on the recipient we normally accentuate the social distance between us, and in some cases this can seem almost like obsequiousness. To a French reader, an official letter without such formal expressions would appear particularly inappropriate, even rude or offensive. The conventions governing 'negative' politeness in French and English are quite similar, but they do not overlap completely.

POLITENESS AND SLANG

You may have noted that what is here being discussed under the heading of 'negative politeness' is conventionally regarded simply as 'polite' behaviour. Many of the conventionally polite formulae we use in both spoken and written language attend to the negative face of the person to whom the language is addressed. However, Brown and Levinson (1987) also apply the term 'politeness' to situations in which we attend to the positive face of our interlocutor, i.e. 'positive politeness'. With many of our interlocutors (e.g. our family, friends, peer-group) we want to play down any distance between us and cultivate feelings of friendliness, equality, in-group membership. Use of expressions that emphasise power or distance (negative politeness) with people such as these would be just as inappropriate or 'impolite' as failure to use them with an important stranger.

It is not just in withholding negative politeness formulae that we express closeness and solidarity in French. We could argue that the whole range of informal vocabulary items in French which we discussed in Chapter 2 exists primarily to express positive politeness. We noted there that French speakers have a very wide choice between words associated with a more informal style and synonyms which are used in more formal settings (see Chapter 2, 2.1.2, 2.2.2). Examples abound of such pairs as *bagnole ~ voiture, fric ~ argent, type ~ homme*. Attempts are often made to associate the former with lower-class speakers and the latter with upper-class. Indeed, French dictionaries frequently give such words the label *pop(ulaire)* (= 'working class'). Such stratification of the lexicon along social lines has little basis in the observed linguistic behaviour of French speakers. Upper-class speakers appear to be quite happy to use *pop.*-labelled items. The difference between the members of these pairs lies not in 'meaning' nor in the social class of the speakers, but in the pragmatic function they are called upon to carry out: the essential value of informal vocabulary and slang to native-speakers of the language lies in listener-oriented utterances and the communication of proximity, solidarity, in-group membership (i.e. positive politeness).

It is for this reason that foreign learners of French should be wary of using slang vocabulary too early in a relationship with a French person or group. Use of positive politeness formulae, presuming in-group member-ship, by a foreigner (who is by definition a non-member of the group), can easily be construed as intrusiveness. It is only when you are confident that you have been fully admitted to the group that you can have recourse to slang without fear of being 'called to account'. Conversely, it is quite normal for groups in society to cultivate slang vocabulary with the express intention of excluding outsiders. One of the most interesting characteristics of slang is its capacity to generate an endless sequence of synonyms (see Guiraud 1973: 56–59). A clear example of this is the use of *verlan* which we discussed earlier (see Chapter 9, p. 159). The rapid turnover of slang words in certain social groups (especially teenagers) can be linked, on the one hand, to the desire to keep one step ahead of the uninitiated (slang words can become known to non-members of the group), and, on the other hand, to competition among group-members to demonstrate their centrality within the group by their mastery of the lexical code.

Conclusion

In this chapter we have seen how we use our cultural knowledge to produce appropriate talk in speech situations. Our communicative competence in French is made up not only of our knowledge of the abstract phonological, lexical and grammatical systems of French, but also of the knowledge about how we use language in specific speech events. Although it is important to understand how talk is organised in both formal and informal speech situ-ations in French, one of the most common speech events we will no doubt encounter is everyday French conversation. We have seen how participants jointly construct conversation by taking turns to speak, and how they co-operate to maintain each other's public image, or face. These last two chapters have demonstrated that there is a good deal more to understanding the way a language like French works than considering the meaning of words (lexical semantics) and the ways in which they are strung together in sentences (syntax).

Seminar exercises

1.   What are the formal characteristics of each of the following texts which enable you to allot them to a particular text type?

(a)   Remettre au receveur le nombre de tickets indiqué par l'affiche 'TARIFS' apposée dans les voitures. Le compostage constituera la preuve du paiement et rendra ces tickets valables pour le parcours à effectuer. Ils devront être présentés à toute réquisition des agents du Réseau Routier.

(b)   Attendu que le droit à une quotité de succession implique l'obligation de supporter une quotité proportionnelle des dettes et charges; que ce droit et cette obligation sont des conséquences de tout titre successif universel; qu'il n'y a point à distinguer sous ce rapport entre les successeurs à titre qui sont institués par la loi et ceux qui sont institués par la volonté de l'homme; qu'il n'y a pas à distinguer davantage soit entre le légataire universel, qui se trouvant en concours avec un héritier à reserve, est tenu de demander la délivrance, et le légataire universel, qui, ne concourant point avec un héritier légitime, est saisi de plein droit de la succession, soit même entre le légataire universel et le légataire à titre universel; que ces divers légataires sont, comme les héritiers eux-mêmes, de véritables successeurs à titre universel, ayant les mêmes droits, sujets aux mêmes charges.

(c)   N'attendez pas des mois pour avoir la seule 'Encyclopédie Générale Complète' . . . 35,50 F suffisent.

Oui, dans quelques jours et pour un premier versement de 35,50 F les deux premiers tomes de l'"Encyclopédie Générale Larousse' seront dans votre bibliothèque, à portée de votre main, de vos questions, prête à vous faire connaître tout de la géographie à la philosophie (tome 1) et de la biologie à l'astronomie (tome 2). Dès le mois d'octobre à la parution du dernier volume de l'"Encyclopédie', VOUS posséderez la seule encyclopédie française complète en 68. Vous pourrez enfin feuilleter ses 3 000 pages, regarder ses 5 200 photos, graphiques ou cartes en noir et en couleurs, lire ses nombreux articles signés des plus éminents universitaires. Pour 14 versements de 35,50 F seulement, offrez-vous les trois volumes en couleurs de l'"Encyclopédie Générale Larousse', votre seconde memoire! Hâtez-vous de profiter du prix de faveur actuel de souscription.

2.   Identify the linguistic features used to create 'cohesion' in the following text:

Les textes en présence adoptent un schéma proche d'analyse des problèmes de communication et de culture à notre époque. Ils constatent un état de crise et proposent des solutions. Mais, ils le font de manière sensiblement différente, selon des choix personnalisés.

La crise culturelle est d'abord relationnelle. On admet qu'on ne sait plus se parler authentiquement. Guyard montre que des instruments technologiques comme la CB ou le walkman, tout utiles qu'ils soient pour conjurer l'angoisse vitale, isolent l'individu, le coupent de tout contact vrai avec autrui.

Elle est ensuite institutionnelle. Harris et Onimus relèvent l'échec de la politique culturelle de Malraux au cours des années 60-80. On n'a pas su ouvrir à ces lieux de dialogue et de créativité que sont les Maisons de la culture. On s'est renfermé dans un élitisme frileux.

Pourtant, les mêmes auteurs font état d'une demande en matière de communication. D'énormes besoins sont à satisfaire, mais comment?

Les solutions avancées sont variées mais nullement contradictoires. Harris, pour qui les moyens financiers sont primordiaux, chiffre l'accroissement nécessaire du budget de la culture de 7 à 15%, et Guyard, lui-même, qui privilégie le relationnel, souligne que celui-ci n'est pas sans incidence sur la politique économique. L'un et l'autre disent faire fond sur le nouvel outil télématique pour libérer la communication et la culture, les rendre accessibles à un vaste public.

Mais on propose également des réformes de structure, comme la création de lieux 'naturels' d'échanges, pour Guyard, l'exportation de nos modèles culturels, pour Harris, l'ouverture de l'école sur l'extérieur, la définition d'une charte culturelle avec les communes pour Onimus.

Il s'agirait enfin, comme le suggère ce dernier, d'agir sur la psychologie des gens, en les invitant à ne plus s'isoler, et à rechercher ensemble les moyens d'exprimer leur pleine adhésion à la vie.

3.   Make your own recording of a stretch of French conversation and make a careful transcription of the recording, paying close attention to overlapping talk, pauses and non-verbal sounds such as laughter. See how the talk is organised in comparison with (a) a stretch of written French discourse and (b) a stretch of English conversation.

4.   Analyse the politeness strategies in the letter below. Explain whether you would expect to see the same formulae used in a letter to a French friend and why.

Monsieur,

Notre maison, établie depuis einquante ans commercialise dans une vingtaine de pays des produits de parfumerie et de savons.

Désireux de nous introduire sur le marché vénézuélien, nous vous serons reconnaissants de bien vouloir nous communiquer la liste des sociétés importatrices-distributrices de ces produits dans ce pays. Nous souhaiterions également connaître les marques qu'elles représentent, ainsi que les noms et adresses des sociétés intéressés par cette importation.

Veuillez trouver ci-joint le catalogue de nos articles.

Vous en remerciant par avance, nous vous prions d'agréer, Monsieur, l'expression de nos sentiments distingués.

[Taken from Vivien and Arné 1996: 123]

Glossary of linguistic terms

Terms given in bold in the definitions are defined in a separate entry. This glossary makes ample use of Crystal 1991, to which the reader is referred for fuller explanations.

accountability. In conversation analysis, the principle which states that co-conversationalists are considered to be responsible for their behaviour in interactions.

acoustic phonetics. The branch of **phonetics** which studies the physical characteristics of speech sounds (wavelength etc.) using instrumental techniques. Compare **articulatory phonetics**.

adjacency pair. Paired utterances that form an organisational unit in conversation, consisting of a first and a second part, as in *ça va? – très bien*. The response or second part may be preferred (or **unmarked**) or dispreferred (**marked**).

affrication. A term used in phonetics to refer to a process whereby plosive consonants like [t] and [d] are combined with a fricative element like [ʃ] and [ʒ] to form [tʃ] and [dʒ] respectively, as in English *church* and *judge*.

allomorph. Variant realisation of the same underlying **morpheme**, depending on the context in which it appears.

allophone. A unit of sound which is the concrete realisation of the more abstract **phoneme**. Allophones are pronounced differently according to their phonetic surroundings; thus the French /R/ phoneme, usually represented as a voiced uvular trill, is pronounced as a voiceless uvular fricative following another voiceless consonant, as in *être*: [ɛtʁ]. An **allophonic transcription** is enclosed in square brackets, as in the example given.

allophonic (or 'narrow') transcription. A transcription which incorporates a certain amount of allophonic detail which a **phonemic (or 'broad')** **transcription** would leave out.

alveolar. In the articulation of **consonants**, involving the 'alveolus', or ridge of gum behind the top teeth. The French and English **fricatives** /s/ and /z/ are produced at the alveolus. The term alveolar is one of the **place-of-articulation** criteria used to classify consonants.

anaphora. A grammatical process involving back-reference to a previously occurring **phrase** or **sentence**. Several word **categories** may be used anaphorically, as in *Il le fait ici,* where each word has anaphoric reference. Compare **cataphora.**

antonymy. A term used to denote oppositeness of meaning.

articulator. A part of the **vocal tract** which is involved in the production of speech.

articulatory phonetics. The branch of **phonetics** which studies speech sounds from the point of view of how they are produced or 'articulated' by the **vocal organs.**

assimilation. A term used in **phonetics** to refer to the way some aspect of a **phoneme** is 'copied' by another when they occur in sequence, e.g. in French *médecin* the sequence [ds] (voiced consonant + unvoiced consonant) is often pronounced [ts] (unvoiced conconant + unvoiced consonant).

aspirated. The articulation of a sound accompanied by the exhalation of an audible breath.

back. In the classification of vowels, back vowels are those pronounced with the tongue root retracted to the back of the mouth. Examples are the French vowels in *tout, cône, botte.*

blade. The part of the tongue immediately behind the **tip.** The tongue blade is involved in the production of /t/ and /s/.

borrowed words. A term used in **lexicology** to refer to words which come into the language from another language, e.g. *le weekend* in French.

cataphora. A grammatical process involving reference forward to a subsequent **phrase** or **sentence,** as in for example: *mes remarques sont les suivantes.* Compare **anaphora.**

category. In **syntax, words** and **phrases** are classified as belonging to different categories (or classes). Word categories correspond more or less to the 'parts of speech' of traditional grammar (nouns, verbs, adjectives, etc.). As in traditional grammar, words and phrases are assigned to categories using the tests of **substitution** and **distributional analysis,** but contemporary linguists have created some new categories to replace more traditional ones: see **determiner.**

clause. A unit in **syntax** which is intermediate between **phrase** and **sentence.** Some clauses can function in a syntactically independent way, similarly to sentences, as for example *Marie quitta la maison.* A 'main' clause like this can be supplemented by a dependent or 'subordinate' clause, such as *lorsque le taxi arriva.*

coherence. In **pragmatics** and textual analysis generally, the term coherence refers to the logical character of a stretch of language; a text is coherent if its various 'propositions' or statements are organised in a development which 'makes sense'. Coherence may or may not be explicitly marked using **cohesion** devices.

cohesion. The way in which the different units making up a stretch of language are explicitly linked together using linguistic items, often referred to as **connectors**. Cohesion is important in marking clearly the relation of the different units to each other; relations may be of contrast (marked by *mais, cependant*), continuation (*en plus, d'ailleurs*), etc.

collocation. A term used in **lexicology** to refer to the habitual neighbours of a word, i.e. the words which the word in question habitually occurs with.

communicative competence. Knowledge incorporating both cultural competence and knowledge of the phonological, lexical and grammatical systems of language; speakers need to use both types of knowledge to communicate successfully.

complement. An element of **syntax** which 'complements' or completes the sense of a verb. The complements are in capitals in the following examples: *Je croyais QU'IL ETAIT PARTI; Elle mangeait DES FRITES.* These examples are designed to make clear that without a complement, the sense of the verb is incomplete. Contrast **modifier.**

complementary distribution. The fact of two **allophones** of a **phoneme** occurring in mutually exclusive phonetic contexts. Thus French /l/ is voiceless when a follows a voiceless consonant, as in *siffle,* but voiced elsewhere. Complementary distribution also operates on the level of the **morpheme**: thus in French, the prefix *in* is realised as [in] before vowels (*inadmissible)*, but as [ɛ̃] before consonants (*incroyable).*

connectives. Items whose function is to link linguistic units, such as conjunctions like *et, puisque* and adverbs like *d'ailleurs.*

connotation. This term is used in **semantics** to contrast with the term denotation, referring to different types of meaning. It indicates the emotional associations which are suggested by a word, whereas denotation indicates the relationship between a word and the 'thing' to which it refers.

consonant. A speech sound which is produced with a degree of constriction or narrowing of the **vocal tract.** Compare **vowel.**

constituent. A linguistic unit, a **word, phrase** or **clause,** which combines with other units of the same **category** to make up a **sentence.**

context. The total environment in which language occurs, including the spatial, social and linguistic environment. This latter is sometimes referred to as the **co-text.**

contextualisation cues. Signals which speakers use to understand language by inferring meaning from them. Contextualisation cues are not necessarily communicated intentionally by a speaker. For example, a yawn may convey tiredness or boredom independently of a speaker's intentions. Contrast **implicature.**

continuer. A particle, often non-lexical, such as 'mm' 'hmm', etc, placed in such a way that the person currently holding the **floor** in conversation is encouraged to continue speaking.

conversational maxims. In Grice's theory of language (1957), conversational maxims are general principles which speakers observe in order to ensure efficient communication; these maxims govern the quality, quantity, relevance and manner of what is said. Thus, according to the maxims, speakers should ensure that their contribution is true (quality); speakers should not say more than is required (quantity); speakers should ensure that their contribution is relevant (relevance); and speakers should avoid ambiguity and obscurity (manner). Speakers may of course wish to violate these maxims, for instance when lying, being ironical or playful, etc. Much conversation is apparently obscure and ambiguous because speakers often assume background knowledge in their hearer and imply what they wish to say, rather than stating it explicitly. See also **implicature, inference.**

co-operative principle. The principle proposed by Grice (1957) to account for the fact that speakers when conversing manage to achieve effective communication, despite apparent ambiguity and obscurity. According to this principle speakers co-operate so as to negotiate meaning out of conversation; Grice suggested that to do this, they generally observe four **conversational maxims.**

co-text. In **pragmatics**, the linguistic context with which **utterances** are surrounded. Contrast **context.**

created words. A term used in **etymology** to refer to new words created on the basis of words already present in the language (e.g. by derivation or composition).

cultural knowledge. Our knowledge of how to act in and interpret our environment, shared to some extent with fellow members of our culture but influenced by individual experience and abilities. Cultural knowledge is used in the interpretation of **utterances.**

deictic. 'Deixis' literally means 'pointing' and a deictic is a word or expression which refers to some element in a situation which is determined by the context in which the language is produced; deictics may indicate aspects of person (*moi/toi*), place (*ici/là*), time (*maintenant/alors*). A deictic may also be used to refer forwards or backwards in a **co-text**; see **anaphora** and **cataphora**. Thus deixis is an umbrella term which covers reference both within and outside a stretch of language.

dental. Involving the teeth in the articulation of **consonants**. French /t/ is a dental **plosive**. The term dental is one of the **place-of-articulation** criteria used to classify consonants.

derivational morphology. The morphological process which creates new words by combining **morphemes**, as in *nation + al ⇒ national*.

determiner. A non-traditional **category** of **word** which 'determines' or indicates some **feature** or features of the following word; for instance, the

French determiner *la* indicates number, definiteness and gender in the following noun.

determinism (linguistic). This term expresses the notion that our thought processes are determined to a greater or lesser extent by the structure of our native language.

dialectology. This is the branch of linguistics concerned with the study of dialect. A dialect is normally seen as the form taken by a language in a particular region.

diglossia. A term used in **sociolinguistics** to refer to a situation where two very different language varieties co-occur throughout the speech community, each with a distinct range of social functions.

diphthongs. These are combined vowel sounds, as in English *cow, buy* and *boy*, where the point of articulation of the vowel shifts from one position to another, within the same syllable.

discourse. A term used to refer to a stretch of spoken or written language which is longer than a single grammatical unit.

dispreferred. See **unmarked**.

distributional analysis. A test used in **syntax** to assign a **word** or phrase to its appropriate **category**. Thus we can define the linguistic unit *le garçon* as an noun **phrase** in terms of its distribution; for example, it can occur before a verb phrase (e.g. *partira*), and this is a feature of French **syntax**. See also **substitution**.

elision. The dropping of certain sounds in connected speech, for example *les autres*, frequently pronounced *les aut'*.

ethnography of communication. A theoretical framework which focuses on the study of the **communicative competence** of speakers, using the insights of several disciplines, notably anthropology, sociology and sociolinguistics.

etymology. The branch of linguistics concerned with the origins and history of words.

face. In **pragmatics**, the term face is used similarly to the colloquial sense, as in 'to lose face': the self-esteem and self-image which all competent adult members of a society possess. A distinction is made between negative face, our need to stress our individuality and be unimpeded in our actions, and positive face, our need to belong to a group and for certain of our wants to be appreciated by others. Negative and positive face in turn trigger negative and positive **politeness**.

face threatening acts (FTAs). Acts which potentially fail to attend to the **face** wants or needs of oneself and others: requests, apologies, etc. The degree of threat in a given FTA depends on several factors: the degree of power that speakers possess relative to each other; the social distance between them; and the weightiness of the particular FTA.

face wants. The requirements in terms of negative and positive **politeness** which our negative and positive face impose on us and our interlocutors.

feature. In **morphology**, a feature is a linguistic element in a **word** or **morpheme** which indicates semantic attributes such as tense (past, present, future), number (singular, plural) and gender (masculine, feminine, neuter).

felicity conditions. In **speech act** theory, the criteria which have to be fulfilled for a speech act to be 'felicitous' or successful. Several kinds of felicity conditions have been distinguished, both social and linguistic: for example, speakers have to be sincere when they perform a speech act such as making a promise; and a police officer has to utter a precisely correct formulation to arrest a suspect.

floor. In **pragmatics**, the rights and obligations associated with being the speaker in a conversational encounter and holding the attention of the other participants in the encounter.

free variation. In **phonology** and **morphology**, a linguistic element is said to be in free variation if it occurs randomly in the same linguistic context as another, without any linguistic motivation: thus for example, English speakers may pronounce 'either' as [i:ðə] or [aiðə] (although non-linguistic factors such as speech style, or a speaker's belonging to a particular social or regional group, may be determining factors). Similarly in morphology, it may be possible to add to a **word** one affix from a choice of two or more: for example, in standard French the ending of -*er* verbs in the past historic tense is -*a* (e.g. *chanta*), but in various northern French dialects the ending is -*it* (e.g. *chantit*). Contrast **complementary distribution**.

fricative. A **consonant** produced using audible hissing or friction. Friction is produced by bringing two **articulators** close together; for example, an **alveolar** fricative is produced when the tongue **blade** is brought close to the gum-ridge behind the teeth. The term fricative is one of the **manner-of-articulation** criteria used to classify consonants.

front. In the classification of **vowels**, front vowels are those pronounced with the tongue **blade** advanced to the front of the mouth. Examples are the French vowels in *qui, mes, lait*.

functional analysis. In the study of **sentence** structure, it is possible to analyse a **phrase** from the point of view of its function in a sentence (**subject, predicate, complement**) as well as of its behaviour or structure in a theory of **syntax**: these two viewpoints need to be kept distinct.

fusion. A process in **morphology** which 'fuses' or combines more than one **feature** in a single form, as in the French pronoun *leur*, which contains the features 'plural' and 'indirect object' in a form which is difficult to separate out into distinct **morphs**.

grammar. A term which has several senses in linguistics; in this book it is used to designate the system of rules that native-speakers internalise as children and operate to produce **grammatical** sentences. Grammar generally embraces **morphology** and **syntax**, although some linguists also include **phonology**.

grammatical. A sentence is said to be grammatical if it is judged by native-speakers to be well-formed according to the rules of **grammar** which they intuitively recognise and operate. Such a judgement is not to be confused with a prescriptive pronouncement on grammaticality, such as 'don't end a sentence with a preposition'.

head. The indispensable core element in a **phrase.** The heads are in capitals in the following examples: *le BOURGEOIS gentilhomme; le TYPE qui parlait.*

high. In the classification of **vowels,** high vowels are those pronounced with the tongue held above its **neutral** position. Examples are the French vowels /i/ and /y/, as in *qui* and *du.*

homonymy. A term used when one form has two or more unrelated meanings, e.g. *air* (= air), and *air* (= tune). Cf. **polysemy.**

homophony. A term used to describe two or more forms which have the same pronunciation, e.g. *saint* and *sein.*

hyponymy. A term used in lexical **semantics** to refer to cases where the meaning of one form (with specific meaning) is included in the meaning of another (with a more general meaning), e.g. *carotte – légume, moineau – oiseau.*

idiolect. The personal dialect of each individual speaker of a language.

implicature. In **pragmatics,** an implicature is something which is implied but not said explicitly, and which a hearer needs to understand in order to respond successfully. Thus for example, the **utterance:** *Il fait froid ici* may imply a directive or request for the window to be closed.

inference. The process (and result) of inferring or working out what is meant by an utterance by focusing on the appropriate features or 'contextualisation cues' which the utterance contains. Note that in contrast to **implicatures,** not all inferences which can be made from a given utterance are necessarily intentionally communicated by the speaker.

inflectional morphology. The morphological processes which change the form of a word to fit its **grammatical** function in a sentence. For example, English plurals are generally formed by the addition of the -s morpheme, as in *pack* ⇒ *packs.* By contrast, French generally changes the form of the article: *la table* ⇒ *les tables.* These examples illustrate the fact that morphological processes are represented differently in speech and writing.

informative signals. This term refers to signals about ourselves which we give to other people unintentionally (e.g. by having unbrushed hair, a strange accent, by shifting around in our seat), whereas communicative signals refer to the signals we give with the intention of conveying a specific meaning (e.g. by language).

inherited words. A term used in French **etymology** to refer to words which have been in the language since Latin, i.e. Latin words which have been in unbroken use in France since Roman times. Their form and meaning may well have changed substantially over this time, but they remain the direct continuators of their Latin source.

inter-speaker variation. This refers to the way lingustic differences develop between different speakers (or groups of speakers).

intonation. This term is used to refer to contrastive changes of pitch (or melodic note).

intra-speaker variation. This refers to the way linguistic differences exist within one and the same speaker, according to the different situational contexts in which they find themself.

larnyx. The 'voice box'; the part of the windpipe or trachea containing the **vocal cords.**

lexical semantics. The study of the meaning of words, as opposed to the meaning of sentences and utterances.

lexicology. This is the branch of linguistics concerned with the study of a language's vocabulary. It is associated with the subject of lexicography (the art/science of dictionary-writing).

liaison. This term refers to the pronunciation before a following vowel of certain word-final consonants which are silent in other phonetic contexts (e.g. the final *s* in *les* is not normally pronounced (*les parents*), but surfaces when the next word begins with a vowel (*les enfants*)).

low. In the classification of **vowels,** low vowels are those pronounced with the tongue held below its **neutral** position. An examples is the French vowel /a/, as in *patte.* Also referred to as open vowels.

manner of articulation. One of the criteria used to classify **consonants** which refers to how the **articulators** are brought together to produce a speech sound. Examples of manner-of-articulation criteria are **fricative, plosive** and **nasal.**

marked. See **unmarked.**

mid-high. In the classification of **vowels,** mid-high vowels are those pronounced with the tongue in an intermediate position between **neutral** and **high.** Examples are the French vowels /e/ and /ø/, as in *thé* and *peu.*

mid-low. In the classification of **vowels,** mid-low vowels are those pronounced with the tongue in an intermediate position between **neutral** and **low.** Examples are the French vowels /ɛ/ and /œ/, as in *lait* and *peur.*

modality or **mood.** Terms used to refer to attitudes of fact, wish, possibility, etc. expressed by a verb, e.g. subjunctive versus indicative versus conditional, *pouvoir, vouloir,* etc.

modifier. An element in **syntax** which provides additional but non-indispensable information about what has gone before, as in (modifier in capitals): *elle est partie chez lui EN MOTO.* Contrast **complement.**

morph. A concrete realisation of the more abstract **morpheme.** Thus the English plural -s morpheme is realised phonetically by various forms: {-s}; {-z}; {iz}. As these examples show, morphs are conventionally represented in brace brackets.

morpheme. The smallest meaningful unit in language, found at the level lower than the **word**. A single morpheme may constitute a word, as in the French *bon;* morphemes also combine to form words, as in *bon + té* ⇒ *bonté*. This example illustrates the distinction between 'free' morphemes, which may occur in isolation as words (*bon*), and 'bound' morphemes, which can only occur in combination with others (*té*).

morphology. The branch of **grammar** which studies the structure or forms of words, as distinct from **syntax** which studies the way those forms are strung together in longer sequences (**phrases, clauses, sentences**). **Derivational morphology** is concerned with the way in which new words can be created by adding affixes to existing words. **Inflectional morphology** is concerned with the way one and the same word modifies its shape according to its grammatical function.

nasal. Involving the nasal passage in the articulation of consonants and vowels. Nasal consonants are produced by lowering the **velum** to release air through the nose; the French nasal consonants are /m/, /n/, /ɲ/ and /ŋ/. The term nasal is one of the **manner-of-articulation** criteria used to classify consonants.

natural meaning. Meaning that is conveyed unintentionally through non-linguistic means: gesture, facial expression, etc. Contrast **non-natural meaning**.

neutral. In phonetics, the 'speech ready' position where the tongue is neither **high** nor **low**, **front** nor **back**.

non-natural meaning. Meaning that is conveyed using language. The use of the term non-natural reflects the conventional nature of language; there is in general no natural connection between a word and what it refers to. Even 'iconic' words which appear to mimic what they stand for, such as *chuchoter*, vary greatly across languages. The relation between language and the world is therefore arbitrary.

phoneme. A unit of sound which produces meaning when it contrasts with another sound. Thus for example, /b/ and /k/ are phonemes of French because they can be substituted in a sequence which is otherwise identical, to produce a meaningful contrast: *bar ~ car*. Phonemes are represented in oblique brackets, as above. See also **allophone**.

phonemic transcription. A systematic transcription of the speech sounds of a language which takes account only of the language's **phonemes**, i.e. those sounds which serve to distinguish meaning. Contrast **allophonic transcription**.

phonetics. The study of the production of human speech sounds. Phonetics is concerned with describing and classifying the sounds of speech; these sounds may be described, among others, from the point of view of how they are produced by speakers (the **articulatory** viewpoint); or of the physical properties of the sounds (the **acoustic** viewpoint).

phonetic transcription. A systematic method of transcribing the speech sounds of a language, using a notational system; the International Phonetic

Alphabet (IPA) is the most commonly used. The IPA is based on the **articulatory** features of speech sounds. A phonetic transcription is conventionally enclosed in square brackets, and incorporates more phonetic detail than a **phonemic transcription**. See also **allophonic transcription**.

phonology. The branch of linguistics which studies the relatively abstract way in which languages arrange speech sounds into patterns to produce meaning. Phonology uses as its database the more concrete findings of **phonetics**.

phrase. In **syntax**, a **word** (*Marie*) or word group (*le type avec qui je discutais*) which functions as a **constituent** of a larger unit (a **clause** or sentence). A phrase does not have the **subject–predicate** structure typical of the clause or sentence, and hence is not autonomous.

place of articulation. One of the criteria used to classify **consonants** which refers to the place in the **vocal tract** where the consonant is produced.

plosive. A **consonant** produced by momentarily blocking the airflow and then abruptly releasing it: /p/, /t/ and /k/ are plosives in French. Also referred to as a **stop**. The term plosive is one of the **manner-of-articulation** criteria used to classify consonants.

politeness. In **pragmatics**, the linguistic expression of politeness across languages has been the object of much study, in an attempt to formulate universal principles which might transcend the cross-cultural differences which are very salient.

politeness principle. The principle which states that people engage in rational behaviour so as to attend to their own and other people's **face wants**.

polysemy. A term used to refer to words with a range of different but related meanings, e.g. *poser* = (1) put down, (2) pose (for a photograph), ask (a queston) etc. Cf. **homonymy**.

pragmatic principles. Principles to which speakers generally adhere in communication. Examples are the **co-operative** and **politeness** principles.

pragmatics. The branch of linguistics concerned with language in the real-life situations in which it is used, as opposed to the study of language divorced from its surrounding linguistic or social context. This latter study is the concern of most other branches of linguistics.

predicate. In **syntax**, a **sentence** can be argued to consist of a **subject** and a predicate, that is something which is asserted about the subject. The predicates are in capitals in the following examples: *Jean EST MALADE; la fillette S'EST EVADEE.*

preferred. See **unmarked**.

presupposition. The information that a speaker assumes that the hearer knows already.

productive. A linguistic process is said to be productive if it can be applied in an indefinite number of new cases; thus the French suffix *-ation* can be added to a verb to produce a new noun, as in for example *privatisation*. Contrast **suppletion**.

proform. A word which can replace another word or **phrase**. The term proform has wider application than the traditional 'pronoun', as a proform can replace not only nouns and noun phrases, but also other **categories** of words such as adjectives, as in the last of the following examples (proforms are in capitals): *j'ai vu Jean – IL va bien?; où est ta mère? – ELLE est dans le jardin; il devient gaga – il L'a toujours été.*

pronominalisation. A term used to refer to a rule which replaces a noun or noun phrase with a pronoun.

psycholinguistics. The study of the relationship between language and the mind.

register. In this book the term 'register' refers to the dimension of language variation governed by the different uses to which language is put. It covers a spectrum of **intra-speaker** variables, notably speech **style**.

relativity (linguistic). This term expresses the notion that all languages have their own linguistic structure, which is peculiar to them and which is quite different from the structure of other languages.

repair. A correction (or attempt at correction) made to talk by either of the participants in a conversational interaction. A repair made by the speaker is called 'self-repair', as in: *J'ai vu Jean, je veux dire John.* 'Other repair' is initiated by the hearer, as in: *T'as vu qui?*

replacives. A term used in French **morphology** to refer to forms created by replacing an element present in a base-form with something else, e.g. *belle > beau.*

Sapir-Whorf hypothesis. This hypothesis states that we dissect nature along lines laid down by our native languages – by the linguistic systems in our minds.

semantic change. This term refers to the process whereby words change their meaning over time, e.g. in medieval French the word *bureau* referred to a type of cloth often used to cover the table in a counting-house. In time the meaning of the word was extended to mean the table itself, and eventually the whole office.

semantics. The study of meaning, asserted in modern linguistics to be independent of **syntax**. This principle is illustrated by the famous **sentence**: 'Colorless green ideas sleep furiously', which although deeply problematic semantically, is recognised by native English speakers as being **grammatical**.

sentence. The largest unit recognised in the analysis of **syntax**. Various definitions of the sentence have been proposed, all more or less unsatis-factory: for instance, a sentence has been defined as a unit of meaning (but a **word** is too). Perhaps the most useful definition of the sentence refers to its structural autonomy: a sentence is 'the largest unit of grammatical descrip-tion' and is independent of other sentences for the purposes of description or analysis, even though reference to other sentences in the surrounding co-text may be necessary for full understanding.

simple sentence. This refers to the structure of sentences containing just one clause. The term contrasts with complex sentence which contains more than one clause.

sociolinguistics. The study of the relationships between language and society.

speech act. An **utterance** considered in relation to the intention of the speaker and/or its effect on the hearer. Several kinds of speech acts have been distinguished: a speaker uses a 'directive' to attempt to get a hearer to do something, as in *ferme la porte*; a 'declaration' brings about a new state of affairs, as in *I now declare you man and wife.* See also **felicity conditions.**

speech event. A type of **discourse** which has distinctive characteristics: for instance, an interview is a speech event which has clearly defined turn-taking rules and distribution of speaking rights.

speech situation. A social occasion, formal or informal, which lays upon the participants varying conventions and expectations concerning their speech production: for example, the speech situation in a French courtroom will impose such expressions as *Mon éminent confrère, Monsieur le Juge, plaider la légitime défense.* A speech situation provides the context for **speech events**, which in turn are composed of **speech acts.**

standard language. An abstract set of norms, usually enjoying official status, against which speakers of a language judge what is and what is not correct in their pronunciation, **grammar** and vocabulary.

stop. See **plosive.**

style. In this book the term style is used to refer to the dimension of language variation along which the in/formality of a **speech event** may be situated. Formality in turn essentially depends on the relationship of the participants in a speech event; the less intimate the speakers, the more formal the occasion, and conversely. See also **register.**

stylistics. The branch of linguistics which studies the different varieties of a language which arise from the different situational uses to which it is put, and tries to establish principles capable of accounting for the particular choices made by individuals and social groups in their use of language.

sub-category. Within a **category**, a **word** may be further defined according to more detailed criteria, or sub-categorised. Thus a word may be categorised as a verb, and sub-categorised as transitive, requiring a preposition, etc.

subject. The element in a **sentence** about which something is said or 'predicated', as in the following example (subject in capitals): *LE GARÇON est tombé.* See also **predicate.**

subordinate clause. This term refers to a clause which is dependent upon another (usually main) clause: *Paul est arrivé QUAND MARIE ÉTAIT PARTIE.*

substitution. A test used in **syntax** to assign a **word** or **phrase** to its appropriate **category**. Thus we can define the linguistic unit *vélo* as a noun in terms of its being capable of being substituted for other words in the same linguistic context; for example, it can occur in the same slot as *marché* in the phrase *le marché*, i.e. after a **determiner**, and this is a feature of French syntax. See also **distributional analysis**.

subtractives. A term used in French **morphology** to refer to forms created by removing an element present in a base-form, e.g. *grande* ⇒ *grand*.

suppletion. In **morphology**, a process which supplies irregular or 'one-off' linguistic forms, as in some French present ⇒ future forms: *va* ⇒ *ira*. This process is not **productive**.

syllable. A unit of rhythm intermediary between an individual sound and a word. A syllable consists typically of a **vowel** (or vowel-like sound) which may or may not be preceded and followed by **consonants**.

synonymy. Synonyms are two or more forms with very closely related meanings, e.g. *véhicule – voiture, argent – fric*.

syntax. A term used both by traditional grammarians and by contemporary linguists to refer to the study of the rules which govern the combination of **words** into **grammatical sentences**. A further sense of the term refers to the system of rules which native-speakers have stored mentally and which enables them to understand and produce an indefinite number of new sentences. In this sense native-speakers have in their head the syntax of their language.

tip. The frontmost part of the tongue. The tongue tip is involved in the production of **trilled** [r], which is still sometimes heard in French.

transformational grammar. A 'transformation' is a formal linguistic operation that shows a correspondence between two structures (e.g. active and passive structures like *Marie aime Pierre* and *Pierre est aimé par Marie*). A grammar which uses such transformations is called a 'transformational grammar'.

transition relevance place. In **pragmatics**, the point at the end of a unit of conversation when it is appropriate for another speaker to begin speaking.

trill. A **consonant** produced by rapidly tapping one articulator against another, as in French trilled [r], where the tongue tip is tapped against the **alveolar** ridge. The French /r/ may also be pronounced as a **uvular** trill, transcribed [R]. The term trill is one of the **manner-of-articulation** criteria used to classify consonants.

turn-taking. The rules or mechanisms which participants observe in order to share out the **floor** in conversation.

unmarked. A linguistic item is considered to be unmarked if it forms the 'basic' or 'normal' member of a set of items. Thus a singular noun is analysed by linguists (and intuitively felt by non-linguists) to be the unmarked member of a singular–plural pair, because plural seems to derive from singular rather than the other way round. In **pragmatics**, the response of an **adjacency pair** is said to be unmarked or 'preferred' when it conforms to speakers' expectations of what is required. So for example, the stimulus *ça va?* will usually be expected to elicit a conventional reply such as *ça va*, rather than a detailed description of one's health or personal situation. As the example shows, an unmarked response tends to be shorter than a marked (or 'dispreferred') one.

utterance. A stretch of spoken language between two silences, as opposed to the more abstract, syntactic notion of the **sentence**. An utterance may be a sentence, part-sentence, or something which occurs in place of a sentence such as a non-lexical vocalisation like *uh-huh*.

uvular. In the classification of speech sounds, relating to the uvula, the small fleshy extension of the soft palate or **velum**. French /r/ is generally pronounced as a uvular **fricative**. The term uvular is one of the **place-of-articulation** criteria used to classify **consonants**.

velar. In the classification of speech sounds, relating to the **velum** or soft palate, the moveable muscular flap behind the hard palate. The French and English **plosives** /k/ and /g/ are velar. The term velar is one of the **place-of-articulation** criteria used to classify **consonants**.

velum. The soft part of the palate located at the back of the mouth.

vocal cords or **folds.** The muscular folds, situated in the **larynx**, whose vibration produces audible sound. This sound is then modified in the throat, mouth and nose to produce speech sounds.

vocal organs. Those organs and anatomical features which are involved in the production of speech: the lungs, trachea, **larnyx**, mouth, nose, etc.

vocal tract. The part of the air passage above the lungs which is involved in the production of speech: trachea, **larynx**, mouth, nose, etc.

voicing. Vibration of the **vocal cords** or **folds**. All **vowels** are voiced. Voicing is the feature that distinguishes the **consonants** /b/, /d/, /g/ from /p/, /t/, /k/.

vowel. A speech sound which is produced with relatively little constriction or narrowing in the mouth. Vowels always have **voicing**. Compare **consonant**.

word. A linguistic unit which, though intuitively recognised by speakers, is difficult to define rigorously. Two criteria which have been suggested as necessary for a linguistic unit to fulfil in order to be considered as a word are: 'positional mobility' (the word is mobile within a **sentence**, as bound **morphemes** are not); and 'uninterruptability' (no other linguistic unit may be inserted within a word; thus *chemin de fer* is a word by this criterion, since *chemin beau de fer** is unacceptable).

zero morph. This term refers to cases in **morphology** where an underlying **morpheme** is expressed not by the presence of a particular morph, e.g. the French plural morpheme on adjectives is realised as /z/ before following vowels (*petits enfants*) but by a 'zero morph' (*petits garçons*) before following consonants.

Bibliography

Adamson, R. *et al.* 1986: *Le français en faculté* (2nd edition). London: Hodder and Stoughton.

Ager, D. 1990: *Sociolinguistics and Contemporary French.* Cambridge: CUP.

Aitchison, J. 1981: *Language-change: Progress or Decay?* Cambridge: CUP.

Aitchison, J. 1987: *Words in the Mind.* Oxford: Blackwell.

Aitchison, J. 1992: *The Articulate Mammal.* (3rd edition). London: Routledge.

Anderson, R. 1988: *The Power and the Word: Language, Power and Change.* Glasgow: Paladin Grafton.

Armstrong, L. 1982: *The Phonetics of French.* London: Bell & Hyman.

Battye, A. and Hintze, M.-A. 1992: *The French Language Today.* London: Routledge.

Bernstein, B. 1971: *Class, Codes and Control*, vol. 1: *Theoretical Studies towards a Sociology of Language.* London: Routledge and Kegan Paul.

Bloch, O. and von Wartburg, W. 1991: *Dictionnaire étymologique de la langue française* (9th edition). Paris: PUF.

Bremner, G. 1986–1993: *Aberystwyth Word Lists.* Published privately by the author.

Brown, P. and Levinson, S. 1987: *Politeness. Some Universals in Language Use.* Cambridge: Cambridge University Press.

Brown, R. and Gilman, A. 1971: The pronouns of power and solidarity. In J. Laver and S. Hutcheson (eds), *Communication in Face to Face Interaction.* Harmondsworth: Penguin.

Byrne, L. S. R. and Churchill, E. L. 1993 (completely revised and rewritten by G. Price): *A Comprehensive French Grammar.* Oxford: Blackwell.

Catach, N. 1993: Reform of the writing system. In C. Sanders (ed.) 1993: 139-54.

Catford, J. C. 1965: *A Linguistic Theory of Translation.* London: Oxford University Press.

Coveney, A. 1990: Variation in interrogatives in spoken French: a preliminary report. In W. Ayres-Bennett and J. N. Green (eds), *Variation and Change in French*. London: Routledge.

Crystal, D. 1991: *A Dictionary of Linguistics and Phonetics* (3rd edition). Oxford: Blackwell.

Dubois, J., Lagane, R., Niobey, G., Casalis, D., Casalis, J. and Meschonnie, H. 1971: *Dictionnaire du français contemporain*. Paris: Larousse–Bordas.

Durand, J. 1993: Sociolinguistic variation and the linguist. In C. Sanders (ed.) 1993: 257-85.

Encrevé, P. 1987: *La liaison avec et sans enchaînement*. Paris: Seuil.

Etiemble, R. 1964: *Parlez-vous franglais?* Paris: Gallimard.

Farrington, B. 1980: *Le français en faculté* (Audio Course). London: Hodder and Stoughton.

Fasold, R. 1984: *The Sociolinguistics of Society*. Oxford: Blackwell.

Fasold, R. 1990: *The Sociolinguistics of Language*. Oxford: Blackwell.

Gadet, F. 1989: *Le français ordinaire*. Paris: Colin.

Gadet, F. 1992: *Le français populaire*. Paris: PUF (Que Sais-Je?)

Giles, H. 1970: Evaluative reactions to accents. *Educational Review*, 22: 211-27.

Goffman, E. 1963: *Behavior in Public Places*. New York: Free Press.

Grevisse, M. 1986: *Le bon usage* (12th edition, rewritten by A. Goosse). Gembloux: Duculot.

Grice, H. P. 1957: Meaning. *Philosophical Review*, 67: 377-88.

Grundy, P. 1995: *Doing Pragmatics*. London: Arnold.

Gueunier, N., Genouvrier, E. and Khomsi, A. 1978: *Les français devant la norme*. Paris: Champion.

Guilbert, L. 1975: *La créativité lexicale*. Paris: Larousse.

Guiraud, P. 1973: *L'Argot*. Paris: PUF (Que Sais-Je?).

Gumperz, J. J. 1982: *Discourse Strategies*. Cambridge: Cambridge University Press.

Halliday, M. A. K. 1964: The users and uses of language. Reprinted in J. Fishman (ed.), *Readings in the Sociology of Language*, 1968: The Hague: Mouton.

Hartley, D. (ed.) 1987: *Travaux pratiques*. London: Hodder and Stoughton.

Haugen, E. 1950: The analysis of linguistic borrowing. *Language*. 26: 210-32.

Hawkins, R. 1993: Regional variation in France. In C. Sanders (ed.) 1993: 55-84.

Heritage, J. and Greatbatch, D. 1991: Institutional talk: news interviews. In D. Boden and D. Zimmerman (eds), *Talk and Social Structure*. Oxford: Polity Press.

Higgins, I. and Hervey, S. 1992: *Thinking Translation*. London: Routledge.

Hope, T. E. 1971: *Lexical Borrowing in the Romance Languages*. Oxford: Blackwell.

Hudson, R. 1984: *Invitation to Linguistics*. Oxford: Martin Robertson.

Hymes, D. 1971: On communicative competence. Reprinted in J.B. Pride and J. Holmes (eds), *Sociolinguistics*. Harmondsworth: Penguin, pp. 269-93.

Labov, W. 1972: The study of language in its social context. Reprinted in J. B. Pride and J. Holmes (eds), *Sociolinguistics*. Harmondsworth: Penguin, pp. 180-202.

Ladefoged, P. 1994: *A Course in Phonetics* (3rd edition). New York: Harcourt Brace Jovanovich.

Lass, R. 1984: *Phonology: An Introduction to Basic Concepts*. Cambridge: Cambridge University Press.

Levinson, S. 1983: *Pragmatics*. Cambridge: Cambridge University Press.

Lodge, R. A. 1989: Speakers' perceptions of non-standard vocabulary in French. *Zeitschrift für Romanische Philologie*, 105: 427-44.

Lodge, R. A. 1993: *French: From Dialect to Standard*. London: Routledge.

Lyons, J. 1981: *Language and Linguistics*. Cambridge: Cambridge University Press.

Martinet, A. 1970: *Eléments de linguistique générale*. Paris: Colin.

Massian, M. 1985: *Et si l'on écrivait correctement le français?* Paris: Hachette.

Matoré, G. 1968: *Histoire des dictionnaires français*. Paris: Larousse.

Mey, J. L. 1993: *Pragmatics: An Introduction*. Oxford: Blackwell.

Milroy, J. and Milroy, L. 1991: *Authority in Language*. London: Routledge and Kegan Paul.

Müller, B. 1985: *Le français d'aujourd'hui*. Paris: Klincksieck.

Nunan, D. 1993: *Introducing Discourse Analysis*. Harmondsworth: Penguin.

Ochs, E. 1979: What child language can contribute to pragmatics. In E. Ochs and B. B. Schieffelin (eds), *Developmental Pragmatics*. New York: Academic Press.

Offord, M. 1990: *Varieties of Contemporary French*. London: Macmillan.

Ouhalla, J. 1994: *Introducing Transformational Grammar*. London: Arnold.

Palmer, F. 1971: *Grammar*. Harmondsworth: Penguin.

Pinker, S. 1995: *The Language Instinct*. New York: William Morrow.

Price, G. 1991: *An Introduction to French Pronunciation*. Oxford: Blackwell.

Rat, M. 1968: *Dictionnaire des locutions françaises*. Paris: Larousse.

Sacks, H., Schegloff, E. A. and Jefferson, G. 1974: A simple systematics for the organization of turn-taking for conversation. *Language*, 50: 696-735.

Sanders, C. (ed.) 1993: *French Today*. Cambridge: Cambridge University Press.

Saville-Troike, M. 1982: *The Ethnography of Communication*. Oxford: Blackwell.

Schiffrin, D. 1994: *Approaches to Discourse*. Cambridge, MA: Blackwell.

Spence, N. C. W. 1976: Le problème du franglais. In *Le français contemporain*. Berne: Francke, pp. 75-103.

Stubbs, M. 1983: *Discourse Analysis*. Oxford: Blackwell.

Toubon, J. 1994: L'esprit des langues. *Le Monde* 24.2.94.

Tranel, B. 1987: *The Sounds of French*. Cambridge: Cambridge University Press.

Trudgill, P. 1995: *Sociolinguistics*. (3rd edition). Harmondsworth: Penguin.

Ullman, S. 1969: *Précis de semantique française*. (4th edition). Berne: Franke.

Valdman, A. 1976: *Introduction to French Phonology and Morphology*. Rowley, MA.: Newbury House.

Vivien, G. and Arné, V. 1996: *Le Parfait Secrétaire*. Paris: Larousse–Bordas.

Walter, H. 1988: *Le français dans tous les sens*. Paris: Laffont.

Walter, H. 1997: *L'aventure des mots français venus d'ailleurs*. Paris: Laffont.

Williams, R. 1976: *Keywords*. London: Collins.

Yaguello, M. 1978: *Les mots et les femmes*. Paris: Payot.

Yaguello, M. 1988: *Catalogue des idées reçues sur la langue*. Paris: Seuil.

Yule, G. 1985: *The Study of Language*. Cambridge: Cambridge University Press.

Index

Entries indicated in bold are defined in the glossary